BLUES ALL AROUND

THE AUTOBIOGRAPHY OF
B. B. KING

"For almost 50 years, King has let his guitar, Lucille,
do the talking. Now the celebrated bluesman tells
his own gutsy story."
—*Buzz*

"A classy book from a classy man...straightforward,
frank, unaffected, and breezy, with many funny,
insightful stories and anecdotes."
—*Seattle Times*

"King tells his very American success story with
the lyricism and leisurely pace of a born storyteller...
with warmth and sincerity."
—*San Francisco Examiner & Chronicle*

"The name B. B. King is synonymous with the blues,
and *Blues All Around Me* documents the experience
behind that hard-earned reward."
—*Rolling Stone*

"This is one of the best recent pop-music bios.
King speaks straight from the soul, it seems,
just like he plays the guitar."
—*Booklist*

"Excellent...provocative...King comes off in print not
unlike he does in his music: warm and polite, down home
and sophisticated, expressive and tasteful."
—*Orlando Sentinel*

"The thrill is never gone."
—*USA Today*

Avon Books are available at special quantity discounts for bulk purchases for sales promotions, premiums, fund raising or educational use. Special books, or book excerpts, can also be created to fit specific needs.

For details write or telephone the office of the Director of Special Markets, Avon Books, Inc., Dept. FP, 1350 Avenue of the Americas, New York, New York 10019, 1-800-238-0658.

blues
ALL AROUND ME

THE AUTOBIOGRAPHY OF B.B. KING

b.b.king

with
DAVID RITZ

SPIKE
AN AVON BOOK

AVON BOOKS, INC.
1350 Avenue of the Americas
New York, New York 10019

Copyright © 1996 by B. B. King
Page 337 is an extension of this copyright page.
Inside back cover author photo by Michael Steele
Interior design by Kellan Peck
Published by arrangement with the author
ISBN: 0-380-80760-2
www.spikebooks.com

All rights reserved, which includes the right to reproduce this book or portions thereof in
any form whatsoever except as provided by the U.S. Copyright Law. For information
address Avon Books.

Library of Congress Cataloging in Publication Data:

King, B. B.
    Blues all around me; the autobiography of B. B. King / B. B. King with David Ritz.
        p.   cm.
Discography: p. 315.
1. King, B. B. 2. Blues musicians—United states—Biography. I. Ritz, David. II. Title.
ML420.K473A3   1996   96-27773
781.643'092—dc20   CIP

First Spike Printing: December 1999
First Avon Books Mass Market Printing: September 1997
First Avon Books Hardcover Printing: November 1996

SPIKE TRADEMARK REG. U.S. PAT. OFF. AND IN OTHER COUNTRIES, MARCA REGISTRADA, HECHO
EN U.S.A.

Printed in the U.S.A.

OPM 10 9 8 7 6 5 4

If you purchased this book without a cover, you should be aware that
this book is stolen property. It was reported as "unsold and destroyed"
to the publisher, and neither the author nor the publisher has received
any payment for this "stripped book."

For my children:

Shirley Ann, Patty, Ruby, Rita, Michele, Claudette, Riletta, Karen, Big Barbara, Little Barbara, Gloria, Robert, Willie, Leonard, and Riley, Jr.

ACKNOWLEDGMENTS

Thanks to Lou Aronica, Sid Seidenberg, Mel Berger, Aaron Priest, Lisa Vance, Lupe DeLeon, Jennifer Hershey, Kathleen Oga, Sherman Darby, Norman Matthews, Etta James, Jerry Wexler, Isaac Hayes, Robert Gordon, Charles Keil, Michael Lydon, Josh Sklair, David Snyder, Bobby Murray, Peter Guralnick, Andy McKaie, Roberta Ritz, Alison Ritz, Jessica Ritz, Joel Dufour, Tina France, Helena Hopper, Floyd Lieberman, Marc Norberg, Ray Baradat, and Erina Siciliani, loyal friend for thirty years.

CONTENTS

CONTENTS

CONTENTS

CONTENTS

1

Memory of the Heart

I struggle with words. Never could express myself the way I wanted. My mind fights my mouth, and thoughts get stuck in my throat. Sometimes they stay stuck for seconds or even minutes. Some thoughts stay for years; some have stayed hidden all my life. As a child, I stuttered. What was inside couldn't get out. I'm still not real fluent. I don't know a lot of good words. If I were wrongfully accused of a crime, I'd have a tough time explaining my innocence. I'd stammer and stumble and choke up until the judge would throw me in jail. Words aren't my friends. Music is. Sounds, notes, rhythms. I talk through music. Maybe that's why I became a loner, someone who loves privacy and doesn't reveal himself too easily.

My friendliness might fool you. Come into my dressing room and I'll shake your hand, pose for a picture, make polite small talk. I'll be as nice as I can, hoping you'll be nice to me. I'm genuinely happy to meet you and exchange a little warmth.

I have pleasant acquaintances with thousands of people the world over. But few, if any, really know me. And that includes my own family. It's not that they don't want to; it's because I keep my feelings to myself. If you hurt me, chances are I won't tell you. I'll just move on. Moving on is my method of healing my hurt and, man, I've been moving on all my life.

Now it's time to stop. This book is a place for me to pause and look back at who I was and what I became. As I write, I'm seventy years old, and all the joy and hurts, small and large, that I've stored up inside me . . . well, I want to pull 'em out and put 'em on the page. When I've been described on other people's pages, I don't recognize myself. In my mind, no one has painted the real me. Writers have done their best, but writers have missed the nitty-gritty. Maybe because I've hidden myself, maybe because I'm not an easy guy to understand. Either way, I want to open up and leave a true account of who I am.

When it comes to my own life, others may know the cold facts better than me. Scholars have told me to my face that I'm mixed up. I smile but don't argue. Truth is, cold facts don't tell the whole story. Reading this, some may accuse me of remembering wrong. That's okay, because I'm not writing a cold-blooded history. I'm writing a memory of my heart. That's the truth I'm after—following my feelings, no matter where they lead. I want to try to understand myself, hoping that you—my family, my friends, my fans—will understand me as well.

This is a blues story. The blues are a simple music, and I'm a simple man. But the blues aren't a science; the blues can't be broken down like mathematics. The blues are a mystery, and mysteries are never as simple as they look.

2

Her Words Are Music

Her hair fell all the way to her shoulders. I loved running my fingers through it, loved the way it felt. Back then, black women wore their hair short, but Mama was different. She was beautiful, wise, and kindhearted. Those are my memories. I close my eyes and see her coming in from the fields. She has a radiant face, luminous brown skin, and a shapely body that weighs around 120 pounds. It's raining and her hair is glistening wet. She hands me a towel and asks me to dry her off. Our little cabin—you could call it a servant's cabin—is cold and Mama is shivering. I'm afraid she's sick. "Are you all right?" I ask. "Fine," she answers. I work hard drying her hair, all the while loving the way it looks in the late-afternoon light, the way it feels so silky and soft. Mama turns toward me. She stops shivering and starts to smile. "Riley," she asks, "would you like to learn how to braid my hair?" I nod my head.

Patiently she shows me how to take the strains of her hair and carefully weave them together. I'm pretty good with my hands, and it doesn't take long to get into the rhythm of braiding. I want to do it right. Want to do it so good that when she walks out among all the workers who sharecrop Mr. Flake Cartledge's land, everyone will see she's the prettiest woman in the world.

When I'm through, I look to her for approval. "Beautiful job, son," she says. "You make me proud." Her words are music. "Now you can go out and play."

The rain stops. Outside the land is wet and soggy. Clouds race across the sky. Early spring in Mississippi, smelling fresh and clean. The hard fields of winter have been hoed and seeded. The hills around Kilmichael glow with the light of a golden sunset. Suddenly a rainbow appears out of nowhere and arches across the world. I stare at the colors and wonder about a pot of gold. The rainbow is too far away; I'll never reach it before dark. I think about my little brother, who died when he was just a baby. I was crazy about him; I wish he were here, wish I had someone to play with. I don't understand death. Death is a cold chill, frightening beyond reason. Where do we go when we die? And why do we have to die at all? I stare at the rainbow, wondering about my brother, when I see someone running up the country lane toward me. It's Peaches and her mom.

Peaches is my girlfriend. She's an older lady; she's seven and I'm six. But please don't underestimate puppy love. She's my first and best love and, man, I'm mighty glad to see her.

"I'm working at the Cartledges' tonight," says Peaches's mother, "and Nora Ella said she'd babysit Peaches for me."

Nora Ella is my mom. Now I'm a happy guy because I have

4

a playmate. I can relax around Peaches, I like talking with her, and my stutter eases up. She and I go running after the rainbow while our mothers chitchat in the cabin. We watch the sky turn from gold to red to blue to deep black. We try catching frogs, we have footraces to see who's fastest, we tease each other and laugh and scamper inside when we're called to eat.

Because it's Saturday night, Mama's made pork chops with thickening gravy and cooked greens and yams and potato pie. I'm nuts for potato pie. There's no electricity, just the heat of the wood-burning stove to keep us warm. An hour or so after dinner, Peaches's mom comes back saying that Mr. Cartledge can use more help. He has an unexpected guest for dinner and would my mom mind doing some chores? Mama doesn't mind, and neither do I, 'cause that means me and Peaches can be alone.

"You think the kids will be all right?" Peaches's mother wants to know.

"They'll be fine," says Nora Ella.

Being left alone is a thrill. The kerosene lamp casts our shadows against the walls. We're already giggling 'cause we know what we wanna do. We wanna play house. That's where we mimic the adults. We act like we're married. We pretend to go off to work, like we're chopping cotton with all the big folk. We pretend to be working the fields all morning until we come home for dinner—that's our word for "lunch"—and then go back and chop and pick till end of day. Then it's time for supper, and Peaches is pretending to be cooking and fixing something hot to eat. "Well, it's time to go to sleep," she says, all excited. "You ready?" I'm more than ready. We climb into my mom's bed, take off our clothes, and Peaches shows me what she learned by watching her folks; she shows how to put my stiff little penis into her vagina. "Push it in and out," she says. "Push it all the way in." I like doing it. It's a game that feels good—warm and close and different than anything else in the world. I like loving on Peaches.

So much for my innocence. Peaches was my sweetheart for a good two years. She initiated me into the wonders of sex. I had little resistance then. Truth is, I've had little resistance most of my life. To explore a woman's body while satisfying a woman's desire is a unique pleasure. Nowhere else have I found that special combination of stimulation and relaxation. I was sad, in fact, when Peaches put a stop to our lovemaking without explanation. Of course it didn't help that a year earlier Mama had caught us in the act. In a blind fury, she snatched me off Peaches, threw me across the room, and beat the living hell out of me. I mean, whipped me raw. But Mama didn't touch Peaches. I'd seen Mama hit her when Peaches disobeyed, so why not now? " 'Cause you know better than to do a thing like that, Riley" was Mama's only response. I didn't understand why Peaches didn't get whipped like me.

I didn't understand some other things about Mama. She had her ways and her ways weren't always clear. Leaving Daddy, for example. That's one of my first memories, and one of the first mysteries in my life.

I was born in the great Mississippi Delta, that part of America that someone called the most Southern place on earth. Born on September 16, 1925, on the bank of Blue Lake, between Indianola and Greenwood, near the tiny villages of Itta Bena and Berclair. Daddy was Albert Lee King and named me Riley B. The "B." didn't stand for anything, but the "Riley" was a combination. Daddy had lost a brother called Riley, but Daddy also drove a tractor for a white plantation owner named Jim O'Reilly. When Mama went into labor and Daddy went looking for a midwife, O'Reilly helped him find the right woman. O'Reilly was there when I was born and asked Daddy what he was calling his baby boy. Seeing that O'Reilly was a fair and good man, he wanted me to have his name. Years later, when I asked Daddy why he dropped the "O'," he said, " 'Cause you didn't look Irish."

My early memories of Daddy are blurry. He only comes into focus when I see him waving goodbye. He's standing still, but me and Mama are moving. I'm four or five years old. We're in the back of an old beat-up truck that's taking us away. One of her uncles is driving, a man I don't know. Daddy is growing more and more distant until he finally disappears. It's a gray day and the roads are bumpy and I'm not sure what's going on, except I've never been on a trip like this. What's only seventy miles feels like seven hundred. We're riding through the long, flat Delta. The Delta goes on forever. The cotton's been picked and the land looks barren and bleak and I'm a little scared, a little uncertain, until Mama puts her arm around me.

"It's hard for you to understand," she says. "But your daddy and I, well, we're not living together no more. That doesn't mean he don't love you. And that don't mean I don't love you. We love you lots. But we're going separate ways. You and me, we're going back to my people. My people live in the hills."

The hills start outside Greenwood. When we arrived in Kilmichael, we got out of the truck and into a rickety old wagon pulled by a horse that went deeper into the hills, deep into the country to a plantation owned by Edwayne Henderson. Mr. Henderson was a handsome and flamboyant guy who had a happy outlook on life and, given the times, treated us okay.

His plantation provided our livelihood. Plantation may be the wrong word, but that's the word we used. Maybe "farm" is a better word. Either way, these were places where my mother's people worked as sharecroppers—first the acreage owned by Henderson, then at George Booth's farm, and finally the land of Flake Cartledge. All white men.

My grandmother was part of the world of the Kilmichael hills, and she reminded me of Mama. Pretty face, soft-spoken voice, kind eyes. Her name was Elnora Farr. Mama also had a younger sister and an older brother, William Pulley, who could be a little mean, a right-to-the-point kinda guy. Uncle William's thing was: "If you don't do like I say, boy, you got trouble." So I did what he said. He was the main man in the family. I loved him but was afraid of him.

Pop Davidson was Mama's grandfather, and I'd have to call him a little crazy. He was a stutterer who talked with his shotgun and liked to ride his mule while swigging moonshine whiskey out of a jug. He also called himself a preacher, but someone else might call him a jackleg preacher. That means his preaching was a little less than legit; he talked the talk but didn't always walk the walk. Pop had been born a slave, but you couldn't tell it by his attitude. No one got in Pop's way, especially me. When I saw him coming, I'd duck.

My great-grandmother, who'd also been a slave, talked about the old days. She'd talk about the beginnings of the blues. She said that, sure, singing helped the day go by. Singing about your sadness unburdens your soul. But the blues hollerers shouted about more than being sad. They were also delivering messages in musical code. If the master was coming, you might sing a hidden warning to the other field hands. Maybe you'd want to get out of his way or hide. That was important for the women because the master could have anything he wanted. If he liked a woman, he could take her sexually. And the woman had only two choices: Do what the master demands or kill herself. There was no in-between. The blues could warn you what was coming. I could see the blues was about survival.

Great Grandma spoke with quiet authority. She'd put me on her lap and, up close, I'd notice wrinkles around her mouth and over her lips. Her eyes would twinkle and her voice was steady. I believed her every word. Unlike some of the men, she didn't exaggerate or fib to build herself up. She was sincere. She told me a story about Houston, Mississippi, where a black boy fell in love with the master's daughter. When the moon was slim and the night was dark, they'd meet undercover and steal a kiss. I pictured them in the woods, holding hands and falling in love. As Great Grandma said it, I saw it. But someone caught them and told the master, who flew into a murderous rage. He tied the boy to a tree trunk and had him tarred and feathered. He was going to burn this boy alive. But the girl came a-running; the girl was hysterical and pleaded, "Father, it's not his fault. He didn't rape me, I let him take me. I love him." "Well, what do you want me to do?" asked the father. "Don't let him suffer," said the girl. "It'd be kinder to shoot him."

The story ended there, and cold chills ran up my spine. *That was a strange kind of kindness*, I thought. "Couldn't they let the boy go?" I asked. "Never," she answered. "Not in Mississippi." My great-grandmother's stories were warnings to stay out of trouble. That attitude was passed down to her daughter and her daughter's daughter.

If my mother was in her twenties and my great-grandmother was in her seventies, my grandmother was in her fifties. Grandma had some brothers scattered around. Before I knew her, she had run off to Arkansas and had another family and other kids. But something went wrong, so she came back to my mom and me.

I see her on her way to church. Frost is on the ground and she's walking carefully, a little afraid of slipping. She turns around to take my hand; she feels my chest to make sure my sweater is warm enough. Like Mama, Grandma keeps me in sight, makes me feel like I matter.

What mattered most in the Mississippi of my childhood was work. Mr. Flake's land was probably no bigger than twenty acres. I worked the cotton and corn fields beside my mama, eager to feel part of everything happening around me. I was small, a beanpole of a kid, but determined to do like the big folk. When Mama worked up at Mr. Flake's house, cooking and cleaning, I was right there, carrying my share of the burden, sweeping and dusting and scrubbing floors.

When I was only six or seven, I was in charge of milking the twenty cows on the farm. I'd milk ten in the morning and ten at night. Learned to squeeze their tits in a proper way. Manipulating the milk out of the udders wasn't easy, but I knew the maneuvers and I filled the pails.

There were some hungry days when our only food came from our garden, but we made do. White folks didn't eat the head or intestines of pigs, and we would. We'd use the brains, we'd take the bone out of the feet to make hog-head cheese and hog-head salad. We cooked intestines and called 'em chitlins. We also knew what to do with parts of goats and cows that the whites wouldn't touch. Through necessity and ingenuity, we developed a delicious cuisine of our own.

Our world was small. The farm was in the country and the country was cut off from the rest of the state. I didn't know about no stock market crash or Depression. I just knew that after milking the morning cows I'd walk nearly three miles to school, no matter the weather. It was a one-room schoolhouse run by a teacher who taught everyone from pre-primer through twelfth grade. He's the only man who was ever able to knock any sense in my head. I was a slow learner. Never a natural student. But my teacher, Luther Henson, had a powerful influence on my young brain. To this day I feel the light of his lessons shining down on me. I owe this black man more than I can say.

For all the hard times and tough challenges I faced during different periods of my life, I think I was lucky or blessed or both. When things looked bleak, a good guide would appear to set me straight. Someone once asked me about the villains who got in my way, the bad guys who wanted to trip me up or take me out. I don't remember any. Maybe it's my nature to remember the good and forget the bad, or maybe it's my destiny to lock onto the righteous for help. Either way, Luther Henson was the first and maybe the most important man to shape me. More than anything, Mr. Henson gave me hope.

He sat in a chair on a raised podium where he ruled as master of the Elkhorn School way out in the country, just across from the Elkhorn Baptist Church. One teacher for forty or fifty kids. Not sure whether Mr. Henson even went to college, but he was a wise and wonderful human being. He had vision. He'd tell us, "Y'all see how the white kids have school buses and y'all don't. Well, that's going to change one day. One day soon. Y'all hear about lynchings"—there'd been lynchings and cross burnings all around us—"where our people are punished for something they didn't do. Remember, not all the whites are behind this. If the whites wanted to, they could kill every one of us. But there are good men among the whites, just like there are bad men. Crazy people come in all colors. And one day soon the good people will win over the crazy people. One day the courts will listen to our side of the story. And one day this law separating coloreds from whites will be thrown out. Because one thing is certain: No matter how bad things seem now, change is on the way. That's the law of nature. Justice is coming. And justice is a powerful force—more powerful than evil. Justice can't be stopped."

These were mighty words sailing into the ears of a little know-nothing country boy. I wanted to believe him, and I did. Not that I was a goody-goody. I had my problems with reading and writing. In a class of ten or eleven students, I'd put myself near the bottom. I was more drawn to the girls than the books. One girl in particular.

She sat in front of me and I'd twist and turn and stare at her overdeveloped breasts. Her breasts fascinated me. I had to touch them, and finally I did, putting my arms around her and giving her a gentle squeeze. I loved her softness. I tried to sneak the feels when Mr. Henson was grading papers, but he usually caught me. Man, he'd be pissed. He'd run out the door, snatch off a stiff twig from a tree, come back, and whip me hard. If that wasn't bad enough, the girl with big boobs would also bite my hand. You'd think that was enough to stop me from doing it again. Well, you'd think wrong.

Mr. Henson had me thinking in good ways. He seemed part of a bigger world. He had a nephew named Pervis Henson, who played with Buddy Johnson's famous big band. That excited me—just to know someone with connections to a famous black orchestra. Mr. Henson was also the first to show me a black newspaper, the *Pittsburgh Courier*. He had copies of the

Black Dispatch from Oklahoma. He'd point out black people doing good things, getting educations, writing books, winning prizes. Back on the farm, Mr. Flake had subscriptions to the *Greenville Democrat* and the *Memphis Commercial Appeal,* but the news about our people was almost all bad. Mr. Henson showed me the other side.

We'd learn the achievements of blacks—Booker T. Washington, Frederick Douglass, Mary McLeod Bethune—and how hard work, tenacity, and faith were the keys to accomplishment. We followed the fights of Joe Louis like he was fighting for our freedom. At the same time, Mr. Henson taught us not to be aggressive against other people. He believed in getting along with others, learning what they're doing, and then doing it better than them. He'd say, "The world might look cruel and unfair, but it doesn't help to moan. The world will get better only if you strive to make it better." Words might sound corny now, but I believed them then. I believe them now.

I believe my early childhood nourished me. Mr. Henson not only had knowledge to offer, he had wisdom. We had no money for sports programs, but he showed us how to make a baseball out of rags. When he saw me struggling with my stutter, he said, "Riley, just slow down and let your mouth catch up to your mind. Take a deep breath and take your time." But I was prone to panic. I asked, "W-w-w-w-what if I can't g-g-g-get the w-w-w-word out and everyone's w-w-w-w-waiting for me?" Mr. Henson just smiled and replied, "Well, they'll just have to wait, won't they?"

3

Heavenly Music

I was touched by people who spoke with love in their hearts: my mother, my teacher, and my preacher. Church, you see, made a mighty impression on this skinny kid with a thick skull and a yen for the opposite sex. Church was the highlight of the week. Church was not only a warm spiritual experience, it was exciting entertainment, it was where I could sit next to a pretty girl, and mostly it was where the music got all over my body and made me wanna jump. Sunday was the day.

Sunday starts with me running after a chicken. I grab him, wring his neck, pluck off his feathers, and boil him in hot water so Mama can cook him later. Sunday's the best eating day. Mama might even make a chocolate cake or potato pie. She might have a man friend over. For a while, a guy named Edrich Basket lived with Mama. Not sure whether they married or not, but I am sure Sunday is special. Sunday means church. The Elkhorn Baptist Church is next to school, but there's another

15

little country church, a sanctified church, in an area called Pinkney Grove. That's a Church of God in Christ, and that means they'll be doing whatever it takes to praise the Lord, making a joyful noise, even talking in tongues. That's the church where I wanna go, where you exit happier than when you enter. It's also where Uncle William's wife has a brother who preaches. He's Archie Fair. And Reverend Fair does more than preach; he plays guitar.

Slipping into the very first pew, looking around to see which girls are sitting where, feeling happy and tingly up and down my skin, listening to Mama singing with the choir with a voice so sweet it makes me wanna cry, I can't sit still. My eyes dart from here and there, only to land on the one object in the whole church that fascinates me most: Reverend's guitar. It leans against his pulpit and, man, it's beautiful. The body is hollow wood with a cord that plugs into the wall. Its rounded shape and lovely curves remind me of the body of a beautiful girl. I wanna run up and put my arms around the guitar, but I don't dare. I don't know how to play. And besides, here comes the Right Reverend leading the congregation.

Archie Fair is the nearest thing I know to God on earth. He talks like his words have already been written out in a book. Each word carries weight; each sentence carries good meaning. His sermon is like music and his music—both the song from his mouth and the sound of his guitar—thrills me until I wanna get up and dance. He says one thing and the congregation says it back, back and forth, back and forth, until we're rocking together in a rhythm that won't stop. His voice is low and rough and his guitar is high and sweet; they seem to sing to each other, conversing in some heavenly language I need to learn. The choir joins in, and the congregation joins the choir, and I'm right in the middle of a universe of music filled with nothing but pure spirit. There's an old piano and tambourines, hand-clapping and foot-stomping and shouting that starts in your toe and goes through the top of your head. The beat is steady and strong as the beat of your heart. No room for fear in here; no room for doubt; it's a celebration of love that gets even better when, after services, Mama says Reverend and his wife are coming over to visit.

To me, Reverend is a holy man. It's an honor to have him pat me on the head, a pleasure when he smiles in my face. I notice that he comes in carrying his guitar, which he carefully places on the bed. I don't say much in his presence. My stutter and my shyness keep me quiet. Besides, Mama says children should be seen, not heard. So I listen and get hungry as Mama fries up the chicken all crispy and brown. Good smells fill our cabin. I eye the chocolate cake and I also eye the guitar, laying on the bed like a girl waiting be touched. While the adults are busy talking, I ease over to the bed. While they're not looking, I reach over and, oh-so-carefully, touch the wood of the guitar. Just sorta gently stroke her. Touch her strings to see how they feel against my fingers. Feels good. Feels like magic. I wonder: *How do you get her to make those sounds? How do you get her to sing?*

"Go ahead and pick it up." It's the voice of Reverend Fair, who's caught me desiring his guitar. Mama's mad I touched something that don't belong to me, but Reverend calms her down. Reverend understands. He tells me his guitar is called a Silvertone, and it comes out of the Sears Roebuck catalog. When Reverend talks to you, it's like there's no one else in the world around. He hears what your heart is saying. He feels what you feel. He knows your soul. "You can touch it, boy," he says. "Ain't gonna bite you."

He shows me how to hold her, how to take her in my arms. She's bigger than me, but I still put her on my lap. She feels good against my body. Can't plug her in 'cause, unlike the church, we have no plugs, but I can pluck the strings and make a few small sounds.

"Lemme show you a few chords," the Reverend offers. I'm enraptured, hanging on his every word, watching like a hawk while he shows me a one, four, and five chord, simple constructions I use to this day. I can sing a whole multitude of songs with those three chords. "The guitar," says Reverend, "is a precious instrument. It's another way to express God's love."

Well, brother, that's what I wanted at age seven. Wanted to express everything Reverend was expressing. Fact is, wanted to *be* Reverend. Next year I taught Sunday school to some of the younger kids. People looked at me like a church boy, and I was glad to be seen that way. Church had the singing, church had the guitar, church had folks feeling good and happy, church was all I needed. I'd be a guitar-playing preacher like Reverend, except for my stutter and the fact that I couldn't concentrate on my book learning. Still, Mama and Reverend believed I would devote myself to God because I was eager to please and filled with the spirit.

Mama was the strongest spirit. She remained my main teacher in the hard lessons of life. If she was too stern, she'd be the first to say so. That's one of the reasons I loved her so. There's a moment in our life together I've never forgotten, a time when she prepared me for a visit to a grieving family. Their mother had died and the body, on display in their cabin, was to be embalmed the next day. The body had been dressed for viewing. "But don't stare," Mama said, "and don't eat up all the food." Mama liked to dress me real neat. I remember my little sailor suit with short pants. I remember Mama warning me again that if she sees me eating too much, she'd give me a look.

It's creepy in the cabin. The dead body is scary, and I don't know where to look or what to say. My uneasiness makes me hungry. I eat a few cookies but when I see the potato pies on the other side of the table, I go right to them. I'm just about to put that pie in my mouth—it's pipin' hot and smells delicious— when Mama gives me a look. I think it means *Stop eating*, but I want the pie. It's about the size of a saucer, and I slip it in my pocket. I sit down and, man, that sucker starts burning my leg. I can't do nothing but cry; I'm crying like a little baby, tears just streaming down my face.

"What's wrong with you, boy?" Mama wants to know.

I can't say; I just stammer and look down. Mama won't have it. She takes me outside and demands an explanation. I look up and say, "I'm sorry, Mama, I know you d-d-d-d-d-didn't want me to eat no m-m-m-m-more, so I snuck this pie." I take it out of my pocket and Mama sees how it's still burning hot. She has me slip off my shorts and sees how the heat's burned off my skin. I'm in agony. "Oh, baby," she says, "you took my look the wrong way. I didn't mean for you not to eat. You don't need to be scared of your mama." And with that, she apologized. But more than apologized, she started crying along with me. She was as hurt as me. We were deeply connected; our hearts were joined together.

There was a night of jagged lightning, a murderous night that felt like the end of the world. Wind and rain and thunderous commotion. A summer storm that would rage through the Mississippi hill country and tear the trees from their roots. Tornadoes would ride over the land like the devil himself. We could hear the tornado coming from miles away. We couldn't run or hide; we didn't have a car or truck or even a bicycle or wagon. We could only wait and pray. Me and Mama waiting in the corner of that little shotgun shack, her arm around me. I looked in her eye to see her fear, but all I saw was strength, determination. I was shaking. The terrible screaming wind got louder; we could hear the tornado getting closer. I thought of the stories the old folk told of angry funnels that pick you up and suck the life out of your body, tornadoes that level whole plantations and leave death in their wake. This was a deadly funnel; I could feel it outside our door, wind screaming so loud I had to hold my ears, when suddenly it was right up on us— the terror, the tornado, the thing was right there, right in front of us—when the roof was ripped from over our heads and then, mysteriously, unexplainably, the tornado was gone. Just like that. Just like magic. The angry funnel moved on and we stayed put. The rains had been so heavy that the next day we found little fishes wiggling around puddles all over the cotton fields. But that night Mama and I didn't even get wet. Can't explain it, but the storm didn't touch us. It was just me and Mama, standing alone in that corner, thanking Jesus for the miracle.

I saw other miracles connected to Mama. There were lots of great-aunts and uncles around, but the greatest was Great Aunt Mima, short for Jemimah. Her miracles centered on music. Mima lived in a sharecropper's cabin like the rest of us. She was younger than Mama and young-thinking, the most modern of all my relatives. Visiting her was great, except for one thing: She sniffed snuff. Dipping snuff we called it. Snuff was a powdered tobacco you'd pack under your lip and spit into a spittoon, sorta like throwing darts. Some of the snuff sniffers, like Aunt Mima, had deady aim. Never saw her miss once.

Only thing that bothered me about Mima was the minute I arrived, she was all over me with suffocating hugs and kisses. I'd wanna back away, but I didn't wanna hurt her feelings. With pieces of dipping snuff stuck to her teeth and mouth, her kisses weren't too sweet. Some of the company she invited for Sunday dinner wasn't too sweet either. I remember a man named Isaiah Wright.

Well, to us kids, Mr. Wright did everything wrong. The other grown-ups would leave us leftover pieces of chicken. Mr. Wright left us nothing. The other grown-ups liked the kitty cat we called Thomas. Mr. Wright hated him and would kick his butt. Mr. Wright's own butt was usually hanging out of his old torn farmer's overalls. He wore out the seat of his pants, and when he sat in Aunt Mima's cane-bottom chairs, his testicles would hang out and attract flies. Wasn't a pretty scene. The flies would attract Thomas, who Mr. Wright would smack and kick. This went on for months. Until one Sunday when I got an idea.

I got a piece of twine and looped both ends. I put one loop around Thomas's neck and, crawling under the table, the other loop around Mr. Wright's testicles. He was so busy scratching and shooing flies, he didn't realize what was happening. Seeing Thomas, he started scolding and swatting him, saying, "Get outta here, kitty. Get away." When Thomas ran, he nearly took Mr. Wright's testicles with him. Mr. Wright's voice went up several octaves, he started screaming something awful, and I couldn't help but howl. Mama gave me a serious whipping, but seeing Mr. Wright turn beet red was worth the pain.

The most worthwhile thing about Aunt Mima's place was her crank-up Victrola, a machine that changed my life. See, Mima was a music fan. She had the first collection I'd ever seen.

She'd go into town and find records, bring 'em home, and neatly pile 'em next to the Victrola. You'd wind up the record player like you'd wind up a watch. Her first model was a cylinder; later she got a turntable. Her 78 rpm shellac discs were shiny platters that looked like flying saucers. Aunt Mima taught me to gently put on the platter, set down the needle, and watch the turntable spin. A second passed and then—*pow!*—those beautiful scratchy sounds flew in my face, cutting right through me, electrifying my soul.

Now I'd heard shouting in the fields ever since I could remember. My daddy could sing him some blues. Big husky voice. And I had an uncle—Mama's sister's husband—called Jack Bennett. You could hear Uncle Jack singing from miles away. No matter where you went, walking behind the plow or picking cotton, you'd be hearing beautiful voices, singing about the sun high in the sky or the gathering storm clouds or the long, hard day or how good the food would taste once work was done. Seems like the songs were made up by the heart, nothing written or rehearsed, music meant to take the ache out of our backs and the burden off our brains. Some of this music you might call blues.

Blind Lemon Jefferson was as close to the field shouters as anyone else. Aunt Mima had his records, and later I learned he came from Texas. He had a big burly voice—like Daddy and Uncle Jack—and put so much feeling into his words until I believed everything he sang. He had power. Like all the great bluesmen, Blind Lemon sang for sinners. When he sang "Rabbit Foot Blues" or "Shuckin' Sugar Blues" or "That Crawlin' Baby Blues" or "Mosquito Moan," I moaned along with him. It was like him and his guitar were part of the same being. You didn't know where one stopped and the other started. Blind Lemon was strong and direct and bone-close to my home.

Lonnie Johnson was different. Mima loved Lonnie Johnson and soon I learned to love him even more. It took a minute longer to appreciate Lonnie than Blind Lemon. Lonnie was definitely a bluesman, but he took a left turn where Blind Lemon went right. Where Blind Lemon was raw, Lonnie was gentle. Lonnie was more sophisticated. His voice was lighter and sweeter, more romantic, I'd say. He had a dreamy quality to his singing and a lyrical way with the guitar. Unlike Blind Lemon, Lonnie sang a wide variety of songs. I liked that. I guess he found the strict blues form too tight. He wanted to expand. When he sang "Tomorrow Night," probably his most famous ballad, I understood that he was going to a place beyond the blues that, at the same time, never left the blues. Later I'd learn that Lonnie performed with Louis Armstrong and Duke Ellington. As my life went on and my passion for blues grew, it hurt me to see that Lonnie never got the critical acknowledgment he deserved. The scholars loved to praise the "pure" blues artists or the ones, like Robert Johnson, who died young and represented tragedy. It angers me how scholars associate the blues strictly with tragedy.

As a little kid, blues meant hope, excitement, pure emotion. Blues were about feelings. They seem to bring out the feelings of the artist and they brought out my feelings as a kid. They made me wanna move, or sing, or pick up Reverend's guitar and figure out how to make those wonderful sounds. Blind Lemon and Lonnie hit me hardest, I believe, because their voices were so distinct, natural, and believable. I heard them talking to me. As guitarists, they weren't fancy. Their guitars were hooked up to their feelings, just like their voices.

Scholars also like to talk about the Delta bluesmen and how

they influenced each other. They break down the blues according to different parts of Mississippi and say each region gave birth to a style. Well, as a Delta boy, I'm here to testify that my two biggest idols—guys I flat-out tried to copy—came a long way from Mississippi. Blind Lemon was from Dallas and Lonnie from Louisiana. I later learned about Delta bluesmen like Robert Johnson and Elmore James and Muddy Waters. I liked them all, but no one molded my musical manner like Blind Lemon and Lonnie. They entered my soul and stayed. Sixty-five years after hearing them on Aunt Mima's precious Victrola, hardly a day goes by that I don't listen to them. When Lonnie sings from "Bow Legged Baby," "She's got big bow legs, wears her dress above her knees," I'm laughing like a little kid discovering blues for the first time.

But the discoveries at Aunt Mima's entailed more than the blues. There was Bessie Smith and Mamie Smith and Ma Rainey, to be sure, blues ladies who tore off the top of my head. I still hear songs like "Empty Bed Blues" and "Crazy Blues" and "See See Rider Blues." Mima also loved gospel. Among her collection of forty or fifty records were things by J. M. Reverend Gates, who sang songs like "Death's Black Train." There were jazz bands like Duke Ellington's, whose rhythms, more complicated than the beat of the blues, still fired my blood. Mima also had Jimmie Rodgers, a yodeler who happened to be white but who sang songs like "Blues, How Do You Do?" They called him the Singing Brakeman and I sang along with him.

Not all my musical impressions were made by Aunt Mima's records. At a tender age, I was fortunate enough to get next to a true-life bluesman. I'm talkin' 'bout Bukka White, my mother's first cousin. Booker T. Washington White was the real deal. He had cut phonograph records for Victor and Vocalion with his name printed on the label, and he lived in a glamorous place called Memphis, Tennessee. He'd come to visit my mom and her family a couple of times a year: midsummer and Christmas. He knew how plantation owners hate for strangers to come 'round when the workers are busy, so he'd pick the off-times and show up looking like a million bucks. Razor-sharp. Big hat, clean shirt, pressed pants, shiny shoes. He smelled of the big city and glamorous times; he looked confident and talked about things outside our little life in the hills. He was a big-boned man, big head, big fists, big arms, flashy teeth, and a beautiful smile when you looked him in the eyes. He always had a good word and candy for the kids, a real happy-go-lucky guy, joking and stroking everyone with compliments and charm. He lit up my world. He could have been a con man because you believed every word he said, but he wasn't; he was a bluesman. I knew that because of the guitar he carried. His guitar was as much a part of his person as his fancy big-city clothes.

He'd saw off a short piece of pipe just big enough to slip his fat finger inside. Or sometimes he'd use a bottleneck, maneuvering that sucker in his left hand, sliding up down up the strings. Man, you talk about the prettiest sound this side of heaven! His vibrato gave me goose bumps. Cousin Bukka was king of the slide guitar and a spine-tingling storyteller whose songs like "Aberdeen Mississippi Blues"—he came from Aberdeen—and "Shake 'em on Down" were popular with people all over. He'd talk about playing roadhouses in Tennessee, Arkansas, and Georgia where people gambled the night away. He had to explain to me what gambling was. For a while, he'd lived in Chicago with tall buildings and railroad trains running right through the city. It was like hearing a fairy tale; it was too much for a little country boy to understand.

Like Reverend Fair, Cousin Bukka would let me touch his instrument. I tried like hell, but was frustrated by the size of the instrument and my own impatience. Didn't make much progress. I tried to maneuver the bottleneck like he did, but my fingers were too stupid. Truth is, they still are. I never copied Cousin Bukka's songs or his style. Much as I appreciated his musical manner, I was more attracted to the open cry of Blind Lemon and the sweetness of Lonnie Johnson.

Visits were treats, ways to break up the routine of schoolwork and fieldwork. And one of the most wonderful treats was when Mama had us catch the Greyhound back down to the Delta for a few days to see some of Daddy's people. The family I loved most were actually called the Loves. Uncle Major and Aunt Kathleen Love were Daddy's adopted family. Daddy said he was an orphan, that his blood family had been killed—I never knew how—and he'd been separated from his brother. The Loves were all he had.

Uncle Major was my favorite. He had the worst speech impediment of anyone I'd ever known, so bad he couldn't get out a word. Probably because I stuttered too, the way he suffered with his speech broke my heart and made me love him even more. There was a silent bond between us. Unlike the others, I could feel what he wanted to say and sometimes said it for him. But beyond his crippling stammer, Uncle Major had cataracts that covered both eyes until he could barely see light from dark.

He wouldn't let everyone lead him around, but he did let me. "B-b-b-b-b-boy," he'd stutter, "f-f-f-f-f . . ." and I knew that meant he wanted to go fishing. I'd take his arm and walk him to the creek, making sure he didn't trip over any rocks or twigs. Without talking—talking was just too frustrating for him—he'd show me how to fix up a fishing pole with a line and a hook and grig worms that we'd find in rotten old trees. The grig worms were firm and big as a finger. We'd sit and wait. If we were lucky, we'd catch a cod or a buffalo fish or a big channel catish. But I had to be patient. Uncle Major showed me patience. Without being told, I'd describe things I knew he wanted to see. "Well, Uncle Major," I'd say, "the sky is sure blue today and the clouds look all puffy and white and the grass is starting to grow and the cotton blossoms are coming up everywhere you look." Painting the picture for Uncle Major made me appreciate the scenery and helped me to love the land around me. I saw simple nature—a field of wildflowers, the markings of a redbird—through the eyes of a man who'd been robbed of sight. On the way home, Uncle Major would lean on me heavy, trusting that I'd steer him clear of harm. That trust made me even stronger. I'd call the trust love.

Funny, but during those visits down to the Delta, I don't remember Daddy as much as Uncle Major. Daddy was usually off driving his tractor. Fact is, he had really driven out of my life. My life consisted of Mama and her family, mainly Grandma Elnora, back in the hills of Kilmichael on the farm owned by Mr. Flake. Mama's character was my main guidepost. I believed what she said when she said the Golden Rule was the only rule. Treat others how you wanna be treated. She lived those words and I prayed she'd live forever. There were times when she'd get sick and I'd get scared. There were other times, still sketchy in my mind, when Mama went off to live with a man and I stayed with Grandma.

Grandma might take me to a relative's house where the old

folk would talk late into the night while they put me in the next room to curl up on the bed and go to sleep. But I couldn't sleep, I couldn't help but hear them tell spooky stories about headless bodies being carried off in open coffins. They were probably lying or exaggerating, but these tall tales painted such frightening pictures of ghostly death that when they turned off the kerosene lamps I found myself shivering with fear. They told the stories with such emotion and in such detail that, in the eyesight of my imagination, I saw dead bodies coming after me, dripping blood, breathing down my neck. The dark became a tomb. Today as an old man I still carry the fear of a little boy; I can't sleep in the dark; a light must be burning in my bedroom.

Maybe I feared more than the dark. Maybe I sensed in the distance between me and Mama that something was wrong. Maybe I saw in her eye the coming of a change, a slowing down, a sickness. I don't know. I can't remember the sequence of events probably because I don't want to remember. But by the time I was eight years old, three or four years after leaving the Delta, things were changing. Mama's energy was being sapped. Her eyesight was failing. Worried that she lacked the strength herself, she asked Grandma to take care of me. I didn't understand what was happening and was afraid to ask questions. I was afraid of the answers. But a feeling of terror deep in my gut wouldn't go away. I prayed to God to lift the fear, but the fear remained. Darkness was creeping over me.

4

Dawn

Not sure whether I'm awake or dreaming. Grandma is standing over my bed and shaking me gently. "Get up, Riley," she says. Maybe it's a dream within a dream, maybe it's not happening at all. The gray light of morning is pouring in the window. The light feels harsh and cold. My feet are cold and my eyes drowsy. Grandma's eyes say something isn't right. I already know. I ask, "Are we going to see Mama?"

"We'll go in the wagon," says Grandma.

Fear is in my throat. I get dressed. A morning chill cuts through my clothes and I feel naked as me and Grandma climb into a wagon pulled by a horse. It's winter and nothing is growing and the fields are empty and I wonder how many people have died between this winter and last. I don't say anything and neither does Grandma. The sound of the horse's hoofs striking the ground strike my heart like a clock that won't stop ticking. My throat is dry and my nose is runny and freezing cold. I smell

29

fresh manure; here and there, the rising smoke from a furnace or fireplace turns the gray sky muddy brown. The sun is a million miles away. I wonder if I'll ever be warm again.

I don't know how long we ride—an hour, maybe two. When we get off the wagon, I'm scared to enter the little shack where no kerosene lamps are burning. Inside it's dark. A man stands beside the window, but I can't remember his face. I can't remember his name. I just remember the coldness and fear moving from my throat to my stomach. My stomach is upset and I need to use the outhouse, but I can't leave. I'm walking into the bedroom, where I can already smell the natural fragrance of my mother's skin. I know that smell so well that tears come to my eyes. Mama's eyes are half-closed; her eyes seem to be covered by a film that gives her a hazy faraway look. When I stand above her, her gaze does not meet mine. That's when I realize she's gone blind.

I think of Uncle Major and how I'll take her hand and lead her outside. I'll let her lean against me; I'll make sure she doesn't trip. We'll get in the wagon and go back home and walk to church and see Reverend Fair, who'll pray for her recovery. The whole congregation will pray and sing and the spirit will heal her body and the film leave her eyes and she'll see and laugh and live with me like she used to. I start to say this, but something inside knows better. I understand the blind don't suddenly see. I realize my mother is sick and dying. Her arms are thin as toothpicks, her body so frail it looks as though she'll break in half. She breathes heavily, and when she speaks it's with tremendous effort. When she holds out her hand to me, I take her hand in mine. Her palm is perspiring, her fingers limp. If she could squeeze my hand, she would, but she can't. As her lips move, no sound comes. She lacks the strength to push out her words. I bring my head down to her chest so I can hear her whisper. Her voice is hoarse and filled with pain.

"Kindness . . ." she says. Then her voice cracks and I can't hear the rest of her words. I want her to save her breath and not speak, but she's determined. A long time passes before the half-spoken words fall from her mouth. "People will love you if you show love to them . . . Just remember that, son . . ."

Her blind eyes can't see me, but somehow they see through me. I feel her love covering every inch of my being. I put my cheek next to hers, my ear next to her mouth. I hear her saying, "I love you, Riley." I hear myself saying, "I don't want you to go away . . . I don't want you to leave." And then she says, "I'll never leave . . . I'll always be with you . . . I'll always be your mother."

I sobbed all that morning and all that day. The man next to the window went away and Grandma stayed with me. Mama was too weak to speak anymore and Grandma urged me to leave. But I couldn't, wouldn't. I wanted to stay with her until . . . until forever.

"We need to get back," Grandma said. "It's going to be dark soon."

It stayed dark. All the lights in my life went out. I can't remember details. My mind blocked; pain and fear have dulled my memories. Mama died. They said she was twenty-five. Grandma came and told me—maybe the next day, maybe the next week. I'm sure the relatives rallied around, but I can't see them, I don't recall their words. The funeral is a blur. I've shut out the sight of my mother in a coffin being lowered in the ground. I've shut out the church service, the eulogy, the sorrow and sobbing and concern over my welfare. I just remember being with her on that gray day when she spoke those last words to me, words which feel like they're written across my heart.

What was the disease that killed my mother so young? Six years ago, when I was diagnosed with diabetes, I wondered whether Mama had the same condition. In the country, of course, modern medical care was minimal. For blacks, it didn't exist. Losing my mother left me bewildered, lost, and afraid. I felt like the world might do anything bad to me at any time. I felt unprotected. I kept seeing Mama in different ways—first as the healthy hardworking woman I'd known most of my life, then blind and weak and dying in bed. The church was a comfort—being surrounded by the music and the warmth of the congregation—but the church couldn't fill the void. Nothing could.

Grandma tried her best. But then, what seems like only a year or so later, Grandma grew weak and sick and came down with pneumonia. My memory is that she died just a little over a year after my mom. A writer looked up the records from the farm that show Grandma didn't die until five years after Mama, so maybe my memory is wrong. Or maybe those old records are wrong. Maybe someone wrote it down wrong. The memory of my heart is clear: I lost both those ladies within a very short period of time. My memory says that from ages ten until thirteen I lived alone.

This was a powerful period in my life. I'd call it a turning point. There were people who would take me in, relatives to feed or house me, comfort me as best they could. Mr. Flake's farm was a community where everyone knew everyone else and you couldn't say I was left alone. But I was alone. I was alone in my mind and alone in my spirit. I didn't want to live with relatives, didn't want to live with anyone except the memory of my mother and her mother. Couldn't stand for people to feel sorry for me—still can't—and all their pity hurt me even more. Truth is, I wanted to be alone. I wanted to stay in the little sharecropper's cabin where I'd been living since Mama moved us from the Delta. That was the only home I knew, and it was good enough for me. Anything else would feel strange.

Maybe I'd been a loner before Mama died. Maybe I was born with that temperament. But when Mama died, seems like I decided to be even more of a loner. I believe that's how I dealt with her death. I remember going over to Aunt Mima's and sitting on the floor with my ear against her Victrola. Something in the music kept pulling me in. The blues was bleeding the same blood as me. The blues didn't have to explain the mystery of pain that I felt; it was there in the songs and voices of singers like Lonnie Johnson and Blind Lemon Jefferson, in the cries of their guitars. I'd also listen to the spirituals of Sam McCrary of the Fairfield Four gospel quartet. For hours on end, I'd lose myself in the music until Aunt Mima would worry my mind wasn't right.

"Stay here, Riley," she'd say. "Live here with us."

"I can't."

"Why not?" she'd want to know.

"I just can't."

Staying in the cabin was like staying with Mama. Her smells and her memories were in the walls and the floors, in the wash-tub and the wood-burning stove. Leaving the cabin would be leaving Mama. When I think back now, I see how I could've moved in with a relative or been adopted by a family. But that felt phony. I couldn't impose on anyone else. Mama's death cut me off from the world. I had my family once and my family had been destroyed. I'd rather live with the destruction than deceive myself. As a ten-year-old, I decided to go it alone.

I had help from an unlikely source—Mr. Flake Cartledge. He was a fair-minded and liberal man. Looked like a combination of John Kennedy and John Dillinger. Handsome guy. Never heard him once use the world "nigger" or witness him abuse a worker. He'd keep evil forces like the Klan off his land. The Cartledges were respected. We were powerfully lucky that way; other plantation owners were cold-blooded racists. But Mr. Flake, seeing my attitude, helped me maintain myself. He let me live in that cabin by myself, keeping an eye on me, asking me to do personal chores for him, just like Mama had done, and to take meals with his family. His wife Thelma and his son Wayne treated me right. I was a houseboy, but he also had me working the cotton and corn fields. I'd help him grade the roads with horses—in those days, he didn't have tractors—and I never missed a day milking ten cows in the morning and ten at night. Looking back, I see I put my grief in hard work. That impressed Mr. Flake, and it allowed me to keep from crying. I hid my pain, a pattern that set me on a course for life.

I stayed busy, but I also stayed lonely. I kept loneliness close to my heart, like a secret or a shame. I felt too wounded from Mama's death to get close to other kids. Funny, but it was easier making friends with animals. Seemed like squirrels and rabbits and birds and even cows were characters I could talk to. And I did. When the empty silence of the cabin got to me, I'd go outside to a little thicket overgrown with trees and grass and bushes. I'd bring little bread crumbs and feed the field mice, who'd normally scamper away. But they were never frightened of me, and I loved lying on the ground watching 'em nibble on food while I'd tell 'em how much I missed Mama. I felt like Tarzan as a baby. Sometimes a bird would settle on my shoulder or a bunny would hop right up to my nose. Sometimes I'd give them names or make up stories like Mama made up stories for me. I might fall asleep and wake up to find a purring kitten on my stomach. No one knew I was carrying on these conversations, and that made them even more special. The animals were my buddies. I felt like they understood me.

I also learned to play alone. I'd find arrowheads in the woods that Mr. Henson said came from the ancient Indian tribes that once lived on the land. That inspired me to make up adventures about the Indians and the cowboys and secret hideouts and skirmishes and chases over the hills and through the valleys. I entertained myself with imaginary stories in a world that was completely unreal.

I was also hearing more about the real world. It was 1935, and in school I'd hear the word "Depression" and was taught that President Roosevelt was trying to do something for the poor. Having always been poor, the poverty in the rest of the country didn't mean much to me. But without Mama or Grandma around, staving off my personal poverty meant depending on myself. In the past, I'd wanted to work to please my mother and be by her side; now my motivation was pure survival. No work, no food.

I grew up fast. I learned about the wages of a sharecropper. You get your house and rent for free, and you get an allowance called a furnish, an advance against the crop you'd bring in. A big family might get $25 a month; me and Mama were getting around $10. You cultivate the land, you work the fields, you plant the seeds, you pray for a good crop. The growing season stretches from March to July, and when you start picking the cotton you split your haul fifty-fifty with the plantation owner, who's keeping all the records.

If a family made $2,000 a year, that was big money. Lots of them made nothing because lots of owners were crooked. If you were real hungry or hardworking, you could be hired out to work someone else's crop, chopping or picking for 75 cents a day or 35 cents per hundred pounds of cotton. As the years went on, I grew into a skilled cotton picker.

I also saw how the plantation was a world unto itself. The owners would tell their hands—the black folk who worked the land—that not even the law could touch them if they did their work and stayed on the plantation. Plantation bosses were absolute rulers of their own kingdoms. Sheriffs didn't like to violate their boundaries, even if it meant giving up a criminal. It gave you a double feeling—you felt protected, but you also felt small, as if you couldn't fend in the world for yourself. I could feel the old link to slavery; I knew the sharecropper system was a thousand times more fair-minded—after all, we were free citizens—but I also knew that, in some ways, sharecropping continued the slavery mentality.

When my great-grandfather Pop Davidson told stories of being a slave, he pictured himself as a hero, sassing the bosses and standing up for his rights. I always wondered whether that was just his homemade whiskey talking. Then one day I saw for myself. Seems like one of his daughters, my great-aunt, went off and married a guy who moved her to the plantation where he was working. She and her husband fought, as newlyweds often do, and she came running back home. Well, her husband didn't like that, and rather than go after her himself, he went to the most powerful man he knew, his plantation boss, to retrieve his wife.

I remember the day it happened. It was a rainy afternoon and I'd just trudged those three miles back from school. I was 'bout to start my chores up at Mr. Flake's when I heard this commotion. Folks were running over to my great-granddaddy's, talkin' 'bout how Pop Davidson had his gun and was about to blow off some boss's head. Had to see this for myself.

Well, it was quite a scene. This big white boss standing in front of Pop's shack with my great-aunt's husband by his side, not asking, but *demanding* that Pop release his daughter. She was somewhere hiding in the house. Remember, Pop had a tough time talking. Like me, he had a stutter, and he also had a temper. So when he finally did appear at his doorway, he had a Winchester in his arms and rage in his eyes.

"That woman belongs on my land," said the white boss.

"G-g-g-g-get the hell off my pr-pr-pr-property," Pop ordered.

"You ain't talkin' to no white man like that," said the white man.

And with that, Pop aimed his rifle and blasted a shot that barely missed the top of the white man's head. We ran behind trees and hid in the thickets to see what would happen next.

The white man was stubborn and kept on coming. But Pop was even more stubborn and fearless and gave him another blast, this time barely missing his feet. When the boss looked up, he saw Pop was actually foaming at the mouth. That's when he backed down.

I saw it as a victory. Made me think that a man, even an old former slave like my great-granddaddy, could keep his dignity. Sometimes I wondered about Pop's stuttering, which, like Uncle Major's, frustrated him like crazy; I wondered if a speech impediment has to do with boiled-up fury inside. Why did I stutter? Classmates were cruel and called me stupid, teasing me something fierce. But I never saw anyone tease Pop Davidson. They were scared he'd shoot 'em dead.

Later I asked Pop about the shooting incident. He said he'd be damned if anyone was gonna tell his daughter where to go. According to Pop, she was a free woman who could make her own choice without no white man giving her orders. Funny part was that she did decide on her own—to go back to the plantation with her husband.

There were times when my relatives hurt me. My cousin hurt me in a way I'll never forget. We're coming back from school, making that long walk, feeling tired and cranky and especially hungry. You know how hungry kids get after school. We stopped at his house and he asked his mom, my aunt, if he could have his dinner. "Your food's in the safe," she said. "Safe" was a closed compartment, something like a closet, where the insects couldn't get in. He reached in, grabbed his dinner, and began to eat. I waited a few seconds, hoping there'd be food for me, when he asked, "Where's your dinner?"

"Where's your dinner?" is a question that's haunted me all my life. I keep hearing it in my mind. The question cut me deep. My cousin knew there was no one at my house except me. He knew I didn't have any dinner waiting in any safe. It was his way of reminding me that I was stone alone, and too bad. I could have killed him. I could have cried. I could have complained to my aunt and screamed and sobbed and stormed outta there. I could have fallen on the floor and pounded my fists; that's how wounded and injured I felt. But me being me, I did nothing. Didn't say a word to my cousin or my aunt. Didn't give either of 'em the slightest notion that I felt like the most useless, worthless thing on earth. I watched him eat and left. I

kept the hurt inside for the rest of my life. I feel it now, sixty
years later, like it happened yesterday.

A lifetime later, I'd hear Billie Holiday sing "God Bless the
Child." The song says, "God bless the child that's got his own."
Kinfolks may offer you a crust of bread, but, baby, don't count
on it. Don't count on no one but yourself. As time went on, I've
tried to be generous with my family and friends, but I never
looked for generosity in anyone else. If it came, I was grateful;
if it didn't, I was prepared. I never again wanted to ask the
question "Where's my dinner?" and hurt like my cousin had
hurt me. I decided to make my own dinner. Either that, or
starve.

I learned another thing from the hurt my cousin gave me—
never to give that kind of hurt to anyone else. My revenge was
to change a bad feeling into a good one. If I'm working with
you and I sense you're feeling a little insecure, I try to make
you feel great. That's how I get rid of my old hurt. If I don't do
that, my hurt grows and makes me mean and vengeful. But if
hurt can change to kindness—that's something Mama showed
me—the world becomes a little less cruel.

I was good at avoiding cruelty and finding fun. When I got
to be eleven, I'd get a ride into town on Wednesday evenings.
They'd set up a projector in the middle of the main drag of
Kilmichael, close the traffic down to wagons and trucks, and
let the black field hands sit on the street and watch a movie on
an outdoor screen. It was springtime or summer and the
weather was good, maybe a light breeze and a full moon and
me looking around for whatever girl might be sitting away from
her mom or dad. I'd slide over next to her and give her a smile,
hoping she'd reciprocate. Even if I didn't get to hold her hand
or put my arm around her, maybe our knees would touch or

her arm would brush mine. Just being close to her—just feeling the heat of her skin and the scent of her body—was enough to make me weak and happy at the same time.

The movies were mainly cowboys, and I loved them. I loved Gene Autry because he did more than shoot straight and ride fast; he sang songs and played the guitar and, best of all, he got the girls. I related to Gene. When he started strumming, ladies started swooning. This was different from the raw feelings of the blues or the godly feelings of gospel; Gene showed me how music charms through softness. Cowboy music might have been white and coming from a world far from my own, but I could feel its soul. And when the girl sitting beside me would sigh and maybe rub up against me, I silently thanked Gene and made a mental note associating sensuous music with sensuous women.

Tex Ritter was also a cowboy and a singer to boot. I liked him and Wild Bill Elliott, who played Wild Bill Hickok. His serial adventures had me running to town in the middle of every week to see how he'd escape the rustler's knife or save the luscious cowgirl from the jaws of a wildcat. No one read me stories when I was a kid, but the stories on the screen did the trick; they hooked me for life. They had me loving the escape of living someone else's adventure. I liked losing myself in characters and settings a million miles away from the reality of the Mississippi hill country. During the week, I'd think about the people in the moving pictures—Dick Tracy or Fu Manchu or Tarzan—and count the days till I caught up with them again.

Music did the same thing for me. It took me away. Ever since I laid eyes on Reverend Fair's guitar, I wanted one for myself, just like I wanted a girl to call my own. Turned out guitars were cheaper. My first guitars didn't cost a cent. I copied what I'd seen other dudes do—take a strand of any kind of wire and tie it on a broom handle. When I tightened or clamped down on the string, the sounds would change and I'd think I was making music.

I got my first real guitar when I was twelve. Bought it from a man who lived around Kilmichael. Later I learned I'd overpaid—$15 was the price—but I didn't care. I was in love. It was a cherry-red Stella, an acoustic model with a short neck and a good solid sound. Mr. Flake advanced me the money. Fifteen dollars happened to be my monthly wages for working as a houseboy. So he took out $7.50 one month and $7.50 the next.

Never have been so excited. Couldn't keep my hands off her. If I was feeling lonely, I'd pick up the guitar; feel like talking, pick up the guitar; if something's bugging me, just grab the guitar and play out the anger; happy, horny, mad, or sad, the guitar was right there, a righteous pacifier and comforting companion. It was an incredible luxury to have this instrument to stroke whenever the passion overcame me, and, believe me, the passion overcame me night and day.

I'd like to say that I was able to copy my heroes, Blind Lemon Jefferson and Lonnie Johnson, and became a distinguished disciple. The truth is that I tried to copy them but couldn't. Their styles escaped me. It wasn't that their techniques were overly difficult; they were so deeply individual that imitation didn't work. I didn't sound good—or believable—as a warmed-over Blind Lemon or Lonnie. Besides, the blues isn't like painting by numbers or following the dots. The blues, I would soon learn, is something you live.

My guitar gave me new life. It helped me cope. And gave me a little discipline. Other men played the guitar—my cousin's husband, James Farr; Mama's boyfriend Edrich Basket—but they never gave me lessons. For 50 cents, though, I ordered an instruction book by Nick Manaloft from the Sears Roebuck catalog. He mainly featured country songs like "You Are My Sunshine," but that was okay. Least I had some learning method; slowly I was reading notes and playing scales.

I was also still tied to the church and didn't quite give up the notion of preaching or at least singing the gospel. I was a strong voice in the choir and was learning to use my guitar to accompany spiritual songs. Me and my cousin Birkett Davis and two classmates, Walter Doris, Jr., and Dubois Hune, started a vocal quartet. I sang lead tenor. We called ourselves the Elkhorn Jubilee Singers and tried to sound like the great Golden Gate Quartet, but didn't. We also wanted to sound like the Ink Spots, but couldn't. Their harmony was perfect and ours was shaky. We tried to recreate the parts we'd learned in church— the sound foundation of an alto, tenor, baritone, and bass—but our voices were changing. When we sang "Precious Lord" and "Working on the Building," the parishioners would wave their hands in appreciation. The church is a great support for young singers, but I had too many records at Aunt Mima's to fool myself. I knew we had a long ways to go. Rehearsals were our form of entertainment, though, and we worked hard to forge a sound that would be pleasing and true to the only tradition we knew: soul-satisfying gospel built on smooth harmonies.

Three or four years had passed since I lost my mother, and though the pain was not gone—I still feel the pain as I write this book—I wasn't crumbling or turning into a recluse. I wasn't going off the deep end. I had the normal urges of a teenager whose hormones had started to rage.

More than ever, me and the boys were eyeing the girls. That's another reason church was attractive. All the pretty girls went to church. To me they looked like angels walking the earth. And even though an angel was usually chaperoned by her mama, you might be able to walk her home after church. You might arrange a secret meeting back in the woods. Once in a great while, you might even convince her to give you a little—maybe a little feel, maybe a little more. It was rare for me to find a girl who'd agree to intercourse. And if she did, she wouldn't let me climax inside her, which is the part I liked best. Most of the sex revolved around masturbation. The boys would gather in a circle and see who could come first. I'd usually be last.

My passion for the guitar never died. When it was stolen out of the cabin a year after I bought it, I felt like I'd been whacked in the head with a shovel. Why would someone take something that wasn't theirs? I was so heartbroken, it was a long time before I got another. I didn't want to take another chance of losing something so precious. I hated living with the bitter feeling that I'd been wronged.

In the tiny universe of Mr. Flake's farm, Mr. Henson's school, and Reverend Fair's church, I was this hardworking kid trying to stay out of trouble and do right. Didn't get into many fights and didn't sass my elders. In some ways, even without parents to protect me, it was a safe world. I would have gone along for a long time without changing a thing. I like routine. I like knowing what the day will bring, what to expect and when to expect it. The one thing I wasn't expecting was my father. Yet one day, out of the blue, Albert Lee King appeared. Daddy had come to get me.

5

"You All Right, Jack?"

That was the first thing he asked.

"I'm okay," I answered.

I liked it when he called me "Jack." That was Dad's way of being affectionate. Never once in my life did he tell me he loved me. But when he said "Jack," I took it as a sign of love. He said it with warmth in his voice. "Jack" was his boy; "Jack" was someone special.

Men don't always do a lot of talking, especially between fathers and sons. Between me and my father hung a heavy silence. I don't know why, but we never had a lot to say. He was a big strong muscular man, weighing about 250, who went about his business—driving a tractor—without a word. He liked to drink but never got drunk. Never did know another man who held his whiskey like Daddy. I wouldn't call him an alcoholic because he never got raunchy, mean, or crazy behind booze. He kept his distance from me and, for that matter, from the rest of the world. Later in our lives, when I made a name for myself, I never heard him say he was proud of me. He'd brag about his son to my friends, but not to my face. He'd claim to play guitar better than me, which really wasn't true, and he'd sing the blues—always in private—in a powerful voice I admired.

Daddy was different. I'd call him a mystery. I didn't know what had happened to him during the years I lived with Mama and the years after her death. I didn't even ask him. Later I learned that he simply lost touch. He didn't know where I was. I didn't challenge him or express anger. That's not my way. And besides, Daddy wasn't the kind of man you challenged.

"You're gonna come live with me now," he said.

I was? I was gonna leave Mr. Flake's farm and everything I'd ever known for the past nine years? I guess I was. Daddy said I was. Was I excited? Sure. But I was also nervous; I didn't know what to expect.

"Got us a house over in Lexington," my father explained. Lexington was another world away. It was twice as big as Kilmichael. I didn't know a soul in Lexington. But what was I gonna do? Daddy was standing in the middle of my little cabin like the most powerful man in the world—cocksure of himself and ready to move.

"I got a borrowed truck out there," he said. "Just put your things in the back and we'll go."

Just like that? Daddy had no doubts. Just assumed I'd wanna pack up and leave. But what about my goodbyes? What do I say to my teacher and preacher and friends at school? I couldn't tell Daddy that I wanted to say goodbye to the little animals around the cabin who'd become my buddies and looked to me for food. My father wasn't the sentimental type; he didn't have a lot of patience.

So I left.

Course I said something to Mr. Flake, who told me he'd tell the others that my father had come for me. "You come back whenever you want to," Mr. Flake assured me.

I followed my father to the truck, climbed in, watched him slide into first gear and tear off. He drove with determination; he had a sense of direction. I worried about who would do my chores—the milking, the mopping, chopping weeds, and cutting grass—but I knew Mr. Flake would find someone by day's end. But who'd be living in my cabin? And what about the $15 a month I'd been earning? Where would I get money of my own?

"You got a new mama and three sisters and a brother," said Daddy as we headed southwest, winding down through the hills. That sounded great and scary at the same time. A new family waiting for me, but a family I didn't know. Nine years in one place and now everything was turning topsy-turvy. It was even closer from Kilmichael to Lexington—some fifty miles— than that first trip from Indianola to Kilmichael. But this second trip had an even longer feel to it, like I was slowly being pulled away from something close to my heart.

Maybe I expected my father to give me something I'd been missing since Mama died. But Daddy's love was completely different than Mama's. With Mama there was reassurance and comfort and the knowledge I was special. With Daddy there was strong silence, the road ahead, no stopping, no questioning, no touching. We both stared down the afternoon sun and listened as the tires crunched over the dirt road.

Lexington made me uneasy. Daddy's wife made me uneasy.

She was a nice lady named Aida Lee. Later I'd learn to call her Mama King and love her like a mother, but not initially. When the truck drove up to the house and I met her for the first time, I was startled by her resemblance to my real mother. I thought, *Daddy found him another Nora Ella.* But she didn't look at me or talk to me or touch me with Mama's warmth. How could she? I didn't come out of her body. I came on a borrowed truck.

Their house amazed me. They had electric lights; not even Mr. Flake had electricity. For the first time in my life, I was living in a place with a radio. They also had an inside bathroom with a toilet. I felt foolish because I didn't know how to flush and was too ashamed to ask. I felt like the ugly duckling.

The house was super-neat, all spick-and-span. Mama King was ticky in her ways. "Ticky" means lots of rules—your shoes go here, you can't sit there, you must wash behind your ears. Ticky made me feel out of place. Having lived alone for so long, I wasn't used to other people's rules. At the same time, being someone who hates breaking rules, I felt pressure to obey. Mainly I felt mixed-up.

We lived on a street next to white people, and that was also something new. Having a stepbrother and three stepsisters—four people who eventually became close to me—was strange at first. There was William D., Cora Mae, Barnell, and Modie Fay, each with lots of energy and personality. A whole lot was happening in that house. And making things stranger was the fact that the man who'd brought us all together was usually gone.

Daddy drove his tractor on a plantation outside of Tchula, fifteen miles away. He'd be gone all week, leaving in the dark of Monday morning and not getting back till late Friday night. Maybe he'd check on us on Wednesday night and maybe he wouldn't. If my brother and I were messing up, Daddy would grab the switch in a hurry. But William D. was better with words than me. He could talk himself out of a whipping; I never could. If I messed up, Daddy would say, "Your heart belongs to God, but your butt belongs to me." I never could talk to my father like I wanted to. On the weekends, he'd go drinking with his friends. There wasn't much time for just me and him.

Sometimes he'd take me with him to a lady who'd sell him liquor. Seems like he spent lots of time at this woman's house. I remember how she didn't shave the hair on her legs and arms, and I wondered why. Daddy would only say, "One day you'll find out about women for yourself." He never explained the birds and bees; he'd only say, "Don't get the girls pregnant." That was his approach to sex education. Sometimes he'd add, "Jack, a hard dick has no conscience."

I don't want to give the impression that I fault my father. I don't. The truth is that he's one of my heroes. He's monumental to me. I believed—and still do—that a man must stand in the door of his home and let the wolf get him before the wolf gets his family. The wolf never got my father *or* his family, and I admire Daddy's guts. He never slacked off work or lied to me or shrugged his responsibilities. He dealt with his family from a distance, but was available when needed. Eventually I'd do the same. I don't know whether I was copying him or whether, by coincidence, my work, like Daddy's, simply kept me away. All I know is that in many ways, big and small, I've followed my father.

If Kilmichael had only a couple of thousand residents, Lexington must have had five thousand. To me that was big. I enrolled at the Ambrose Vocational High School, another difficult adjustment. Elkhorn had been my only school and Mr.

Henson my only teacher. Elkhorn was tiny; Ambrose was huge. Ambrose had dozens of teachers and hundreds of kids brought in from all over. I'd never seen black kids on a school bus before. I thought we'd always have to walk to school. Only a few years before, Mr. Henson had predicted it, and now I saw it with my own eyes: black kids riding the bus.

As a stuttering boy from the backwoods, I felt like a hick. My accent was country, my clothes were torn. Had nothing but one pair of denim overalls. Same clothes I wore to work I wore to school. Other kids, with their clean shirts and nice trousers, talked clearly and expressed themselves well. I was tongue-tied. I was secretly scared of not being able to do the work. In my hidden heart, I felt over my head. If the kids belittled me, I'd let it pass. I wasn't a brawler. I remember Mama saying it's better to be used than to use someone else.

I'd escape through the radio. Two stations out of Nashville came through loud and clear. WSM played country, and I loved listening to those weeping steel pedal guitars. But it was WLAC that kept me wrapped up in the radio. They played black music. I'd sit enthralled, listening to the original Sonny Boy Williamson—Sonny Boy #1—who had a stutter worse than mine and a harmonica style that gave me goose bumps. There were no empty spots between his human voice and his harmonica voice; they were inseparable. Plus his rhythm was so rocking, you'd forget the blues he just gave you a minute ago. Those were precious moments.

There were other moments, though, of shock and pain that can't be erased from my memory. A sunny Saturday afternoon and I'm walking to the part of Lexington with the stores and the main square, I'm running an errand for Mama King, feeling the summer heat along my skin, feeling halfway happy. At least there's no school today. I'm delivering a big basket of rich folks' clothes Mama King has washed and ironed. Suddenly I see there's a commotion around the courthouse. Something's happening that I don't understand. People crowded around. People creating a buzz. Mainly white folk. I'm curious and want to get closer, but my instinct has me staying away. From the far side of the square, I see them carrying a black body, a man's body, to the front of courthouse. A half-dozen white guys are hoisting the body up on a rope hanging from a makeshift platform. Someone cheers. The black body is a dead body. The dead man is young, nineteen or twenty, and his mouth and his eyes are open, his face contorted. It's horrible to look, but I look anyway. I sneak looks. I hear someone say something about the dead man touching a white woman and how he got what he deserves. Deep inside, I'm hurt, sad, and mad. But I stay silent.

What do I have to say and who's gonna listen to me? This is another secret matter; my anger is a secret that stays away from the light of day because the square is bright with the smiles of white people passing by as they view the dead man on display. I feel disgust and disgrace and rage and every emotion that makes me cry without tears and scream without sound. I don't make a sound.

I was raised to be a good boy. In the hill country of Kilmichael, segregation was born into my blood. My mother had been strict to tell me where to go and where not to go. Lexington was even stricter. My father had pointed out a service station with three doors—one said WHITE MEN, one said WHITE LADIES, and the third said COLORED. "That's the way it is," said Daddy. He didn't explain or excuse or say anything else. That was the way of the world and I was expected to accept it.

I wasn't taught to hate white people. That dead body hanging from the platform broke the heart and wounded the spirit of every black man and woman who passed by. But I suspected that it also hurt right-thinking white people. Both parents had spoken well of fair-minded white people—my namesake, Jim O'Reilly, and Flake Cartledge—so I knew better than to blame a whole race for the rotten deeds of a few. When some blacks talked about whites as the devil, I could see the source of their wrath. I could still see the dead man outside the courthouse on the square. But I couldn't turn the fury into hatred. Blind hatred, my mother had taught me, poisons the soul. I kept hearing her say, "If you're kind to people, they'll be kind to you."

I worked off my fears. During the season, trucks would pull into town and take kids out to the fields. I picked and chopped cotton, I pulled corn, I did whatever chores came my way. I wanted money. I also wanted to do better in school, but school still made me uneasy. The principal was Professor Seal, the first man I'd seen who shaved his head clean. He was a short guy with big muscles like Joe Louis, one of my first idols. Professor Seal would talk nice while he whacked the hell out of you. He'd get a couple of the brawny football players to hold you down, lay you across a wooden barrel, pull your pants down, and beat your butt red while saying, "I hate to do this, but even a mule can learn something."

I avoided Professor Seal and stuck to Miss Thomas. She was a beautiful black woman who reminded me of Mr. Henson, patient and loving and full of information I could understand. I had a crush on her that stayed locked in my heart. No one knew. There was an older black man who had a little farm outside Lexington where I'd go work and be paid in used clothes. He'd give me some of his old shirts and pants. I'd wear them to school, hoping to impress Miss Thomas, but the shirts would swallow me whole and the pants would sag and drag and I never did feel right.

I never thought of discussing my unhappiness with Daddy or Mama King. In those days, kids didn't talk to their parents about problems. Kids weren't seen as having problems. Kids were kids. Do what you're told. Obey. Keep quiet. Looking back, I see myself as an obedient kid programmed to please. So how do I explain the fact that, after only six months of living in Lexington, I got on my bicycle and sped out of town like a bat out of hell, never to return again?

I didn't leave a note. No one—not my father or Mama King—had the least warning I was leaving. I'm not sure I knew what I was doing till I did it. Looking back, I see me like the guy who heard the train whistle blow and said, "Sorry, but I'm gone."

What was on my mind that day in the early fall of 1938? I heard a whistle in my head. I wasn't complaining or crying or bemoaning my fate. I was just moving back to where I wanted to be. Home. In my mind's eye, I always kept a vision of home, the cabin, Mr. Flake's farm, the places where I felt comfortable. The pressures of Lexington had been building: living in a ticky household where I was scared of breaking rules; living with an instant family who were really strangers to someone like me who was deeply shy; going to a school that seemed big as a factory and just as cold; feeling poorer and shabbier than the kids around me; stammering through my lessons; never liking the Lexington that displayed a dead body in front of the court-house.

The more I thought, the harder I pumped the pedals. I'd bought the bike with money earned doing chores. Other than the clothes on my back, it was my only possession, my ticket out of misery. The countryside was hilly and the ride wasn't smooth, the dirt road covered with rocks and pebbles. I was huffing and puffing and soon hungry as hell because I had only enough money for a few crackers. The trip took two days. I stopped the first night when I saw a herd of cows wander into a barn. I felt friendly toward cows and figured I could sleep there with peace of mind. Animals seemed more comforting than people.

I snuggled up and thought of what I was doing. The barn was filled with the smell of hay and manure and clean night air. I was excited to be on the move, realizing this was the first time someone hadn't moved me. Mama had said back in the Delta, "We're leaving here; we're going to Kilmichael." Then Daddy had said, "We're leaving here; we're going to Lexington." Now I was the one deciding where to go. Now I was really on my own.

I don't remember dreams, but that night my dreams had to be scrambled. The harsh light of day woke me up and had me on my way. Goodbye to the barn and cows and hello to hunger; the morning hunger was bad. I wanted to buy some crackers, but my bike needed a dime's worth of grease, which only left me enough for a bottle of Barg Big Grape soda. My stomach was empty and growling and I was feeling faint. Had to keep pedaling, though, had to make it home and move ahead with my plan to go back where I was wanted. Had to fight the aching in my legs, the shortness of breath, my heart hammering against my chest, wondering whether I'd pass out 'cause I need more than a bottle of soda pop to get me up these hills. I think of the Bible story of the prodigal son. I think I'm about to lose it and fall on my face when I remember Reverend Fair saying that

God may not come when you call Him, but He's always right on time.

Must be three, four o'clock when I see a little old black woman on her porch, just sitting and rocking. She looks so calm and gentle and I'm so hungry, I make myself get off my bike, walk up to her, and say, "Excuse me, ma'am, but I was w-w-w-w-wondering . . . well, if you have s-s-s-s-something to eat . . ."

She looks at me for a second or two. I feel her reading my eyes. Then she gets up and walks in the house and comes back with a platter of buttered biscuits and a whole quart of buttermilk. I'm here to say that no one has tasted better food anywhere in the world. The biscuits are fluffy and light and the milk thick and rich and I wolfed it down and to this day thank that woman with all my heart. Now I can make it home in nothing flat. I can deal with the hills.

Six decades later, I'm haunted by the fact that I could never find this woman again. At different times in my life, I went back to that spot on the road between Lexington and Kilmichael, looking for the lady who fed me. I wanted to thank her, give her something, tell her I hadn't forgotten. But the house was gone and the lady probably deceased. I've wondered whether she was an angel—the way she appeared out of nowhere, the generosity of her offering, the sustenance of her gift. She got me where I needed to go. If she hadn't been in that place at that time, I surely would have passed out. They'd have to find my father, and my father would have dragged me back to Lexington. The kind lady allowed me to follow my own destiny.

That destiny was—and is—more complicated than I'd imagined. Mr. Flake's farm had changed in the six months I'd been gone. He was happy to see me, but I was unhappy to learn that someone else was living in my cabin. So I thought that my great-aunt Beulah Belle Davis and her husband John Henry would take me in. Their son, Birkett Davis, had sung with me in the Elkhorn Jubilee Singers. But they were all gone, moved down around Indianola in the Delta, leaving me stranded.

I could have panicked, but didn't. Could have ridden that bike back to Lexington, but that seemed wrong. It seemed right to find my aunt and cousin in the Delta. The Delta, after all, was my original starting point, land of my birth. So it made some sense to take a reverse trip all the way back to the beginning. I was returning to my roots.

I asked Mr. Flake to get word to Daddy King that I was all right. Didn't want him to worry. I doubted if he did. We were so much alike, he probably figured where I went. At the same time, I didn't want to face him and explain. Silence suited me fine. Silence was easier than words.

Moving was easier than standing still. I worked in the fields and, within a few days, earned enough to buy bus fare. I was on my way. Once we got a little past Greenwood and the hills gave way to the flatlands, I was back in the Delta. I felt the heat of the bright sun in the big sky that spread over the fields that extended far as the eye could see. The cotton blossoms, all fluffy and white, covered the land like a carpet.

"Cotton pays good down here," said my cousin Birkett shortly after I arrived. "Stay around and you can make some money."

So I did.

6

King Cotton

n the Mississippi Delta of my childhood, cotton was a force of nature. Like the sun and moon and stars above, it surrounded my life and invaded my dreams. I saw it, felt it, dealt with it every day in a thousand ways. It's how I beat back the wolf. Cotton turned me from a boy to a man, testing my energy and giving me what I needed—a means to survive. But I did more than cope with the crop. I actually loved it. It was beautiful to live through the seasons, to break the ground in the chill of winter, plant the seeds against the winds of spring, and pick the blossoms in the heat of summer. There's a poetry to it, a feeling that I belonged and mattered. Hoeing and growing cotton has a steady rhythm; it's a study in patience and perseverance. You sweat and strain and sometimes curse the elements. The Delta mud—we call it gumbo mud—gets so damp and thick, it'll suck the soles off your shoes. It's stronger than tar, but fertile enough to make farmers rich.

Cotton didn't make me or my people rich. But cotton got us through. It moved me from one part of my life to another, and sometimes, even today, when I'm riding on a bus and gazing out over an open field, I see myself back on the plantation owned by Mr. Johnson Barrett where I worked from "can" to "can't." That's from break of day till God turns off the lights, forcing me to quit or trip in the dark. In the hills, I was out there picking with Mama and Grandma on Mr. Flake's farm, but that was child's play compared to Mr. Johnson's spread. His land was so vast, you could start walking in the morning, walk all afternoon, and still be walking while the sun set on his property. Plus, he leased another huge plantation adjacent to his own. Maybe a thousand acres in all.

I lived with my aunt and uncle, Cousin Birkett, and his sisters. Their sharecropper's house on Mr. Johnson's land, some eight miles outside Indianola, had three bedrooms and a kitchen. Still no electric lights. They let me into their life at a time when I was yearning for something stable. Maybe I wanted to show Daddy that, when it came to farming, I could work hard as him. Or maybe I just wanted to prove my independence to myself. No matter why, I was moved, motivated, and raring to go. "Put me to work, Mr. Johnson. Let me show you what I can do."

Some of my relatives wondered what happened to my religious leanings. Some asked whether I was still going to preach. Part of me still yearned to serve in the army of the Lord. But the truth is that I never got the calling. I'd heard ministers testify how they've actually heard the voice of God urge, "Come and do my work." I've never heard that voice. If I had, I wouldn't have argued. But without hearing it, I couldn't fake it.

I still wanted to do good in the world, even if Bible study didn't call to me like the cotton fields.

Mr. Johnson introduced me to those fields and proved a trustworthy teacher. There were dark-hearted racists running all over the Delta. Indianola is the birthplace of the White Citizens' Council. We were surrounded by people blinded by hatred. Yet God blessed me by putting me in the hands of another good man. Mr. Johnson was in his late forties or early fifties. He wore khaki pants, all starched and ironed, like he was on his way to church. He was Jewish and proud to tell you so. He didn't have a lot to say, but I alway felt him thinking. He wasn't the kind to yell or scold or abuse his workers, but if you did something wrong he'd eye you until you felt shame. Mr. Johnson had quiet strength. In my memory, he treated me like a son. And he did something no other owner would dare do. He hired a black man as his foreman. This was Booker Baggett.

All the other plantations had a white overseer. But for some ten years Booker ran the show for Mr. Johnson. He knew everything there was to know about planting. He also ran the supply stores, where you'd buy clothes or flour or anything else you needed. When I first met him, I was a little scared because he had a solemn face and no smile anywhere in sight. I thought, *Oh, man, this dude's gonna fry me for breakfast.* But soon I learned he was honest and fair. What impressed me most, though, was Booker's ability with a tractor. He handled that big machine like a kid's toy. I'd watch and dream about the day I could drive a tractor.

Those dreams were fueled by the mule. Me and the mule got to know each other real good. The mule was a primitive version of the tractor. I followed the mule for four long years— six months a year, six days a week, twelve hours a day. They say you average about five miles an hour walking behind the mule. Well, I've clocked a million mule miles, and I'm here to say it ain't no picnic.

I'm following the mule because the mule is plowing the land, turning the soil. The mule will shit, piss, and fart in my face—he'll do it all—and I'll keep holding him steady by the ropes. I've got him harnessed and I've got him trained. I've taught him that "Whoa" means stop; "Gee" means turn right; "Ha-hee" means left; "Git up" means go. I keep him from stopping to chew on a bush or a plant. Ever so often, I stop to give him water and food. I hate it when others abuse their mules, beating them or kicking them unmercifully. I try to be gentle but decisive. Me and the mule are in this thing together. I feel for him, and I have a feeling he feels for me.

The odors coming out of a mule could be worse. Because the mule eats only vegetation, his waste doesn't carry the stink of meat-eaters like cats and dogs. The mule is a hard worker who learns to take orders and helps me through the day. We're breaking the ground and preparing for planting, digging out the bugs and worms that'll ruin the crop. Soon as the soil is turned, birds will fly down and start picking at the worms. I like the whole cycle. I like seeing the soil go from hard to soft, ready to receive the seeds like a woman receiving a man.

No matter where I was, I looked for women—in the fields or church or school, where I studied during the months when the planting was light. Women seemed to take the edge off the roughness of life and the toughness of work. Once in a while, I'd find a female who'd be open to intercourse, but few would let me ejaculate inside. That's what I wanted. Coming inside gave the act its warmth and completion. Coming inside was the perfect climax. I had heard about rubbers, but paid them no mind and never used them. Later that bad habit would change the very nature of my life.

I fell in love at fourteen. I'll call her Angel. She was a dark-skinned beauty with big laughing eyes, a smile that lit up my day, and a body that fired my blood. We never had sex, but we kissed and hugged and took walks after church and everyone knew she was my gal. If any other dude talked to her, he was in trouble with me. Don't even tell Angel hello. I was jealous over her beauty and sweet baby ways.

Young as we were, we even talked about getting married. She said she wanted to have my babies and I said I'd love her right or die trying. I was romantic that way. Her folks liked me 'cause they saw I was a hard worker. Maybe they felt sorry for me, knowing my mama had passed on so young. Angel's mama would make potato pies that had me thinking of my own mother. It was going so well, all this love and affection, that I figured it was too good to be true. I figured right.

It was another one of those nights. A Sunday night. I'd gone up to church expecting to meet Angel. But she wasn't there, and neither was her family. I knew something was wrong, but guessed that they were sick. We had church. Preacher preached and me and my cousin sang. I prayed that Angel would arrive before the end of service, but she didn't. I felt like the others knew something I didn't, but were scared to tell me. Finally, after the benediction, someone broke the news.

Coming back to the plantation from Indianola, riding in the back of a truck, there was an accident. A car plowed into the truck, engines exploded into a fire, vehicles overturned, and Angel and her whole family were crushed to death. The news crushed me. At first I didn't believe it. It had to be another family—a case of mistaken identity. Or maybe they were simply in the hospital, where Angel would recover and be back to normal in no time. Soon, though, I saw that there was no mistake at all. Angel was gone. Her body and those of her mom and dad and brothers were brought back in bags. They'd been mutilated and placed in closed coffins so nobody could see the disfigurement. No one could know the pain I felt inside.

I don't do well with loss. Don't know how to absorb the blow. Can't figure out this mourning process: when to start, when to stop, when to pray, and when to cry. When I started crying over Angel, I couldn't stop, and I felt ashamed. Men ain't supposed to cry like babies. But I called her my baby, and now she's gone and I'm back living in a world where you could lose anyone anytime, just like that. Like my little brother. Or Mama. Or Grandma. Or Angel. Doesn't matter. Can't think about it too long or I'll die of grief. Just keep working. Keep moving on, turning the soil and readying the earth so when the burning heat of summer comes, those cotton flowers will burst open like new life, offering up blossoms ripe for plucking. Think of cotton, not of Angel. Keep the pain down. Try to forget. Work. Pick.

Picking cotton did get me back on track. On Mr. Johnson's plantation, I was one of the best. I'd get out there, work up a head of steam, and pick like crazy. I'd be excited; it was the culmination of the long growing season and also a feast for the eyes, this world of white blossoms. Around Indianola we had a kind of cotton called Delta Pinelent. The planters liked it 'cause it was good for oil, and the pickers liked it 'cause it carried a heavier seed. More weight meant more money. Me and my cousin Birkett Davis would pick side by side, both of us raw bundles of energy. We'd have contests. In one day I might pick 480 pounds. But my cousin was even better; he'd go over 500 pounds. That means we'd each make about $1.75 a day, a buck more than the flat rate. After a while we got a little cocky and, instead of heading to the fields at 6 A.M., we'd wait till the morning dew dried off the plants and start picking at eight and still wind up with 1,000 pounds of Delta Pinelent between the two of us. We were cotton-pickin' fools.

I'd been watching the cotton mature since early summer. Been plowing, chopping weeds and grass that could choke off the plant. Time had come, as the farmers say, to "lay the crop by." That's means I'd done all I could do. Cotton, you see, is fragile. I'd been protecting the crop and praying it'd come up good. From day to day, I'd noticed the itty-bitty buds expanding and forming an X before turning into flowers and then busting open into full-grown blossoms. The cotton is in the blossoms, and the cotton is the victory, the money, the success of the cycle.

I did more than work the cotton fields. I helped grow corn and soybeans. I baled hay with a combine pulled by a mule, maybe the toughest job of all. I did that, say, from July through August or September, while waiting for the cotton to mature. The cattle loved eating hay—we'd store it up as their winter food—but, man, twisting and tying raw baling wire around that stuff was murder. Later on, machines did it. Later on, in fact, machines did everything. But in the Delta of my coming up, it was still human hands getting scratched and cut and bloody and sore.

In this same late-summer down period, after we lay the crop by and before the blossoms grew, I looked for other ways to earn money. I cut wood in a sawmill. I was still a scrawny kid, but learned to pick up big logs by leveraging them with thin sticks. Older guys showed me how brains make up for brawn.

I had energy to burn and the will to work. Work seemed to keep the problems inside my head from getting any bigger. I missed Mama less when I worked; I thought less about Angel and the way she died. Work kept me sane.

I also worked hard at music. I saved up, bought myself a guitar for $20, and joined a group called the Famous St. John Gospel Singers. We weren't famous, but we wanted to be. We wanted to be like the famous Golden Gate Quartet. I traded tenor leads with N. C. Taylor. Along with the Matthew brothers—John and O. L.—and my cousin Birkett, we worked up five-part harmonies and started singing in a few churches outside Indianola. If they found out we had a guitar, some churches would cancel our show. To some, the guitar made us look like a rebel group. Later, though, when they saw our music was drawing crowds, they'd reconsider and invite us back.

Gospel music was going through a change then, just like now. Many black churches are about old-time religion; many black churches are conservative and slow to change. But gospel singers are influenced by the modern sounds of the real world. They can't help it. And the groups we loved, the modern groups, were the Soul Stirrers and the Dixie Hummingbirds, who sang "Joshua Journeyed to Jericho" and impressed us mightily. The Hummingbirds had a great guitarist named Howard Carroll and a lead singer called Ira Tucker with a voice as soulful and deep as the Deep South.

If we had the resources, we might have added a drummer or pianist, but guitar and a cappella voices were all we could manage. I thought about those famous gospel groups. I'd hear them on far-off radio stations broadcasting from Helena, Arkansas, or West Memphis, Arkansas, and I'd say to myself, *Why not us?* My first ambition outside farming was for the Famous

St. John Gospel Singers to be truly famous. Seeing it as a way to combine my love of the Lord, my love of music, and my love of money, I tried to convince myself and the other members that we could succeed in a big way. I succeeded in convincing only me.

There was the world of the country and the world of the city. I lived in the country, in the world of Mr. Johnson's plantation, and on Saturday nights I entered the world of the city. Indianola was a place apart. It had a few paved streets and a few stores where you could buy nice clothes. I still only had one set of clothes. The denim overalls with the bib and the suspenders was my outfit—work and play. That didn't make me happy. When I got to town, I longed to wear silky shirts and sharp trousers to get the feeling of the farm off my back. I still felt like an outsider, a backwoods boy who'd come to sneak a peek at city life. I stayed to myself, hardly talking to anyone or even making eye contact. Mama had taught me not to stare. At the same time, I was curious and eager to learn, dying to see whatever was new and different.

As an adult, I've read how Mississippi was the poorest and most racist of all the states. I've heard it described as dangerous and evil. I'm not here to defend Mississippi or argue with the attacks, which are surely justified. All I can do is testify to my emotions as a teenager cautiously looking to widen my experience. I got by in the world of Mississippi.

Indianola, Mississippi, had a movie theater. Whites sat in the balcony and blacks sat below until white kids started throwing candy at our heads. Then the positions got switched to protect us black kids. Sitting upstairs, looking down at the big screen, I was wrapped up in the adventures of my old cowboy heroes, not to mention the Phantom and the Three Musketeers. There might also be a short film—they called them soundies—with black entertainers like Cab Calloway or Louis Armstrong or Fats Waller. They were wonderful. Around town you'd also find the ten-cent vendor, a primitive screen attached to a projector that, for a dime, showed three-minute music pieces. I suppose you could call them early videos.

Ten-cent vendors widened my world by showing me a film clip of a white man playing the clarinet and, behind him, a black man playing the guitar. Standing glued to that tiny screen, my heart thumping inside my chest, my foot stomping the floor, my head nodding, and my ears tingling, I heard Benny Goodman play "King Porter Stomp" and "Sometimes I'm Happy" and "Let's Dance." On certain songs, the guitarist, Charlie Christian, soloed in a manner that blew off the top of my head. His technique went beyond my Sears Roebuck instruction books. He took me to a new place; he played and phrased like a horn—a sax or a trumpet—that, in turn, played and phrased like a singer. Any way I looked at it, I was in love. Christian played free and fast and swung his ass off.

Swing was the thing. Swing got me so excited, I'd put in another dime and watch and listen all over again. Later I'd learn Christian used something called diminished chords, but at the time all I heard was this unusually gorgeous sequence of notes that seemed to stretch my ears. I was amazed, happy, and encouraged to see he was black—a black man in a white jazz band. In a few more years, I'd also learn that another black man, Fletcher Henderson, wrote Goodman's arrangements. Those arrangements fascinated me—the happy play between the trumpets and the saxes, the rhythm riding under and over every inch of the music. Charlie Christian was smack-dab in the middle of it all, a miracle man doing things to a guitar I never imagined possible. He pointed to a musical world outside Blind Lemon Jefferson and Lonnie Johnson.

Jazz was a new world, and jazz came to Mississippi. In Indianola, Church Street was the action street; Church is where Johnny Jones owned a nightclub called the Jones Night Spot. Other than Joe Louis, Johnny Jones was the only black man written up in the white newspaper for doing something good. He donated money to the armed forces. Without knowing it, he also donated to my musical education.

On Saturday nights, Mr. Johnson provided a truck to haul the workers back to the plantation. But the truck left at 5 P.M., and if I wanted to sneak a listen at the Jones Night Spot, I'd have to walk the eight miles home. Trudging eight miles along a dark country road on a sticky night in August or a freezing downpour in December might sound like a high price for a little music, but, man, this boy was more than willing to pay.

It was the end of the 1930s, the start of 1940s, and music was changing. I was fifteen and loved music in any form, from Grandpa Jones's banjo on the Grand Ole Opry to bluesmen like Tampa Red or Blind Boy Fuller or Big Boy Crudup. I played the guitar whenever I could and tried, unsuccessfully, to copy the musicians I admired most. I wasn't very discriminating—then or now. I'm a fan first. I believed Duke Ellington when he said there's no bad music, just some of it is presented badly. As a kid, hanging around Church Street, the presentation of music was so powerful, I couldn't help but jump for joy. I had discovered art, or truth, or whatever you want to call it; I had seen a light I'd follow forever.

I could see the lights in the Jones Night Spot through the cracks in the side wall. Too young to gain admittance, I'd press my head against the slats and peep inside. Women in tight dresses of red and yellow and baby blue dancing with men all decked out in big suits and ties and wide-brimmed hats. Must be three or four hundred people jammed in there. Folks were dancing in the street, even before they walked into the club. Dancing close, dancing sexy, dancing an inch away from my eyeball, where I could see the curve of a hip or the point of a nipple, smell the perfume and the smoke circling the room over the bandstand where—and this was the best part—Count Basie played.

I'd heard Count Basie on the radio; I knew the band came from Kansas City and sounded good. But listen here: This was better than good. With brass blaring and saxes moaning, they played "One O'Clock Jump" and "Jumpin' at the Woodside" and "Taxi War Dance" and had a short man fat as Santa Claus singing "Evil Blues." Later I'd learn the singer was Jimmy Rushing, Mr. Five by Five. He had a high nasal voice that brought home his message. I think of him now as the Henry Ford of the blues, one of the true inventors. I ran my eye over the band members dressed in matching green suits—the saxist holding his horn horizontally was Lester Young, the light-handed rhythm guitarist Freddie Green, the bass player Walter Page, the drummer Papa Jo Jones. In a few years, I'd read these names in magazines. As a teen, though, I could only identify the round-faced man at the piano as Count Basie and the music he projected as modern and swinging and beautifully loud, as bluesy as anything I'd heard in the Delta. I believe I listened harder than anyone in the history of listening.

That was one night at the Jones Night Spot. Other nights brought in boogie-woogie piano players like Pete Johnson. I knew his records with Joe Turner, the great blues shouter from

Kansas City. Some older folk looked down on boogie-woogie as nasty and radical, but I loved its rocking rhythm and amazing technique. Boogie-woogie piano players were virtuosos of the highest order. They were a one-man band, playing percussion, bass, melody, and improvising all at the same time.

On one night I heard another band from Kansas City, Jay McShann, who had a tremendous blues singer named Walter Brown and a fiery alto saxist called Charlie "Bird" Parker. I didn't know then that Parker would reinvent jazz or that one day we'd cross paths. All I knew was that this form of jazz mixed with blues made me happy. Hearing Walter Brown sing "Confessin' the Blues" and "Hootie Blues" got me high.

I also heard the naked blues at Mr. Jones's establishment, even as I mentally undressed the fancy women dancing inside. When Sonny Boy Williamson played—this is Sonny Boy #2, who took the name from the original Sonny Boy—the gals seemed to get more excited. I studied their backsides like a scientist studying a slide under a microscope. They didn't call him King of the Harmonica for nothing. Sonny Boy's real name was Rice Miller, and he was a big dude who blew the blues out of that sucker until there was nothing left to blow. He played sitting down, using his feet like a drum—stomping loud and hard—shouting and inhaling and exhaling on his harp like his life was on the line. He also had a partner called Robert Jr. Lockwood who made the guitar cry and scream. I'd be standing there for hours, unable to move or look away, no matter how sore my head would get from leaning against the slats. I was the cat peeping into the seafood store. Fine foxy women were everywhere.

I'd also see fine foxy women at the rabbit foot shows. They weren't as sophisticated as the jazz or even the blues at the

Jones Night Spot, but, man, they were fun. There'd be pretty black girls with pretty shapes dancing in a tent on the edge of town. There'd be black comics and black bands and food I'd never tasted before—cotton candy and hot dogs with red-hot peppers. There'd be bawdy ladies who looked a little like Ma Rainey or Bessie Smith with flowing scarves and jeweled hats and long feathers and fabulous furs. They'd strut and shake and sing down-and-dirty blues about getting what they want from a man. I might still have been a boy, but these ladies gave me the feelings of a man. The blues were part of those feelings— Count Basie's blues or Sonny Boy's blues or the blues belted out by the sugar mamas at the rabbit shows. Like the soil, the blues were all around me. And on that long walk back to the plantation—all eight miles—I'd still hear those blues; under the glow of a white Mississippi moon, I'd sing the blues out loud, singing to the birds or the squirrels or to God above, singing because my heart was happy.

7

Dream Machine

had dreams as a kid. Wanted to preach, wanted to sing,
wanted to play guitar and travel with our gospel group.
Wanted a woman to love on and a sense of comfort. Wanted
ways to improve my lot in life. But even though my dreams
might be a little lofty, I was down-to-earth. The earth of Mr.
Johnson Barrett's plantation was my means of sustenance. And
along with my dreaming nature, I tried to stay practical. Tried
to apply common sense to problems and predicaments. So
probably my first dream to come true was the most practical,
one that dealt with the land, my first steady source of money.
I dreamt of being a tractor driver.

Because my father drove a tractor, and because I saw him
high in the seat commanding the massive machine, I associated
tractors with big men doing important work. Because Booker
Baggett was our foreman, and because he commanded the
troops from the seat of a tractor, I had another positive picture

of someone I admired behind the wheel. Then there were women. Women looked up at tractor drivers as special men. I wanted to be special and, God knows, I wanted anything to draw females to me. The last—and most important—factor was salary. I was a guy who'd work for less than $1.00 a day, so to hear about tractor drivers making $22.50 a week was another dream.

That dream came true. And it made me feel like a superstar. I had a loftier view of the world, a powerful engine at my control, and a way to work even faster. Driving the tractor, I never forgot the mule. The contrast was amazing. The mule shit; the tractor hummed. The mule plowed one row at a time; the tractor plowed four at once. The tractor had a gearshift and clutch and accelerator that responded to the touch of my foot by crunching forward or grinding back. The tractor was a big toy for a kid who never had toys. The muffler pipe set on top of the engine, and during the summer the exhaust fumes would get burning hot and make me dizzy. In the winter, though, those same fumes were welcome heat; my back would be cold, but my face would be warm.

Tractors were used for everything, not just hoeing and chopping, but hauling feed or fertilizer or giving someone a ride, like a pretty girl, back to her house. Where dozens and dozens of mules had been used before, it now only took nine tractors to plow the big plantation. To be one of the nine drivers was like being in an elite bomber squadron. Booker Baggett was a great guy to have as my leader and teacher. He was patient in letting me learn and precise about how to maintain the machine. I wasn't good at schoolwork, but I did have a knack for picking up mechanics. I could even do some repairs. I was driven to drive.

Even though I appreciated the beauty of the land from the ground up, the landscape of the cotton fields was even more beautiful from the higher point of view. On a frosty February morning, I'd climb up on the tractor and, as far as the eye could see, look over acres and acres of hard soil. I grew excited at the idea that, by sundown, I'd turn the brittle land into something soft and receptive. As I shifted gears and started plowing, I'd watch the earth turn over. I liked the smells of the cold morning air and the hot engine's fumes; I liked looking at the uncovered dirt, the fat worms and the crawling bugs, the hungry birds flying overhead, the clouds in the sky, the changing light of day, the sound of the hardworking motor, this sense of accomplishment sweeping over me. I wanted to be the best tractor driver. I wanted that $22.50 at the end of the week and a pat on the head from Booker Baggett and Mr. Johnson Barrett. "Riley," I wanted to hear them say, "you're doing a helluva job."

As much as I wanted to stay and plow, I also wanted to travel and sing. I wanted both. The Famous St. John Gospel Singers were sometimes hired as opening acts for big-time programs in the area. If the Pilgrim Travelers, for instance, were playing in nearby Leland, we'd sing a song or two before them. When I saw the Travelers, with their matching suits and two-toned shoes and slicked-back hair, I heard them talkin' 'bout being in St. Louis or traveling to Chicago. I saw how gospel groups can get so popular until the members don't need day jobs. Living off music seemed better than living off the land. I'd say to the guys in our group, "Maybe we could take off after the crop's been picked and start traveling." Because saving was practically impossible, the guys were still living hand-to-mouth and were reluctant to leave. So our circle of churches stayed close to Indianola, and I felt stuck.

At the same time, I felt determined to make more money and did something that surprised even me. On some Saturdays, before the action got going at the Jones Night Spot, I'd find a corner off Church Street, sit on the curb, take out my guitar, and play some gospel songs, accompanying myself while singing "Old Rugged Cross" or "Working on the Building" or "I Know the Lord Will Make a Way." I'm looking for a way to draw attention and maybe make a little money. I'm singing with feeling and strumming with convinction. I don't stutter when I sing, so singing is easier than speaking. If people pass by without noticing me, I'll sing or strum a little louder, raise my voice a little higher, hoping someone will stop. A man does. He's dressed nice and clean and listens for a short while. He likes what he hears and hums along. This is going good. I'm feeling good, the song's flowing out of me, and the man is smiling and feeling the spirit. When I'm through, he's pleased. "Praise the Lord," he says. "Praise the Lord," I repeat, looking to see what he'll do next. "You can sing, son," he adds. "Thank you, sir," I say. "Well, keep up the good work," he tells me before patting me on the shoulder and strolling off. No tip.

I keep up the good work. I sing other hymns and spirituals and gospel tunes for other passersby—men, women, blacks, whites. Several folks seem to like me. But, like the first man, their tips take the form of praise. They say my voice is good or my guitar is sweet, but nothing comes out of their pockets. I appreciate their sentiment, but I'm looking for more than goodwill. Then I have this idea.

Change my attitude. Make a slight move from the sanctified to the secular. I strum a little blues I heard Sonny Boy playing last Saturday night at the Jones Night Spot. I remember half the words and make up the other half. Something about my baby done left me and I'm feeling down; yes, she done left me and I'm feeling down; Lord knows, this here is a mighty lonesome town. Then I start singing how when she loved me, she loved me good; say, when she loved me, the woman loved me good; but now I'm the laughingstock all 'round my neighborhood. Thing about blues is that blues are simple. You sing one line; you repeat that line; and then rhyme your third line with the first two. They call it the twelve bar blues 'cause each of those lines is four bars. That's it. In that basic form, though, you can cram a lifetime of stories 'bout the woes and wonders of earthly love. Everything fits into the blues.

"Sing those blues, son," says the same man who earlier praised my gospel song. It's later in the afternoon, but I'm the same and he's the same; only difference is that "my Lord" has turned into "my baby." When I'm through with my blues, he's smiling like he was before, he's patting me on the shoulder, but—and this is one hell of a big "but"—he's reaching in his pocket and looking for change. "Keep singing, son," he says as he slips me a dime.

That was my first lesson in marketing. I saw something about the relationship between money and music that I'm still seeing today. Real-life songs, where you feel the hurt and heat between man and woman, have cash value. I took note. I started coming to town every Saturday and spent my afternoons on that curb, singing as many blues as I could remember—and making up the rest. From 1 P.M. to nine that night, I might make $10 or even more. Confidence made me a better singer, and people tipped bigger when I sang with more conviction. Before long, I might walk that eight miles home with the loud jingle of heavy coins in my pocket. I was astounded, delighted, and determined to keep it up.

I kept up with church, with the St. John Singers, with my heavy-duty tractor driving, and with whatever extra work I could find. But I did not keep up with school. I dropped out in the tenth grade. I have no excuses, only regrets. My head was swimming with the lure of music and money, with hauling that tractor all over the plantation and eyeing the girls while hoping the girls were eyeing me. School felt like a burden. I knew if Mama was around, she wouldn't approve of my leaving.

Once in a great while, my father came through Indianola. We'd see each other for a quick minute. I wanted him to be proud of me. I'd tell him what I was doing, and if he said, "Glad to see you're working, Jack," that "Jack" told me he cared. He didn't praise, but he also didn't scold me for quitting school.

Years later, I'm still scolding myself. The longer I live, the more I see how I shortchanged myself. Some people have said that I'm even obsessed with my lack of education. I hate that I never went to college. I wish I had had more patience and commitment to improving my fundamental skills. I feel like I'm missing a component—a way of understanding the world— that only more schooling could have provided. But at sixteen or seventeen, I was who I was—an energetic kid whose energy was tied to work in the real world. That meant planting and playing songs, with little time for anything in between.

I was this skinny kid with his own corner on Church Street in Indianola, my hopes in the hat by my side. The sound of coins dropping in the hat kept me singing and thinking I might have the right feel for the blues. At the same time, I went with the St. John Singers to Greenwood, Mississippi, where, for the first time, I sang on the radio. T. M. Mitchum, who owned a furniture store, had his own Sunday program. We'd advertise the store and sing gospel for fifteen minutes. It was nothing but a bare room with a microphone in the middle. We were nervous, but we must have been effective because soon we were selling the Lord as well as furniture for Mr. Mitchum every Sunday at 3 P.M. It was more prestigious than singing on the streets, and when we sent our flyers to the churches, they said: STARS OF RADIO STATION WJPR.

On my own, I was reading music a little better than before, studying my practice books and expanding my circuit. If you think of Indianola as the hub of the wagon wheel, the other little towns lay out along the spokes. Riding the bus or hitching to Sunflower or Belzoni or Berclair, I'd see the chain gangs and feel lucky I hadn't fallen into trouble. Playing and singing blues on the streets and going home with halfway decent change, I was grateful. On the other hand, I didn't feel that a blues singer, especially someone with his hat in his hand, got any respect, even though I myself respected the music and musicians who played blues best. I considered them geniuses.

My mother had filled my heart with a love for a compassionate God. Gospel songs sang of that love. And, God knows, I loved singing gospel. I've heard that black folks are supposed to have this big conflict between singing for the world and singing for God. Some of them surely are divided. I am not. I liked Robert Johnson, the blues singer from Mississippi who they claim traded his soul to the devil for musical talent. But I consider that story bullshit. I would never trade my godly feelings for anything. And in my mind, no blues artist ever has. That myth also makes it seem that blues talent is tainted talent. I don't believe that. I believe all musical talent comes from God as a way to express beauty and human emotion.

Robert Johnson died in Greenwood in 1938. They say he

was messing with the woman of another man, who poisioned him. Johnson wasn't even twenty-seven. His legend has grown. I know his music touched many people like Elmore James and Muddy Waters and Johnny Shines. Because his music was made so close to my home—and exactly during the age of my growing up—you'd think I'd be under his spell. But I wasn't. He didn't speak to me with the power of Lonnie Johnson or Blind Lemon. I listened to Robert Johnson and I liked him, but that was all.

We all have our different paths. Mine would follow blues, but never at the expense of personal beliefs. I played blues first because I love blues, second because people love blues, and third because blues began loving me. When blues began paying, and when the other St. John Singers still wouldn't go to a big city like Memphis to find fame, I gave the blues even more of me. Then something happened that changed my musical life: I heard T-Bone Walker.

I loved how Lonnie and Blind Lemon and many others played guitar. I was—and still am—a student of the instrument. I was fascinated by the sound. I liked most everything I heard. But when I heard Aaron "T-Bone" Walker, I flat-out lost my mind. Thought Jesus Himself had returned to earth playing electric guitar. T-Bone's blues filled my insides with joy and good feeling. I became his disciple. And remain so today. My greatest musical debt is to T-Bone. He showed me the way. His sound cut me like a sword. His sound was different than anything I'd heard before. Musically, he was everything I wanted to be, a modern bluesman whose blues were as blue as the bluest country blues with attitude as slick as those big cities I yearned to see. Later I'd learn that, as a kid, T-Bone had led

Blind Lemon Jefferson around Dallas. I liked knowing that two of my idols were linked so tight.

"Stormy Monday" was the first tune. "They call it Stormy Monday," sang T-Bone, "but Tuesday's just as bad." Yes, Lord! The first line, the first thrilling notes, the first sound of his guitar and the attitude in his voice was riveting. I especially loved "Stormy Monday"—and still sing it today—'cause it's the true-life story of a workingman. He talks about the week-long routine, payday ("the eagle flies on Friday"), partying on Saturday, and falling down on your knees and asking the Lord's mercy on Sunday.

T-Bone had a single-string style that, like Charlie Christian's, reminded me of a horn. His blues approach was deadly, but you could tell he knew jazz. Jazz was in his blood. He'd cut off the notes and leave spaces between phrases that took my breath away. When he played, you felt his personality: edgy, cool, and a little dangerous. His guitar could cut you like a lethal weapon or stroke you like a sweet-talking love letter. And when he sang, he made you feel the story was strictly between you and him.

Mostly, though, T-Bone's guitar had a voice of its own. The voice was high-pitched, sweet, sassy, and sexy as a slinky woman. Just as surely as if he were talking to you, T-Bone spoke through the strings and amplifier attached to his guitar. He was electric in more ways than one. Electricity coursed through my body when I heard the man play. His sound was branded in my head. And his arrangements—a sax or muted trumpet whispering in his ear, a couple of quiet horns repeating a haunting refrain—were models of simple grace.

T-Bone was from Texas, and I didn't get to see him when I was a kid. I studied his pictures, though, and saw that he held the edge of his guitar against his stomach and played with an outward stroke. I held it flat against my stomach. I tried to change to T-Bone's style, but it didn't work. Felt awkward. T-Bone was also a showman, doing splits onstage and playing behind his back, tricks I could never manage. He was a short guy—handsome, sophisticated, and self-assured—who wore elegant clothes. I imagined he lived the life I wanted to live.

Like many guitarists coming up in the late thirties and early forties, I tried to copy T-Bone's sound. I couldn't. And because I couldn't, I had to keep working until, by accident or default, I developed a sound that became me. I'm not entirely settled with that "me" sound today. See, T-Bone's sound was completely individual. Couldn't be no one but him. It was as much part of him as his liver. I've strived for that feeling. I've heard a sound in my head something like a whining Hawaiian or country-and-western steel pedal guitar. I've attempted to duplicate that twang or vibrato or cry. I've been haunted by it, but I'm not certain I've been able to capture it. I've also been haunted by the harmonies I first heard in Reverend Archie Fair's sanctified Church of God in Christ in the hills of Kilmichael. I've tried to integrate all those sounds into my music. But style is a funny thing. If I saw it walking down the street, I wouldn't know it till I heard it. When I heard T-Bone, though, I knew that nothing about guitar blues would ever be the same. I didn't know this man—I wouldn't meet him till years later—but I felt T-Bone Walker leading me into the future.

8

War and Peace

've learned love can be war. The love between a man and woman can be hell. Misunderstandings and jealousy can run wild. But love can also be heaven. I believe in love and have lived my life accordingly—chasing after it, falling in front of it, tripping over it, getting it right, but just as often getting it wrong. As a teenager, I'm not sure I did a great job of separating love from lust. As an adult, I've had the same problem. As a man, I believe that the two are mixed together. Sex is the drive that led me to love. I've loved sex as much as anything in this world. Far as I'm concerned, if there's anything better than sex, they haven't brought it down here yet.

As a tractor driver, sex was always on my mind. It didn't take much to get me going. If I drove past a girl picking cotton, I'd notice the way she bent down. The way her buttocks outlined the back of her dress could fire me up for hours. On a scorching summer day, the sight of beads of perspiration on a soft feminine neck would arouse my imagination. Sometimes it was obvious—a woman with excitingly large breasts. And sometimes it was subtle—a lady with a pretty smile. The lady with the prettiest smile I'd ever seen was called Martha Lee. She was a light-skinned beauty, beautifully built, with big legs, a small waist, and heavy hips. I longed for her.

Martha lived farther up the hills in Eupora, Mississippi, the same region where Cousin Bukka White came from. Her brother John came down to work on Mr. Johnson's plantation and became my friend. When his mother came to visit him, she brought her daughter Martha Lee. We met in church.

Church was a wonderful meeting place. It seemed safe and holy and calm. People felt friendly and blessed; in church you could extend your hand and enjoy a fellowship of the spirit. Women were friendly. Their mothers told them it was perfectly all right to make the acquaintance of a young man, as long as he demonstrated good manners. I like manners. I like greeting women in a gentlemanly way. Feels good to pay them respect. Courtesy smooths out the nervousness of first encounters. And because I sang and played guitar in church, I enjoyed a little status.

As a teenager, I still stuttered, but less so. I couldn't call myself totally confident—I don't feel totally confident even today—but I wasn't hiding in the corner. I'd picked ten thousand pounds of cotton and driven ten thousand miles atop the tractor. I'd accomplished something. After losing my mama and grandma, I hadn't completely fallen apart or starved to death.

I felt starved, though, for love and affection. I couldn't— and still can't—get enough of both. Martha offered me both. Even though I wanted sex, I wasn't insistent with Martha. I couldn't be; she was determined to stay a virgin until marriage.

Besides, we'd never even use the word "sex." Even "funky" would be far too crude an expression. Church kept us in line. And I liked the fact that she was a church girl. Back then, people said church girls made the best wives.

How did I fall in love? What did I know about love? At sixteen or seventeen, I was moved by the way the moon bathed the fields in silver light. It was summertime, and Martha had come down to help her brother gather his crop. During the day, I'd see her picking cotton. She'd nod to me as I drove by on the tractor. I'd nod back and offer a smile. She'd stay on my mind all afternoon. I wouldn't be seeing the rows and rows of white blossoms; I'd be seeing Martha. When night came, I might walk by her brother's house, where she was staying, just to say hello. "Beautiful evening, Miss Martha," I'd say. "It is beautiful," she'd agree. "Care to go for a little walk?" "I wouldn't mind."

At first I didn't even dare to hold her hand. That would have been too bold. She was a shy girl, and I worried that my aggressiveness would scare her away. We walked to a little wooded patch and I watched as she leaned against a tree. Even in a loosely fitting dress, I could see her body was beautiful. "Are you tired from picking all day?" I asked. "I like working with my brother," she answered. We talked about John for a while, about the differences between Indianola and Eupora, about a song I sang in church and the Famous St. John Gospel Singers. I opened up my heart, telling her how I dreamt of playing my music outside Mississippi. I expressed my frustration that the other St. John Singers weren't as willing as me to leave the plantation.

Without speaking, she seemed to understand. Her smile said so much. Her smile seemed to blend with the sweet scent of the evening breeze. I couldn't tell whether I was smelling flowers or the natural perfume of Martha's skin. I walked her back to John's and still didn't hold her hand. "Saturday," I told her, "I'm driving the tractor to town. If you'd care to come along, I'd be pleased." The silence that followed felt like a lifetime. Her answer would tell whether she liked me or not, whether I was someone she only tolerated or actually wanted to be with. I tried to act cool, but the silence went on forever. Finally she said, "I'd love to come." And I walked home whistling.

Saturday came. The sun was boiling hot. I worked the tractor hard in the morning and by noon was ready to roll. I had cleaned myself up and drove the tractor to the spot where other workers would jump on the wagon I was hauling into town. The seat next to me in the cab, though, was saved for Martha. When I saw her coming down the road, I could swear she was skipping. My heart was sure skipping when I saw her smile. Her smile warmed me from the inside out. I helped her into the cab and, as I drove the dirt roads into Indianola, she sat quietly. From time to time, we caught each other's secret glances. I think we were both embarrassed and thrilled and maybe a little confused about how strongly we felt. We tried looking straight ahead, but our eyes kept going back to each other. I wanted to reach out and touch Martha's hand, but I didn't. I was still scared of blowing it. Still wanted to be cool.

We walked around Indianola and looked in the window of the general store. Martha saw a bolt of yellow fabric she liked and went inside to ask the price. It was too expensive. I could tell she was a little down. I had my guitar with me and asked her whether she would mind listening while I played on that corner of Church Street where I'd often performed. I guess I wanted to show off. Even though it was a sunny Saturday, I played "Stormy Monday," trying to sound like T-Bone. To my ears, it didn't come out right, but several folks stopped and listened and dropped something in my hat. Within thirty minutes, I had a nice little pile of money. Walking back past the general store, I went inside. "What are you doing?" asked Martha. "Wait here," I said, "and you'll see." A few minutes later, I walked out with the yellow fabric. "You shouldn't have," she said. "I wanted to," I explained, handing her the pretty material. Her smile was all the thanks I needed.

A month passed. We'd seen each other Sunday nights at church and in the fields during the week. But the best times were Saturday afternoons. On this particular Saturday, we rode in the wagon with the other hands. I wasn't driving. We had a good time in town, sipping on lemonades and looking in the stores. I played on Church Street, earned good money, and, when it was time to head back, decided to ask her, "Would you like to hear some real good music tonight?" "We'll miss our ride," she said. "I told your brother we might be back late," I assured her. "I guess it's okay," she said, and we stayed.

We ate chicken and greens and chocolate cake in a little café where black people cooked and ate and mingled together. I felt grown up. I would have liked to have taken Martha by the arm and escorted her into the Jones Night Spot, but we were still too young. We were only seventeen. We didn't have the right clothes. But I did take her around the side where the holes in the slats of the rickety walls let us peep in. She saw what I saw. And even better, she heard what I heard. That was a special night, not only because Martha was by my side, but because it was the first time I saw Louis Jordan and His Tympany Five. I'd heard his records on KWEM in West Memphis when he played with the Chick Webb big band. I knew about his funny songs and his witty ways, but seeing him through the peephole was incredible—his big bug eyes, his golden alto sax, his strut onstage. He sang "Knock Me a Kiss" and "I'm Gonna Move to the Outskirts of Town" and "What's the Use of Getting Sober When You Gonna Get Drunk Again." Me and Martha, we were laughing up a storm, tapping our feet, having a great time look-ing at all the dancing couples dressed to the teeth, smooching and swinging to the music, when I felt good enough to turn to my girl and kiss her. Her mouth against mine was so soft and sweet that the kiss went on a long, long time.

We found a ride back to the plantation. With Louis Jordan's happy music ringing in our ears, we cuddled close and snuck kisses. We couldn't keep our hands off each other. I wanted her bad, but I understood her character and knew to wait. In front of her brother's house, I said, "Martha, you know I feel, baby. You know I love you." Then she said it: "Well, Riley, I love you too." And then I asked it: "Will you marry me?" This time the silence didn't last long. Her answer was yes.

Six months later, we were married in the courthouse. It was wintertime, and we stood in front of the justice of the peace. Just me, Martha, and a witness. Neither her mom nor my dad were present. No party, no honeymoon. That's how it was done in those days. Many of our friends were getting married, and we wanted to be married too. Marriage seemed like another transition from being a boy to being a man. I wanted to be a man. It didn't matter that we had no money for tuxes or gowns or champagne or fancy white cakes. We had ourselves and our raw love and a little cottage we'd picked out on the plantation. Mr. Johnson helped set us up. Our relatives helped us furnish the place with a bed and a dresser and a table to eat on.

We didn't talk of starting a family, but we naturally assumed we would. We were still teenagers, still naive kids, eager to finally enjoy the physical pleasures we'd so long resisted. And enjoy them we did. Martha was beautiful in bed, and I was beginning to believe I'd found the peace of mind missing since Mama's death. I loved the idea of having kids and being a daddy. Family planning or birth control were foreign concepts. We would let love lead us. We would live happily ever after.

All through the late thirties, I'd heard talk of war. Mr. Johnson would discuss it, and we'd talk about it among ourselves. Even when war broke out in the early forties, it seemed far away. Hitler fighting Russia or Britain bombing Germany didn't have much to do with us on the plantation. But at the end of 1941, when the Japanese hit Pearl Harbor, the war got close. A lot of the guys on the plantations had been drafted or volunteered. Like everything in our world, the army was segregated, but we saw it as a chance to travel. That alone was exciting. Most of us had never been out of Mississippi. We also heard that you could buy cigarettes and beer dirt cheap at the army canteen. I'd begun smoking and drinking a little, so that was good news to me. I switched from roll-my-own cigarettes to Camels.

Beyond the lure of escaping the farm and bargain-priced booze, there was this sense of manhood among the field hands. Men went out and cut timber, even if it was raining and storming. If you mashed your finger, you kept cutting the wood. You didn't complain or cry. If the tractor got stuck in the mud, you pushed it out with your bare hands, no matter how long it took. Your skin might be bleeding sore from picking cotton, but you kept picking. So if you're called into the army, you go.

I registered when I turned eighteen in 1943. In 1944, not

long after I married, I was called to Camp Shelby, which is in Hattiesburg, Mississippi, more than two hundred miles south of Indianola. For me, it was like going to Paris, France. I was ready. Martha was concerned, but she understood. She had patience and faith in our future. She knew I wanted to serve. Some friends said that my marriage would help keep me out of the army, but I wanted in. For years I'd been hungering to see the world, and this was a righteous reason to take off. We'd also been taught that the black soldier enjoyed greater freedom than the black civilian. The uniform was supposed to give you respect. Naive or not, we truly believed that. And as a black man—or, for that matter, as a human being—I wanted respect.

A bus filled with black men filled with expectations pulled out of Indianola early one morning. I looked back and waved to Martha, watching her get smaller and smaller as we headed south. A tractor driver was plowing a field under a cloudy sky. I watched as the metal teeth cracked and turned over the earth. What was I doing on an army bus? Why wasn't I out there myself? My world was changing—hopefully for the better, but processing the change was new and strange. I wanted to see new and strange places, even if they were dangerous. I didn't even consider being killed. Didn't believe it would happen to me. I was on an adventure. My country finally called me; it felt good to know that my country needed me. I thought of Mr. Luther Henson and lessons learned at the Elkhorn School. I thought of the idea of democracy and equality.

A couple of hours later, we passed a field of white workers. A couple of pretty girls were standing close to the road. One of our guys from the bus yelled out in a friendly enough tone, "How y'all doing?" The girls looked up and smiled, not in the least offended. The bus rolled on. In Jackson, we stopped for

lunch at a black café. But before we could get off, a white man
with a rifle got on. His eyes were on fire. He was enraged.
Before a word was spoken, I knew what had happened. He'd
been back in the field when our guy yelled to the white girls.
Now he was looking for blood.

"Okay," he said, "which one of you niggers was screaming
at the girls?"

We looked straight ahead, none of us uttering a sound.

"All right," he went on, "I'll just start shooting you coons,
one by one, till you give up the man."

A couple of white officials were on the bus. They were our
escorts to camp, but they did nothing to interfere. So much for
equal protection in the U.S. Army.

The man slowly made his way up the aisle, jabbing his rifle
into everyone's neck. When he got to me, I felt the cold metal
of the gun barrel against my Adam's apple. I didn't blink. Didn't
swallow. I was sweating bullets inside, but I didn't want to give
him the satisfaction of seeing my fear. I stayed passive. He finally backed off, going to the next guy, threatening him, then
the next guy, then the next. No one budged. There was an
unspoken unity among us. We were solid in our silence. And
when the redneck stormed off without shooting anyone, you
could practically feel the bus deflate from the force of our col-
lective sigh.

From then on, though, nothing was the same. At Camp
Shelby, the greeting officer—a white man—double-timed us to
the barracks, a couple of miles away. While we were still
breathless, he let us know that, just for starters, the canteen,
with its low-priced smokes and drinks, was off-limits. Disgusted, half our company went anyway. I was with those who
stayed behind. When the guys got caught, though, we all got

punished. Ain't no fun scrubbing the toilet with a toothbrush. That made me so mad, I nearly got into a fight, but somehow I stayed cool. Instead I learned to make up my bunk good enough to bounce a quarter off it. After struggling to get it right and tight, some dude came and took my bed away from me. I complained to the officer, who didn't care. That made me wanna fight all over again, but by then I was too tired.

It's easy to get tired of the army. Basic training took a little less than three months. The sergeants were white guys who reminded me of Lou Gossett, Jr.'s role in *An Officer and a Gentleman*. They talked trash—man, they'd say terrible things about your mama, your wife, or your girlfriend—and they were tough as nails. Given all my work on the plantation, I thought I was in shape. But army shape was different. According to the army, I was nothing. They ran me ragged and exercised me so hard until all my bones ached at night. I hung in, though. Men are supposed to hang in.

My only break came because of tractors. My experience with tractors convinced them to let me drive those big ten-gear army trucks, and I liked that. I hauled supplies. Might be menial work, but it gave me a sense of satisfaction. And it was better than washing dishes.

There were no weekend passes during basic training. I was isolated and forced to adjust. I did okay. In new situations, I'm scared, but if you give me reasonable orders, I'll follow them. So the army didn't do me in. The truth is that the army turned me out.

At the end of basic, we learned that the plantation owners in Sunflower County, the land surrounding Indianola, had an agreement with the Selective Service that vital workers—like tractor drivers—would be sent back to the farm after basic training. Crops like cotton and soybeans were considered essential. The troops needed them for food and clothes. I could have chosen to stay in, but decided to go back to my wife. Part of me regretted the decision. I felt like I missed an adventure and had gone through basic training for nothing. Later on, I'd regret it even more. I had none of the veteran benefits. I wasn't eligible under the G.I. Bill and couldn't get a free college education. I would have loved some formal training in music and history. On the other hand, I was alive. I was well. I was back on the plantation.

The trip back was an eye-opener for me. German prisoners of war were on the same train. But unlike us, they weren't forced to sit in separate and inferior compartments. They sat with the white folk. And these were our sworn enemies! Men who, only weeks before, were looking to shoot us dead! It hurt my heart, for example, to see what happened if too many whites got on the train and had to sit in the black section. They'd put up a partition to hide us from view. The train officials were telling the white passengers, "You can look at enemy soldiers who were ready to cut your throat, but you can't look at the black American soldiers willing to die for you." Now ain't that something?

It upset me even worse when I saw how the German prisoners were used to pick cotton in the Delta. We blacks picked till nightfall—seven or eight in the evening. But the Germans were allowed to take off at three in the afternoon. Plantation owners worried about overworking them. That made us feel less than human. We were seen as beasts of burden, dumb animals, a level below the Germans. To watch your enemy get better treatment than yourself was a helluva thing to endure.

As a kid, I was brainwashed by a segregated system. I was

taught caution and strict adherence to society's codes. As a twenty-year-old, fresh out of basic training, I was starting to feel the weight of the system. I felt the injustice. And I felt anger. But I'd be lying to say the brainwashing didn't stick. Years later, when integration came, I still hesitated before entering previously all-white restaurants down South. It was a reflex: *Don't go where you're not wanted.* It saddened me to release my conditioning. The pain of the past is hard to describe. But it's there. It lingers for life.

At Mr. Johnson's plantation, Martha had given up our house and was living with her brother John. That's where we both stayed, her working the fields and doing domestic chores, me driving the tractor. For the first time, the routine was getting to me. I'd done this before. When the war ended later that year—it was 1945—Martha and I found a little house in Indianola. Aside from those few months with my father in Lexington, this was the first time in my life that I wasn't living on a farm.

I'd see Daddy from time to time. He didn't say anything about my getting married, but his silence said a lot. Silence was how he gave approval. I felt I could count on him if I needed him, but I also felt he remained in his own world, driving a tractor like me, working six days a week and taking care of his family in Lexington. When he was around, I felt his care for me. I waited for him to call me "Jack," and then I knew everything was all right.

In my heart, though, I knew everything wasn't all right, at least not in my working life. I felt like I wanted more. I was looking for a way to improve my condition. I kept singing my blues on the streets of Indianola and nearby towns, but that had its limits. I could only earn so much. The Famous St. John Gospel Singers weren't going anywhere either. The other singers were too tied to the plantation. I felt those same ties holding me back, and I kept on keeping on. I had to. Plowing and harvesting and hauling—that was my life. The routine was my comfort and my compulsion, my survival and, at the same time, my source of frustration. Was I really getting anywhere in this mean ol' world? Did I wanna be a sharecropper forever?

Personal frustrations were also mounting. Martha became pregnant, but soon miscarried. That was tough on her, tough on us both. It happened three or four times in the early years of our marriage. I could see the disappointment in her eyes, as though she'd let me down. I supported her as best I could, yet there was nothing I could do to ease the pain. We wanted a baby and a family and, like everyone else, a better life. But we were stuck.

It was a strange day in May. It's payday, and I'm feeling a little antsy, a little more restless than usual. I've been driving the tractor all day and I'm ready to quit. The motor's burning hot and I'm burning to get off work and collect my money. I drive the tractor—the Big M we call it—to the shed to park it for the night. The shed is actually a six-foot space between the ground and the floor of a barn constructed high off the earth because of flooding. I've parked this thing a million times. I can maneuver it like nobody's business. I pull the nose of the tractor under the barn and, hurrying to get out of there, I turn off the engine and jump out of the cab. I'm a few feet away, my back to the tractor, when I hear a backfire. *Pow! Pow!* My heart stops; I freeze, then I run back toward the tractor, but it's too late. I've forgotten that sometimes the Big M does a postignition lunge. Usually I stay in the cab to make sure that doesn't happen. But today I've forgotten, and the result is a disaster. As I watch helplessly, the tractor lunges backward and the smokestack—

the exhaust—that sits atop the engine smashes against the barn and cracks off. The pipe is smashed and part of the manifold is destroyed. Major damage. Hundreds of dollars in repairs. And all my fault.

I do something I usually don't do. I panic. My mind starts racing and my pulse starts throbbing; a million thoughts attack me at once. What can I do? Where can I get the thing fixed? Where can I get the money? How can I keep Mr. Johnson from finding out I've screwed up? I can't. I'm trapped. There seems to be no way out; nothing can save me from humiliation. The more I think, the darker my thoughts. I start getting paranoid, imagining Mr. Johnson will want to shoot me.

I stay in the panic. I'm dazed and half-crazed and acting like I've never acted before. Too much confusion, too much damage. I keep hearing the backfire, keep seeing the exhaust pipe cracking off the tractor, keep fantasizing about Mr. Johnson's rage. This is the man who likes me and treats me like a son, but I'm thinking that he'll be disgusted with me and never trust me again.

The rest of the day is a blur. At some point, I go back to town, go home, and get my guitar. Martha's not there and I'm glad. I wouldn't know what to say to her. Got no explanations for nobody. I ain't good with words and all I'll do is stutter and stumble and never explain nothing. All I wanna do is . . . what? What is it that I wanna do?

Run.

I wanna run.

Wanna leave Indianola and the plantation and the busted smokestack behind. Don't wanna talk or explain, don't wanna cry or feel bad no more. Just wanna move.

So I do.

Grab my guitar. Grab my money—$2.50. And run.

Before the sun goes down, I'm out on Highway 49. Scared to death but on my way. Don't know what I'm doing, except for leaving. I ain't looking back till I get to Memphis.

Gotta get to Memphis.

9

A City Is Like a Woman

She's mysterious until you get to know her. From afar, she's fascinating and glamorous, someone you're dying to meet. You've been dreaming about her, imagining what she's like. You want her to open up to you; you want to explore all her secrets, find her most passionate spots, get inside. You think she might change your life, but you really don't know. A city is like a woman who draws you to her. You're excited and frightened and feel a little out of control. You've got to go to her.

That's just how I was thinking. I had to go to Memphis. My cousin Bukka White stayed in Memphis. I didn't have an address on him, hadn't seen him in years, and didn't even know for sure that he still lived there. I was going on hope. Cousin Bukka was the only relative of mine who stayed in a big city. Even better, he was the only relative who was a professional bluesman. That was enough. Memphis was enough. Memphis was the place where big-time bluesmen performed. Memphis had Beale Street, and going to Beale Street, in the mind of twenty-year-old Riley B. King, was a little like going to heaven.

I made that trip to heaven on the back of a grocery truck. Lewis' Grocery Company distributed food products up and down the state. By luck, one of their drivers picked me up. He said he'd take me to Memphis if I'd help him load and unload on the way. Working my way those 120 miles was fine with me. I've never been comfortable with free rides.

I was confused by the city. Memphis was bigger than I'd imagined, with paved streets and tall buildings and trolley cars and buses carrying people everywhere. I'd never seen anything like it. Never seen factories and plants and stores selling flashy jewelry and smelly fish and silk suits and, best of all, records and musical instruments. Music was in the air. Ladies were everywhere. I arrived in summer and the women, compared to those on the plantation, seemed half-undressed in their frilly dresses and revealing blouses. I didn't know about parks, where you could just sit and relax and enjoy. And then there was the river running along the banks of the city, the wide and mighty Mississippi, with its barges and boats carrying great loads of cotton to the merchant buildings where high finance was conducted by men in starched white shirts.

Mostly, though, I gravitated toward the music. I figured if I found Beale Street, I'd find Cousin Bukka. I found Beale Street to be a city unto itself. It was exciting seeing so many people crowded on the streets. So much activity, so much life, so many sounds. The hot part of Beale Street was only four blocks long, snuggled behind downtown and the famous Hotel Peabody, where the rich businessmen stayed and plotted their fortunes. Beale Street did look like heaven to me. There were three movie palaces, cafés, hotels, pawnshops—I'd never seen a pawnshop before—variety stores, and musicians everywhere. Beale Street was famous, of course, because of W. C. Handy, Father of the Blues, and his composition "Beale Street Blues." He was one of the first to write the blues down on paper so people could buy the sheet music for songs like "St. Louis Blues" and "Basin Street Blues" and "Memphis Blues." I knew Handy was black and that he stayed in Memphis and was known the world over. Even if I never saw him in person, I could feel his esteem. His stature gave the blues pride and his presence made Memphis, at least in my mind, the capital of the blues.

Walking down Beale, noticing the One Minute Café and Mitchell's Hotel, I saw white people shopping the same street as blacks. That was new for me. I heard music coming from a park where men were playing guitars and harmonicas and clarinets and trombones. One man was bowing a violin, an instrument I'd never even seen before. The sounds got me so excited, I started to run. The park is named for W. C. Handy and today there's a statue of the great composer in the middle. But then it was just an open green space where musicians congregated. I stood spellbound. I wasn't about to play; all I could do was listen and learn. I listened for hours and, even though my guitar was under my arm, I never struck a note. All my confidence from all those Saturdays playing all those little Delta towns vanished—just like that. Before Beale Street, I thought I was pretty hot stuff. After Beale Street, I knew I stunk. The cats could play rings around me. The guitarists seemed to have four hands, and I felt like I had all thumbs. Slowly my excitement turned to depression. Man, I'd never be this good. But at least I'd made it to Memphis, and at least one of the guys knew where Cousin Bukka stayed.

Before I left the park, though, I noticed three dudes shooting dice behind a bush. Behind them, sitting on the ground, three other dudes were playing cards. Never seen public gambling before. Everything fascinated me, and I stood there and watched until one of the cats screamed out, "Number One!" Then everyone scattered because a white cop was walking our way and I ran with the rest of them, clinging to my guitar, running past a record shop called Home of the Blues with a picture of T-Bone Walker in the window, my hero flashing in front of my eyes, my eyes soaking in the scene of painted ladies of the night arriving at a nightclub where a fat man was playing boogie-woogie so hard and fast, I thought it had to be Pete Johnson or Albert Ammons. Turned out to be just a local piano player. I'd soon learn Memphis was full of local geniuses.

Memphis at night was hard to negotiate. I didn't know one neighborhood from another, but by asking anyone with a friendly face, I finally stumbled upon Foxwood Street in Orangemound, a section southeast of downtown. I knocked on the door, but Cousin Bukka wasn't there, so I sat on the curb outside his place and must have fallen asleep with my head on the ground and my arm wrapped around my guitar.

"Riley? That you?"

I looked up and saw my cousin, smiling and all happy to see me. He was holding his guitar, except it was in a case. "What you doing sleeping on the street, boy?" he asked. "Better come on in."

He wanted to know what had happened and I told him the story. He listened hard. He seemed to understand, saying that time is the greatest healer. "Mr. Johnson is surely mad as a motherfucker," he said, "but in time he'll cool off. Meanwhile, we better get word to Martha that you're all right."

We did that the next day. But that night I stayed up nearly till dawn. Bukka had just come from playing at a party and was still high from his music. He felt like talking and I loved listening. See, he'd been a boxer and a baseball pitcher and served long time in the famous Parchman Farm Prison for murdering two men. He told me he hadn't gone out looking for them, but fought off these two brothers who'd jumped him. Said he killed in self-defense. And was quick to warn me to stay out of trouble. He was between wives—divorced from one and engaged to another—and had the house to himself. Bukka talked like he sang, simple and down-to-earth, with a rhythm that had me hanging on every word. When we finally fell asleep, my head was swimming with all the scenes of the city I had seen that day and the fabulous stories my cousin had told.

Next day when I awoke and Bukka was fixing coffee, I didn't know what to expect. I felt like I was living in this exotic land of the blues. Even though I wouldn't be the one to suggest it, I thought maybe we'd start playing some blues.

"We'd better start thinking about getting to work," said Bukka.

By work I thought he might mean music, but he meant the Newberry Equipment Company, where he had a job and hoped to find one for me. He did. I was signed on that day. Bukka said, "Don't mess around on this job. Don't be lazy on it." It was a big plant where they constructed underground tanks that service stations use to hold gasoline. We couldn't join the union 'cause it was stone segregated, but some of the workers were helpful and taught me how to weld. I liked welding and adjusted pretty quick to life in a plant. Turned out to be a good job for decent wages, around $60 a week. Best of all, it kept me in Memphis.

I also found extra work at the big McCallum and Roberts mill, operating a machine that spun cotton thread into fabric. I felt like a spider spinning webs. The mechanical part wasn't bad, but the hours killed me—midnight till 8 A.M. After five or six weeks, I had to turn it loose.

I was happy to pay Bukka rent and stay in his place. Like a little puppy, I'd follow him to parties and watch him play his blues. He'd earn maybe $20 a night and show everyone a good time. I'd see him take that bottleneck, slip it on his fat finger, and slide that sucker over the strings, making a haunting sound. Sometimes he'd get slick and use a pipe, and sometimes when he wasn't looking I'd give it another try, but it was no use. I wasn't born to be a slide guitarist.

I could see that Bukka was born to be a bluesman, and I wondered if the same was true of me. I worried that I didn't have his talent—or the talent of someone like Blind Lemon or T-Bone. I felt something beautiful inside Bukka's soul. Even if I didn't follow his style, I was moved by his sincerity. He loved telling stories, simple stories, and used his blues to tell them. His blues was the book of his life. He sang about his rough times and fast times and loving times and angry times. He'd entertain at a party for two hundred people with the same enthusiasm as a party for twenty. Bukka gave it his all. His music had a consistency I admired. Like all the great bluesmen, he said, *I am what I am*. I wondered if I could be that steady and strong.

For the eight months or so that I stayed in Memphis, I was low-key. Just observing. I remembered an old man back on the plantation who used to say, "The Good Lord gave us two of everything, except the one we use too much." I tried to keep my mouth shut and my eyes open. I soaked up the city like a sponge. I was excited being there, but I also had a wife back home and a debt to pay. I hadn't seen her for eight months and missed her something fierce. I reasoned that Mr. Johnson would be in a better frame of mind to accept my apology. My responsible self said, *Go home to Indianola,* even as another voice whispered, *Get back to Memphis soon as you can.*

The bus ride to Indianola wasn't easy. Felt like I was going backward, but I had no choice. It was good being reunited with Martha, although it took us a while to readjust. Maybe we never did. She was jealous of what I might have done while I was away, and I was jealous of her. We were two fools too young to know how foolish we were.

I knew I had to make amends with Mr. Johnson, and I did so. I walked over to his place, knocked, and nervously waited for him to open the door. "Riley," he said, "where you been?"

The tone of his voice told me he was glad I was back. That was a relief. But I was still timid and ashamed of what I'd done. "I'm sorry," I said.

"You know, Riley," he began, "all you had to do was tell me what happened. We could have talked about it. Everyone screws up at least once."

His good attitude almost made me feel worse. I felt stupid for having been gone so long. I'd forgotten he was such a decent guy.

"I want to do the right thing," I said. "I'm gonna pay you for the damages."

"I never doubted you, Riley."

It took only another minute for us to work out a payment

plan. He rehired me as a tractor driver, and let me pay off the $500 cost of fixing the tractor over the next several months. Man, I was relieved. I fell back in my old routine.

And back in the trap. Back singing with the Famous St. John Gospel Singers, who were, more than ever, overripe for national fame. Yet nothing had changed. Because no sharecropper makes any real money, we never had savings, and without savings there was no escape. I was the only one willing to chance it.

In our little house in Indianola, me and Martha finally got electricity. To me, that mostly meant a radio and an amplifier for my guitar. I was still wild about the new T-Bone sound that kept ringing in my ears. But the more I tried it, the more I couldn't do it. Same went for Django Reinhardt. Django is the great Gypsy guitarist from Belgium I discovered when, during the war, a pal was shipped over to France and came home talkin' 'bout this amazing musician he'd heard. In Paris, he'd gone to the Hot Club, where Django played with the violinist Stephane Grappelli. My friend bought some records—those big ol' easy-to-break 78 rpm shellacs—wrapped them up in tissue paper and cloth like they were precious jewels (which they were), and presented them to me when he came home to Mississippi. I couldn't believe what I heard.

Later I'd read how Django had burned two fingers in his left hand in a fire in his Gypsy caravan; they were webbed together in a way that left him with only two free fingers. They called him Three Finger Lightning, and he was. He hit me as hard as Charlie Christian. Django was a new world. Him and Grappelli swung like demons. The syncopation got me going, but the beat was just the beginning. It was Django's ideas that lit up my brain. He was light and free and fast as the fastest trumpet, slick as the slickest clarinet, running through chord changes with the skill of a sprinter and the imagination of a poet. He was nimble like a cat. Songs like "Nuages" and "Nocturne" took me far away from my little place in Indianola, transporting me over the ocean to Paris, where people sipped wine in outdoor cafés and soaked in the most romantic jazz the world has ever known.

I loved Django because of the joy in his music, the light-hearted feeling and freedom to do whatever he felt. Even if I hadn't been told he was a Gypsy, I might have guessed it. There's wanderlust in Django's guitar, a you-can't-fence-me-in attitude that inspired me. It didn't matter that he was technically a million times better than me. His music fortified an idea I held close to my heart—that the guitar is a voice unlike any other. The guitar is a miracle. Out of the strings and the frets comes this personality—whether a blind black man from Texas or a Gypsy from Belgium—of a unique human being.

But guitarists weren't the only instruments talking to me. I loved the big fat sound of Ben Webster on tenor. Ben was a bitch of a player; he worried a ballad to death. And Lester Young, the man they called the President, played that same tenor sax with a laid-back attitude that revolutionized the music. Prez invented cool. Rather than state a melody, he suggested it. He barely breathed into his horn, creating an intimacy that gave me chills. They talk about abstract painters; well, Prez was an abstract jazz man, and he taught me the beauty of modern art. He taught me to use the minimum amount of notes.

I also learned from Johnny "Rabbit" Hodges, Duke Ellington's alto saxist, who had tremendous feeling for songs. If Prez was abstract, Rabbit was concrete. He served up the melody on a silver platter, delicious as dark chocolate. The great jazz instrumentalists taught me how to sing and interpret a song. They showed me how a horn can have as much personality as an actor.

Down in Mississippi, even among the poorest sharecroppers, we could feel the optimism of postwar America. I wanted to feel that optimism; I wanted to believe that things were getting better, that the country's victory meant victory for everywhere. And if my optimism couldn't be justified by my economic condition, at least I could feel optimism in the happy music of Louis Jordan, in Lionel Hampton's "Flying Home," and in the *Jazz at the Philharmonic* concert featuring Nat "King" Cole, Illinois Jacquet, and a fabulous white guitarist named Les Paul, who'd soon refashion the whole instrument. My ears were wide open, even to far-out beboppers like Dizzy Gillespie and Charlie Parker, whose "Back Home Blues" sounded as good and gritty to me as anything by Muddy Waters.

Muddy might have been the most magnificent of all the bluesmen to come out of Mississippi. John Lee Hooker is sure-enough unique and still stands as one of the great poets of the blues. But Muddy became a father figure to generations of musicians, black and white. Muddy became an institution. I've loved Muddy my whole life. Loved his shouting, his songwriting, his wailing guitar. Back in Indianola, we knew that he'd gone to Chicago, where he established a whole school that he'd rule for five decades. Some went to the South Side before Muddy and some went after; there was Big Bill Broonzy and Memphis Slim and Memphis Minnie and Big Maceo and Little Walter and Howlin' Wolf and Junior Parker and dozens more. But no one had Muddy's authority. He was the boss of Chicago and the reason some call Chicago the sure-enough home of the blues.

I was agitated by all this music, everyone moving to different towns, different rhythms reflecting exciting changes in people's lives. But I was never tempted by the Windy City. I'd already been to blues heaven, and it wasn't called Chicago. They say Chicago has the hawk, the ferocious wind that goes whipping 'round in winter and rips off the top of your head. I can do without the hawk. I can do without the freezing snow and sleet. I have my heart set on one destination and one destination only. Long-distance information, give me Memphis, Tennessee.

10

Why I Love Arthur Godfrey

He was relaxed, he played the ukulele, and I believed him when he sold his products. He talked and acted natural, and that was something I liked. He didn't come on like one of those phony announcers in love with the sound of his own voice. You felt like Arthur was your friend, someone to confide in. He was a national personality, a white man, who we heard on the radio all the time. But it didn't matter if you were black or white, man or woman, child or adult, his friendliness was something you trusted. Without trying, he had an easy manner and a winning way. I mention Arthur Godrey now because he had a big influence on the start of my new life when I moved back to Memphis. I'll explain.

In late '48, I was ready to roll out. Finally and permanently, I had to put the plantation behind me. I told Martha, I said, "Baby, I'm going back to Memphis. I'll send for you, soon as I get settled." She believed me. She knew I had to try to make it as a musician. I made it back to the city on another Lewis' grocery truck, helping the driver load and unload all the way. Only this time I didn't stop in Memphis; I went just over the Mississippi River to West Memphis, Arkansas. I had a plan. And at the center of the plan was Sonny Boy Williamson.

See, for years, Sonny Boy #2, the harmonica man I saw at the Jones Night Spot, had a radio broadcast on KFFA out of Helena, Arkansas, called *King Biscuit Time*. Came on every day at noon and all over the South, people loved it. We'd come in from the fields for our noon meal and relax by listening to Sonny Boy. He had him some famous songs like "Fattening Frogs for Snakes," but nothing made him as famous as this show, sponsored by King Biscuit Flour. I'd been listening to it so long, I felt like I knew Sonny Boy personally. So when I heard he'd switched to KWEM in West Memphis, where he was advertising a tonic called Hadacol, I decided to go over and see him. Just like that.

Don't know where I got the nerve. But I found the station, arrived with my guitar about 11 A.M., and asked to see Sonny Boy. He was standing alone in the bare studio, playing his harmonica. He was huge, tall as a basketball player and brawny as a boxer. His face said: *Don't bother me with no bullshit.* He looked like he was ready to brawl at the drop of a hat. I knew he loved liquor, and when he talked, his voice was deep and rough. When he saw me, he took the harp out of his mouth. He seemed to resent the interruption. I took a deep breath and looked him in the eye, remembering all those good times when I'd heard his voice on the radio.

"What do you want?" he asked bluntly.

"I-I-I-I wanna sing a song on your program."

"You do, huh?"

"Yes, sir."

"Go ahead. Lemme hear you."

I sang "Blues at Sunrise," a popular song by Ivory Joe Hunter. "The moon is rising," I sang with all the soul I could muster, "and the sun is sinking low."

I surprised myself 'cause I didn't falter. My guitar hit the right notes and I sang in tune. Maybe those years of church and street-corner blues were paying off. Anyway, Sonny Boy didn't kick me out.

"What do you call yourself, son?" he asked with a very small hint of kindness.

"Riley B. King."

"All right, Riley B. King, you can sing your song at the end of my program. Just be sure you sing as good as you did just now."

I did. I put the song over. When I was through, Sonny Boy told the audience, "The boy ain't bad, but you tell me what you think. Call in if you like him."

When the show was over, a white man came in to say that they'd gotten a good number of calls for me and then whispered something in Sonny Boy's ear.

"Shit," said the bluesman, wrinkling his brow. "I done messed up." Then he turned to me. I thought I'd done something wrong. "Lookee here, Riley B.," said Sonny Boy, "seems like I double-booked myself. I'm working down 'round Clarksdale tonight, but I also got me another date at the 16th Street Grill here in West Memphis. You wanna play the Grill for me?"

"Yes, sir."

I was thrilled beyond reason, giddy and silly and screaming hallelujah inside. First a spot on the radio, now a real-life job.

All within an hour. The blessings were coming. Thank you, Jesus.

"Go see Miss Annie," said Sonny Boy. "She runs the joint."

The joint was just a couple of rooms—one up front for music and sandwiches, one in the back for gambling. West Memphis was wide open. Miss Annie was open to hiring me 'cause she heard me on the radio and liked the song. "I got me a jukebox in here," she said, "but I turn it off 'cause the ladies like to dance to a live man."

Ladies! A live man! I couldn't wait. I was still wearing my old army fatigue jacket. Didn't have nice clothes at all. But Miss Annie didn't seem to care, and all I could think of were those ladies who liked a live man. When the time came, the ladies came pouring in—some escorted, some not, all looking so hot that I tried pouring all my heat into my guitar. The gamblers wandered through to the back, but the dancers stayed up front. For the first time, I played for dancers, played for these ladies who moved so loose and limber that I played better than I'd ever played before. Might have messed up my musical measures or screwed up a lyric or two, but, baby, the beat was there. And these people—all these young people, people no older than me—they loved that beat. They'd forgive me whatever mistakes I made. My voice might crack or my fingers might strike a wrong note, but long as I gave 'em that beat to bounce on, no one was complaining. Soon the club got all steamy and sexy and, man, I would have played all night had Miss Annie said so. Instead, she said, "You got this here job, long as you can get on some radio station like Sonny Boy and mention the 16th Street Grill. Do that and I'll pay you twelve dollars a night, six nights a week."

"Yes, ma'am, I *will* get on the radio."

That night I couldn't sleep for the pictures running through my head. Ladies were in the pictures, for sure. I saw them dressed and undressed, bending over and stretching, grinding and grinning and showing me stuff I ain't ever seen before. My mind was alive with the sound of my own music and the way women had reacted to my voice, their bodies flowing to a rhythm coming out of my guitar. I saw myself coming in them, one with big beautiful breasts, another with a luscious round backside, me kissing 'em here and there and everywhere 'cause I was a bluesman in a nightclub where girls gathered 'round and danced in front of my face. Didn't know whether I was awake or dreaming. Where once I watched Sonny Boy from outside the Jones Night Spot, now I sang on his radio show; where once I peeped through knotholes into juke joints to hear the music and see the foxes, now I was in the spotlight and the foxes were looking at me. My ego was going a little crazy. Man, I felt good. I thanked God and fell asleep.

Morning time and I'm still tingling with energy. I wanna push my luck. Wanna get on the radio so I can mention Miss Annie's place and keep my new job. Gotta do it. Cousin Bukka has been talking about this new radio station, WDIA, playing black music, and I'm heading there now.

I take the bus over to Memphis. It's chilly and rainy, but I'm determined to keep making music on the radio. I got to get somewhere. I get to the bus station and find that WDIA is some twenty blocks away. I walk. The rain comes down harder and, because I don't have a case, I carry my guitar so the strings are against my chest and the wood is exposed to the wet. I hug the instrument to my body like it's my baby. Rain gets worse, my pace quickening, my breath shortening until I'm running down Union Street, looking for this radio station. Finally I'm standing in front of a big plate-glass window. Inside is a black man with super-short hair and super-thick glasses. His name's Nat D. Williams. They call him Professor 'cause he teaches school and he reminds me of Mr. Luther Henson. The red light's on; he's talking into the mike. When he's through, though, when the light goes green, I tap on the window. He gets up and lets me in. In a jovial voice, he asks, "What can I do for you, young fella?"

"I'd like to go on the radio," I say, "and make a record."

He laughs. "Well, we don't make records here, and I'm not in charge of who goes on the air. I'll get Mr. Ferguson."

Mr. Ferguson comes in. He's one of the two white owners. He's a short Jewish man, not much hair, with a serious air about him. He gives the impression of someone in deep thought. He looks me up and down. I'm still this skinny kid from the country. He gives me my first professional interview. Naturally I'm nervous. My stuttering has steadily decreased over the years, but it's still there.

"If I put you on the radio," says Mr. Ferguson, "would you be too nervous to talk?"

"I might do a little s-s-s-stuttering," I answer, "but no more so than the average person. I think the average person will take to me."

He asks me about my background, and I tell the truth. I feel like he's a fair man, and I don't want to give a false impression. I talk about singing on the streets, singing gospel, singing at the 16th Street Grill, singing with Sonny Boy on KWEM. Another guy named Don Kerns comes in to hear me sing. He's the station manager. I do a little Louis Jordan number like "Caldonia."

"You're all right," says Mr. Kerns.

"You seem sincere," adds Mr. Ferguson. "And mentioning Sonny Boy gives me an idea. Sonny Boy's made quite a splash advertising Hadacol. Well, we have a sponsor called Pepticon. It's a tonic like Hadacol. Good for whatever ails you. And we're looking for someone who can sell it. I'm thinking that one way to sell it is through a song. You ever written a jingle?"

"No, sir."

"Willing to try?"

"Sure," I say, cradling my guitar in my arms and playing a few chords. I hum for a couple of seconds and, just like that, start to sing: "Pepticon sure is good . . . Pepticon sure is good . . . and you can get it anywhere in your neighborhood."

Nat D. is smiling and nodding his head. Mr. Ferguson looks at me, almost like a proud relative, and says, "That's okay. That's pretty good. Why don't we give you a try?"

That's how my radio career began.

That afternoon I went on the air from 3:30 to 3:40. Just me and my guitar and my little Gibson amplifier. I sang the Pepticon commercial a couple of times, telling the folks it was good stuff. (Only later would I learn it was 12 percent alcohol.) I sang Louis Jordan's "Somebody Changed the Lock on My Door" and "Buzz Me, Baby." When I talked, I tried to be natural. I thought of Arthur Godfrey, how he sounded like just an average dude, your neighbor or some guy behind the counter at the general store. I was amazed to see that, even if I did stutter, it didn't bother me or anyone else. Stuttering was part of me, and if I was accepting it, everyone else seemed to be accepting it too.

The radio station reminded me of Beale Street in this respect: It was a world apart. In the middle of a strictly segregated South, WDIA was a place where blacks and whites worked together. Bert Ferguson and his partner, John R. Pepper, were starting the first real black radio station. Nat D. was the first black disc jockey in Memphis. He was the granddaddy for all black disc jockeys in the South. Other stations would hire hip deejays like Dewey Phillips, white men who talked black, but blacks talking black on the air to other blacks was something new.

I liked that. I liked working at a place where you were rewarded according to merit. I'm not saying it was perfect. Blacks couldn't be engineers; we couldn't actually spin the records. That was ridiculous and frustrating and made me mad. But the personalities hired by Mr. Ferguson—black deejays like Theo Wade, A. C. Williams, Hot Rod Hulbert, and Rufus Thomas—were told to be themselves. And they were. They set a style for deejaying that influenced radio all over the country, maybe all over the world.

I was still trying to get all over Memphis. Sure, I had my little radio show, and I had my little gig with Miss Annie, but I wanted to get over bigger. That's why I'd enter the amateur contest at the Palace Theater on Beale Street every Wednesday night. Drummer Al Jackson had a big band. (Years later, his son, Al Jackson, Jr., played with Booker T. and the MG's.) Rufus Thomas was the emcee. You'd get $1 if you entered. First prize was $5 and a guarantee of coming back next week. I never won, but I managed to enter every week all the same. I guess I looked so poor and pitiful that softhearted Rufus couldn't turn me away. That's one of the reasons he's still my dear friend today.

Like many of the other black deejays, Rufus had a certain authority and a history behind him I had to respect. Rufus had traveled with the Rabbit Foot Minstrels as a dancer. He was a great all-around showman. You probably know him for his hits in the sixties like "Do the Funky Chicken" and "Walking the Dog," but back in the forties he had a partner. Called themselves Rufus and Bones and, man, they'd joke, dance, and sing up a storm. Rufus did perfect imitations of Louis Armstrong, Fats Waller, and Gatemouth Moore, another great bluesman and Beale Street fixture. Rufus Thomas could flat-out entertain. I also loved him for his wit and wisdom. Rufus would say, "If a white man could be black on Beale Street for just one Saturday night, he'd never wanna be white again." A lifetime later, Rufus testified for me at a dinner when everyone was calling me a star. "B ain't no star," he said, "he's the moon."

At the Rufus-run amateur show, most of the people were there to hear Al Jackson's band, not the amateurs. The band was another proof of the quality of Memphis music. Standing backstage, I'd swear the band was kicking as hard as Basie. Al had a singer named Dick Cole who idolized Billy Eckstine. When Cole sang "Jelly Jelly," you'd turn to jelly.

Martha moved to Memphis only a week after I got my job on the radio. We rented two rooms in a boarding house at 357 North Third Street, north of downtown. Not a fancy place, but clean and big enough for two. Martha found work as a domestic. She cleaned and ironed and tried to adjust to life off the farm. After nearly five years, our marriage was showing signs of strain. The miscarriages made Martha unhappy, and jealousy continued to be a problem. Some of it Martha imagined; but some of Martha's jealousy was justified.

In 1949, I had a son with a woman who lived in Indianola. I didn't tell Martha, but I did tell the woman I'd care for the son. I did, and continued to do so. That's been my way throughout life. If a woman I've been with says the child is mine, I don't argue. I assume responsibility. As I got older, that responsibility grew. Over the years, I'd have fifteen children with fifteen different women. That both enriched and complicated my life. I'll tell you more about that in a little while.

Meanwhile, the birth of my first child came at a delicate time. I was just starting out and still trying to save my marriage. I was excited about my music, always excited about women, and unable or unwilling to hold back that excitement. Along about then, for the first and only time in life, I grew gravely ill and expected to die.

I contracted hepatitis. The doctors didn't know what it was. I lost so much weight that my skin seemed part of my bones. I was too weak to work, too weak even to speak, and couldn't get out of bed for days at a time. I had to call my daddy to sit with me. I wanted both my wife and my father by my side. I stayed in a feverish state, unable to focus or swallow or raise my arms. Every part of me ached. My bowel movements were mixed with blood. I couldn't hold down food. Daddy couldn't say much. He just sat there, a symbol of strength. But strength was something I couldn't regain; I could only visualize the death of my mother and grandmother, imagining that I was going through the same thing. I prayed to God to take me. Wanted to stop suffering. Wanted to just stop.

Then something happened. Hard to explain, but I was looking at my father, looking at my wife Martha, and suddenly I thought, *maybe it's not my time. Maybe I shouldn't be telling God to take me. I don't know God's plan . . . Who does? . . . Maybe there's hope after all.* I started believing things might change. And soon they did. A friend called Boogie Woogie came by with ice cream. For the first time, food looked good. He gave me a taste, and I digested it okay. The doctor showed up with some fish. "Try it," he said. When I did, it went down all right. Seems the doctor understood the nature of my sickness. He gave me medicines and foods that slowly brought me back. I thought of Job in the Bible. The moral of Job's story is patience. Patience has worked for me—in sickness and in health. Patience is the one thing that's seen me through.

11

Faith Is Patience

heard someone say that, and I believe it's true. I believe God created everything. I'm awed by his handiwork, the forests and oceans and sky that surrounds us. I believe God made us. But our nature isn't always godlike. We struggle inside. Our emotions make us jumpy. As a kid, I was always jumping around, from the fields to the church to the street corners. Couldn't stay still. As a young adult, my nature was still restless. That's how I got to Memphis. But once I was there, and once I got over my initial run of good luck, I saw I needed more than talent to stay on course. I needed patience.

It was good being on the radio and playing down at Miss Annie's, but my money was still too funny to buy nice clothes or even a second-hand car. Patience told me I needed to practice my guitar. And patience also said I'd better find extra work if I wanted to stay ahead of the game. So I did. They gave me a second time slot at WDIA from 12:30 to 12:45 in the afternoon.

That meant if I got up early and went over to Arkansas, I could pick cotton till around 11 A.M. and get back in time. Arkansas planters paid better than the Mississippi plantations. I could get as much as $1 per hundred pounds compared to my old rate of 35 cents. So after picking and plugging Pepticon at noon, I'd wait 'cause sometimes they used me to substitute for Maurice "Hot Rod" Hulbert, a deejay with a program called *Sepia Swing Club*. By 4 P.M., I was back in the Arkansas cotton fields, picking for another two hours. That was my routine three or four days a week. It was rough, but it paid.

It paid to hang around WDIA. They constructed a 50,000-watt transmitter that meant on a clear night you could hear us in New Orleans. Locally, people seemed to be liking my Pepticon show. Sometimes on Saturdays I'd go out with the Pepticon salesmen and sing the jingle on the back of flatbed trucks. I was getting a little name in the neighborhood. All the deejays had nicknames, so the station started calling me the Beale Street Blues Boy. That was the three B's, and it was a mouthful. Soon I was getting letters to just the Blues Boy, saying, "Dear Mr. Blues Boy, please play Amos Milburn's 'Chicken Shack Boogie' or Roy Milton's 'Hop, Skip and Jump.' " From Blues Boy it was shortened to Bee Bee, and then B. B. Close friends clipped it off to just plain B.

After seven or eight months in Memphis, I got to be a full-time deejay on the *Sepia Swing Club*. With Arthur Godrey in mind, I developed a believable on-air personality. I was just me. I liked to say I played everything from Bing Crosby to Lightnin' Hopkins. Naturally I played more Lightnin' than Bing, but I do confess to a soft spot in my heart for "Too-Ra-Loo-Ra-Loo-Ra." Bing could sure sing those Irish lullabies. Generally, I soft-pedaled myself as a deejay. Didn't ego-trip. I tried to please the public while, at the same time, educating myself on the new music.

Imagine my situation: Before Memphis, I never even owned a record player. Now I was sitting in a room with a thousand records and the ability to play them whenever I wanted. I was the kid in the candy store, able to eat it all. I gorged myself. Record companies had salesmen who gave me my own personal copies of the newest releases. I hoarded those records like a squirrel hoarding nuts. If I'd been passionate about music before, now I was positively possessed. And blessed.

My blessing, I believe, had to do with the times. I was old enough to have felt firsthand the old country blues. Singers like Blind Lemon Jefferson formed the backbone of the music. I got to see how those blues were modified and modernized by artists like Lonnie Johnson. And then came T-Bone, with his slick single-note styling that copped the cool attitude of jazz without losing a lick of soul. At the end of the forties, it felt like black music was on fire. And sitting in the broadcast booth at WDIA, I felt all the warm, beautiful heat.

The war was over and people were feeling good. Music was making them feel even better. I think it was Louis Jordan who made the real marriage between jump-band jazz and barrelhouse blues. Every musician I knew—singer or saxist, guitarist or drummer—idolized Louis Jordan. First, he was funny. Whether he was talkin' 'bout "Nobody's Here but Us Chickens" or "Reet Petite and Gone," Louis made you laugh. And then he made you dance. He had witty lyrics and irresistible rhythm. Plus, he was novel. He proved you can take the blues in a dozen different directions and keep 'em blue.

Charles Brown was another towering figure of the times. The mention of Charles's name lights up my life. He started off with Johnny Moore's Three Blazers. Johnny Moore was the older brother of Oscar Moore, who played with Nat Cole. The Moore brothers were fine guitarists with an effortless style— equal parts jazz and blues—that provided perfect accompaniment for smooth singers like Nat and Charles. Charles went off and had a string of hits on his own—"Driftin' Blues," "Merry Christmas Baby," "Tell Me You'll Wait for Me"—where you didn't know what you liked more, his piano playing or silky vocals. What I respected most about Charles was his college education. For a high school dropout like me, that was mighty impressive. He also had amazing technique. I loved the idea he could play Bach but preferred blues. Fact is, you could hear a little Bach in Charles Brown's blues.

Roy Brown was another favorite. He had a big-throated, full-throttle way of singing, and a vibrato that went right through me. As a singer, he had balls. He belted out tunes like "Rockin' at Midnight" and "Boogie at Midnight" that everyone wanted to hear. Also loved Wynonie Harris's "Good Rockin' Tonight" and "All She Wants to Do Is Rock." Listening now, these records sound like early rock 'n' roll—but, then again, so does Louis Jordan. Small groups with gutsy singers and screaming saxists were all the rage. And so were a bunch of great instrumentalists.

Lloyd Glenn was a fabulous pianist with a fabulous guitarist, Lowell Fulson. Lowell recorded a song called "Three O'Clock Blues" that would soon change my life. I played it on *Sepia Swing Club* all the time. When Lowell went out on the road in the early fifties, he had another piano player, a blind boy named Ray Charles who had a little hit called "Baby, Let Me Hold Your Hand" and enough musical brilliance to lead Lowell's band. But Lowell was the star. His songs were telling stories to me. When

I finally met him, he said, "B, you the only the deejay spinning my 'Three O'Clock Blues.' I'm gonna give you that song." Lowell also had "Blue Shadows" and a version of "Every Day I Have the Blues" that I loved to death. Loved me some Amos Milburn as well. Those were drinking days—maybe my heaviest—and listening to tunes like "Bad, Bad Whiskey" or "One Scotch, One Bourbon, One Beer" or "Thinking and Drinking" or "Just One More Drink" made me wanna take one more drink. These were also the days of bluesy balladeers like Cecil Gant and, quite naturally, the king, Nat Cole.

Nat was a case unto himself. His jazz trio was the epitome of taste, musicianship, and serious swing. The musicians knew Nat was the next great piano player after Art Tatum and Earl Hines. His technique was a miracle of economy. And when he romped, watch out! I already mentioned that Jazz at the Philharmonic date with Les Paul. Nat's solo on "Tea for Two" is a lesson in invention. I especially loved his own trio, not only because of the space he gave guitarist Oscar Moore, but because the sound was unique.

Art Tatum also had a famous trio with Tiny Grimes on guitar. Tatum had the technique of a Michelangelo, and I was fascinated to see how Tiny worked around him. Tatum played a million notes, Grimes played very few. Tiny's skill was in quietly supporting Art's fireworks. Charlie Christian and Django were more impressive soloists, but Tiny Grimes taught me a lot. His intelligence was about accommodation. He understood dynamics.

So did Nat Cole. The little clubs Nat played didn't have much space for the band, so he eliminated the drummer—just piano, bass, and guitar. Man, that sounded so subtle to me. And when Nat sang "Route 66" or "Sweet Lorraine," it was pure delight. He also did real bluesy stuff like "Mother Told Me" or "Easy Listening Blues." The ease of Nat's approach is the root of his genius. That ease could apply to anything—piano jazz and, later on, pure pop singing. His image also influenced me. Nat was a fashion plate. Wore those pin-striped suits with matching silk ties and handkerchiefs. He was a singing star who dressed as clean as the Chairman of the Board of General Motors. As I was emerging as a public personality of my own, image was important. I looked to certain role models—Duke Ellington was another figure of great stature and impeccable dress—who epitomized class.

Billy Eckstine had him a big band full of boppers: Dizzy and Charlie Parker, Miles Davis and Dexter Gordon. But Billy was also a flashy dresser. He had those long Mr. B collars I loved and always looked like a million bucks. When it came to clothes, T-Bone himself was no slouch. He wore what we called a California jacket—a buttonless model with a belt that wrapped around the waist. Too cool for words.

I wanted to be cool. I was a kid from the country trying to lose the stink of manure. I didn't look like a star. In fact, I never would. Even today I'll walk down the street and get lost in the crowd. But back then I was determined to follow those entertainers who'd developed a sense of style and dignity. Being a bluesman carried a stigma, both from blacks and whites. I fear that's true even today. A bluesman is supposed to be some guy slouched on a stool, a cigarette hanging from his lips, his cap falling off his head, his overalls ripped and smelly, a jug of corn liquor by his side. He talks lousy English and can't carry on a conversation without cussin' every other word. Ask him about his love life and he'll tell you he just beat up his old lady. Give him a dollar and he'll sing something dirty. He's a combination clown and fool. No one respects him or pays him no mind.

I resented that. Still do. That's why looking to role-model musicians was so important. They told the public—and ambitious entertainers like me—that blues-rooted music could be presented with the same class as grand opera. When I saw Count Basie and his men or Duke Ellington's orchestra outfitted in tuxes and tails, that was a beautiful sight to behold. And with his theatrical flair and super-sharp wardrobe, T-Bone was saying that the blues is as sleek as a new Cadillac rolling off the line.

I was saying how my personal guitar style had evolved. The late forties was a critical period for me, not only because I'd soon record my first song, but because I'd flat-out given up copying others. I did it out of frustration, not conviction. Just couldn't pull it off. If I had the chops to become a T-Bone Jr. or a Django Jr., that'd be a thrill enough. But my fingers were too stupid and my mind refused to work that way. I had no choice but, by accident or default, to forge a style that fit my abilities. Elements of my idols surely snuck in. From time to time, you'll hear a small piece of Charlie Christian or Lonnie Johnson. But the single factor that drove me to practice was that sound I heard from the Hawaiian or country-and-western steel pedal guitar. That cry that sounded human to me. I wanted to sustain a note like a singer. I wanted to phrase a note like a saxist. By bending the strings, by trilling my hand—and I have big fat hands—I could achieve something that approximated a vocal vibrato. I could sustain a note. I wanted to connect my guitar to human emotions. By fooling with the feedback between my amplifier and instrument, I started experimenting with sounds that expressed my feelings, whether happy or sad, bouncy or bluesy. I was looking for ways to let my guitar sing.

As a singer, the job was less complicated. I just followed my feelings. I always loved singers—everyone from Uncle Jack hollering in the fields to Doc Clayton to Roy Brown on records—who didn't hold back. I see singing as the most basic musical act. I admired those who used their whole voice, from the falsetto on down, without worrying about being proper. To me, singing is like talking. If it ain't natural, it ain't right.

As time went on, I tried to link my singing voice with my guitar as best I could. In the beginning, when I sang gospel, I used the guitar to complement my voice or even provide rhythm. I'd strum as I sang. But later on, devoting myself to the artistry of blues, I found I couldn't do both at once. I'd solo on my guitar; then sing; then solo; then sing some more. One stopped when the other started. That way I felt a continuity, not a conflict, like a wheel that keeps on turning. Both sounds—guitar and voice—were coming out of me, but they issued from different parts of my soul.

My guitar voice became more individual—more me—when I became more proficient. As a deejay, I gained more confidence as a speaker, which also made me more confident as a singer. For a while, I hooked up with Walter Horton, called Shakey Walter 'cause of how he played harmonica. He and I had a duo along the lines of Brownie McGhee and Sonny Terry, and I liked the interplay between harp and guitar. I felt like I was giving my guitar more personality. But it was one incident in particular that personalized my guitar in a new and permanent way. I'd just got a Gibson L-30. They called it an f-hole, archtop guitar. I added a pickup to make it electric, and it gave me good sound.

In the winter of '49, I'm slowly widening my circle, playing little weekend gigs outside Memphis. Memphis is cool, but I'm learning you have to leave Memphis to spread your popularity. So it's December and I'm in Twist, Arkansas, a tiny town some 35 miles northwest of Memphis. Arkansas can get cold, and this is a December night when even the heat of the music ain't enough to fight back the frost. The nightclub isn't really a nightclub. Just a big room in a chilly old house where the owner has set a tall garbage pail in the middle of the floor and half-filled it with kerosene for heat.

Well, I get to playing and the room gets to rocking, couples get to jitterbugging, snake-hipping, and trucking, and that kerosene is burning hot. I'm up there stoking their fire—the better my beat, the bigger my tips—singing some barn-burning Pee Wee Crayton blues and having a ball. I hear some scuffling, but don't pay no mind, figuring it's only a couple of extra-happy dancers. When voices get loud, though, I know something's wrong. In the thick of the floor, two guys are calling each other names and, even worse, insulting their mothers. The crowd tries to separate them, but it's too late. The dudes are fisting it out, throwing each other to the floor, when they knock over the garbage pail filled with kerosene. *Boom!* Kerosene all over the floor, spreading an incredible river of fire. Flames and screams and panic and running and everyone, including B. B. King, heading for the only door. Bodies crushed and elbows in faces and folks falling down until everyone finally escapes into the freezing night air.

I'm relieved to escape with my life when I realize I don't have my guitar. In my haste, I've left that sucker inside. But the building is burning, it'd be stupid to run back inside, but even more stupid to let my guitar burn, since good guitars are hard to find and I sure don't have the bread for a new one. The flames get higher. I look at that fire and figure I've got about one second to decide. I go for it, dashing back inside. Someone tries to stop me, but I'm gone. Got to. Got to grab that guitar. Fire all around me. Heat unbearable. Burning like hell. Flames licking my feet, scorching my arms. I find the guitar, just as a beam crashes down in front of me. But I got the guitar. Grab it by the neck. Jump back over the beam just as a wall collapses, missing my ass and my guitar by a couple of inches. Can barely see the door for the all-roaring fire. Put my head down, cradling the guitar in my arms, and make a mad dash for the exit. The black night is a welcome sight. I'm burned on my legs, but the guitar is fine. I catch my breath and thank the Lord. "Damn," says one patron to another, "you wouldn't think two guys would near kill each other over a gal like Lucille."

The fight was over Lucille. I never did meet her, though I learned she worked in the club. It was a memorable night, and a memorable name, and I decided right then and there to christen my instrument Lucille, if only to remind me never to do anything that foolish again.

I liked seeing my guitar as a lady. I liked seeing her as someone worth fighting or even dying for. I liked giving her a name and attitude all her own. Truth is, from the time I put a wire string on a broom handle till today, I've turned to Lucille—and there have been seventeen different Lucilles—for comfort and relief. Just to pick her up and stroke her settles me down. Some folks like sitting by waterfalls or meditating in rose gardens. Some people pop pills to relax or hike up mountains. I sit down with Lucille. I put her on my lap and wait until some happy combination of notes falls from her mouth and makes me feel all warm inside. With the possible exception of real-life sex with a real-life woman, no one gives me peace of mind like Lucille.

I've had several Lucilles stolen. That always broke my heart. Not long after the fire at Twist, someone ran off with Lucille. I had booked a gig in Osceola, Arkansas, but couldn't work without a guitar. Herman Green, a fine saxist in my band, said, "B, my father's a preacher and he's got a guitar sitting in his church we could borrow. But we'll just have to climb through the window and take it." I also had to borrow a car from my father, who'd moved to Memphis and was working a night shift at Firestone Tires. Daddy loved Buicks; he had what they called a Buick Straight Eight. Well, we "borrowed" the guitar and made the gig and were coming home when the dude who was driving drove into a bridge to avoid an oncoming car. The Straight Eight engine wound up in my lap, and a big bass fiddle got all busted up. Scared of what'd he say, I had to call Daddy to come get us. I stammered my way through a long, awkward explanation.

"Anyone hurt?" was all he asked.

"No one."

He put down the phone and showed up a few hours later, towed his car away, and made sure we got back to the church so we could return the guitar and leave a little money in the collection plate. Happy ending. My father was able to fix his car and, after a few months of local gigs with borrowed guitars, I bought me a new Lucille. The girl's been with me ever since.

12

Chili, Crackers, and a Big Ol' Belly Washer

On Beale Street, you could get the whole meal for 20 cents. Beale Street had chili, best in the world, thick and rich and spicy delicious. Belly washers were huge quart bottles of flavored soda pop—cream or grape or peach—for washing down the chili. Grab you some chili at Mitchell's Hotel or the One Minute Café. Or go to Johnny Mills' Barbecue on the corner of Beale and Fourth.

Though everyone was poor, doesn't seem like anyone went starving. The street had a spirit best represented by Sunbeam Mitchell, patron saint of Memphis musicians. Sunbeam owned Mitchell's Hotel on the third floor and a lounge, later called the Domino, on the second where he had jam sessions during the week and name bands on weekends. That was the place to hear the heaviest dudes. I call Sunbeam a saint 'cause he'd give you room and board for free if you had a halfway decent story or could play halfway decent blues. Sunbeam loved music and cared for the folks who made it.

There was caring feeling on Beale Street. Musicians would talk to each other, exchange ideas, listen long and hard to each other. I learned so much just hanging 'round the park. Folks were friendly. They sensed your eagerness and opened their hearts, shared their experiences. I made some friends I've kept for life. Bobby Bland was one. He's one of the only people I've stayed close to for over fifty years. He's my favorite blues singer. Man can sing anything, but he gives the blues, with his gorgeous voice of satin, something it never had before. He lifts the blues and makes them his own. I got started a little before Bobby, but when he came 'round Beale Street, I loved having him sit in with those little bands of mine. Bobby was one of the joys of Beale Street.

Beale Street was like WDIA. They were the hot spots for people who loved music and wanted to get somewhere. Seemed like these were the only places where the races really got along. They were islands of understanding in the middle of an ocean of prejudice. Most of the merchants on Beale, like the owners of WDIA, were Jews who'd help you if they could. You could pawn your jewelry for a decent price and buy decent dry goods at Greener's Department Store or Schwab's or Simon Cohen and Sons. Then there were the bands.

Tuff Green's was one of the best. Tuff was a bass player who put together a group with saxist Ben Branch, Phineas Newborn, Sr., a wonderful drummer, and Phineas's two sons— Phineas Jr. on piano and Calvin on guitar. They were both great. Junior, though, was more than great. He was a genius who could play Chopin and Mozart when he was only a child. Folks were calling him the new Art Tatum. Tuff's band never made records but didn't need to. They worked all over, just off their reputation. White people flocked to hear them play country; blacks came for swing or bebop. And Tuff was never ashamed to play the blues. When big names came through to work a week at Mitchell's—say, Cat Anderson from Ellington or Sweets Edison from Basie—Phineas Jr. might sit in and, after a tune or two, the cats would want to take him back to New York or Chicago. But Junior, like many of us, was tied to Memphis and its down-home hospitality.

The more I stayed at WDIA, the more it felt like home. And the more they let me do what I wanted. Naturally I wanted to make records. That didn't come immediately, but I was allowed to form a group and play on the air. Used drummers like Solomon Hardy and Earl Forrest and pianists like Ford Nelson and John Alexander, Jr., a daredevil who later became famous under the name Johnny Ace. I guess you could say this was the first little-bitty B. B. King band.

The first B. B. King record came about 'cause I kept bugging Mr. Ferguson, who'd become something like a father to me. He put me in touch with a man with a transcription firm in Nashville that made commercials: Jim Bulleit. Bulleit also owned Bullet Records, a small operation, and decided I was ready. We used Studio A at WDIA and cut four sides—"Take a Swing with Me," "How Do You Feel When Your Baby Packs Up and Goes," "I've Got the Blues," and "Miss Martha King."

When I hear these songs today, I barely recognize the high-pitched vocalist and stumbling guitarist. But a baby's got to crawl before he walks. The guys behind me—Tuff Green and the Phineas Newborns, both Jr. and Sr.—were already walking tall. And, despite my lackluster performance, I was so thrilled, I would have paid the man for the privilege of recording real records. But nobody bought 'em and, even worse, the company went broke. I teased myself that the sides were bad enough to drive Bullet into bankruptcy.

Miss Martha King, of course, was my wife, and "Miss Martha King" was the best of the four songs. "Yes, I'm sitting here thinking," I sing, "thinking about Miss Martha King . . . I'm in love with that woman . . . I ain't afraid to call her name." But later I change my tune: "Lord, I did everything for you, everything I could, but everything I did didn't do me no good." I'm not saying my blues are strictly true-to-life—I'll make up stories—but this one reflected some of the stress of our marriage. Despite our troubles, I loved that good-hearted lady and wanted her to hear it in song.

I remember once when she went home to Mississippi she got sick and I got worried. I went down to the Delta to visit her, and for a few days our jealous passions subsided. When I left, I had to speed back to Memphis in a borrowed car to make a gig in time. A cop stopped me for doing eighty in a sixty zone. By the way he spoke and looked down at me, I could see he was a stone racist. The man made me feel lower than low. The cop dragged me down to a stone-racist judge who slapped me with a $90 fine. I didn't have $90. All I had was the right to make a call. I called my father. My father is like me; he hates talking on the phone. After I told him the story, all he asked was "You all right?" "Yes, sir," I answered. "Then I'll see you tomorrow," he said before hanging up. I spent the night in jail, but the next day Daddy was down there with the $90.

Martha and I would make up and break up, break up and make up, until it became confusing and finally a little hopeless. My work didn't help. My radio show was carrying my name, and I was finding bookings in a hundred-mile range of Memphis. That meant heavy travel on weekends. That meant separation and more doubts. What was she doing when I was gone? What I was doing? What did I *want* to do?

As a young man, I was divided between a strong notion of loyalty and a large abundance of lust. I could take delight in something as simple as watching a woman slowly wipe on her lipstick. The way she did that reminded me of the way she might slowly remove her panties. In my mind, the power of sexual suggestion was a great pleasure and preoccupation. For the first time in my life, I was in the spotlight. And lots of ladies see the spotlight as sexy. I was just as scrawny and plain-looking as ever, but being on the radio gave me some pull. After a performance in a club, a woman might approach me. That was something new and wonderful in my life. I liked that feeling. It wasn't the reason I played music, but it was a side benefit I couldn't always pass up.

Yet, for all my sexual longing, I believe my musical drive was strongest of all. In my heart of hearts, I wanted to improve my music and be accepted by a larger public. That's always been my dream. I wanted people to enjoy what I sang and played. And I wanted to be paid. The fact that I was now a professional gave me gratification—and also motivation for more money. I was proud I could sell products. I made something of a success out of Pepticon. I've always enjoyed selling products. But my primary product was the blues coming out of my soul.

In the Memphis of my musical coming-of-age, it was easy to be intimidated. I was surrounded by musicians whose technique dwarfed my own. It was the era of cutthroat jam sessions when dudes were sharp and hungry and ready to carve you up. When I think back, I'm surprised I hung in. I could have easily been scared off by everyone else's talents.

I'd listen to records by Barney Kessel, for example, the great jazz guitarist who played at many early Jazz at the Philharmonic concerts, and my jaw would drop. I was awestruck by the structure of his ad-libs. He had the gift of being complicated and simple at the same time. His amplified voice on guitar had a calm beauty that felt like poetry. I followed Barney Kessel's musical stories like a kid following a fairy tale.

In Memphis, the musical stories were just as imaginative. We had our local virtuosos like saxist Fred Ford. He was as good as anyone coming out of New York. After playing across the river in Arkansas, I'd hurry back to Beale Street on a Saturday night just to hear Fred Ford jam. The main dude, though, the man I call the George Washington of Memphis musicians, was Bill Harvey.

Bill was special, not only because of his skill, but his personality. He'd raise my spirits. If I was feeling bad about not being as good as T-Bone or Charlie Christian, Bill would remind me that we're all unique. He was unique. He looked like Louis Jordan and loved his liquor a little too much. That was Bill's only weakness. He had big pop eyes and a quick smile. He was a brilliant bandleader and arranger and tenor saxophonist. His man on tenor was Coleman Hawkins, the daddy of the horn. "B," he'd tell me, "I don't care who's playing tenor today, they all got to go through Hawk." Hawk was his god. Bill's genius was his ability to put a band together in nothing flat. In any band, he made the weakest guy strong by writing parts that fit his strength. They say the orchestra was Duke Ellington's true instrument. Same for Bill Harvey. Bill played a band like Willie Mays played the outfield. He had it covered.

In the early fifties, Bill's bands were all around town, and sometimes they'd back me. That was a thrill and an education. Like Luther Henson, Bill was a patient teacher. He could have written me off as a know-nothing newcomer, but he gave me respect and, even more importantly, taught me to respect my talent.

When Bullet Records went broke, I was discouraged, but I kept on working, sometimes playing with guys like Johnny Ace, saxist Richard Sanders, and Robert Junior Lockwood, guitarist for Sonny Boy #2. Lockwood was the first dude I'd ever heard play "One O'Clock Jump" and make the guitar sound like the whole Basie band. Our circuit was mainly raunchy roadhouses in towns like Birdsong, Arkansas. Arkansas was a gambling state and I was developing something of a gambling habit. I liked betting and naturally I liked winning, but I was mostly losing. The excitement of the nightlife was all over me. I was getting around, which is how I indirectly landed my next record contract.

I'd known Ike Turner from the Delta. I'd seen him in his hometown of Clarksdale, not too far north of Indianola, and I was impressed. Helluva piano player. Plus he could dance and organize a band. He was younger than me, but more advanced. Serious writer. Ike was in tune with grown-up music when he was still a kid. Made you believe he'd been around.

Well, when I was running around with my little group, I booked a date in Clarksdale. I had me a '35 Ford coupé, a two-seater with a rumble seat in the back and a punctured fuel tank. Had to tie a five-gallon can to the running board and attach a hose that ran to the fuel pump. It was a flimsy contraption. Well, I was chugging along this dirt highway just outside Clarksdale when it started to pour. In a matter of minutes, the car stalled and got stuck in a hole in the road. I was late to the gig. I hate being late, and me and the guys had to haul out all the instruments and run to town like thieves in the night. Ike was waiting at the gig.

"Y'all are a mess," he said. "Is this your whole band?" "This is it," I told him. He looked us over again and said, "I better sit in with you." And he did. He played piano and made us sound a whole lot better. Whatever little money I got, I gave some to Ike, who seemed to appreciate it.

And he remembered me. I say that because when I was contacted by the Bihari brothers, owners of Modern Records, I learned Ike was their talent scout. He'd mentioned me. By then Ike had already been playing guitar for Robert Nighthawk. He'd also formed his own Kings of Rhythm that had a big hit, "Rocket '88," with Jackie Brenston on vocals. All this was years before Tina came on the scene. Ike played piano on a couple of my early records. He could romp. Over the years, I followed him closely; I saw him as one of the masters of the tight rhythm and blues band. Ike knew what he wanted and how to get it; he came up with hot grooves and snappy songs that were way ahead of their time. When they talk about rock 'n' roll, I see Ike as one of the founding fathers.

The Biharis were a family-run operation out of L.A. The sisters and brothers ran the show, Jewish people who loved recording and selling black music. As a deejay, I naturally knew their label. Modern Records artists included John Lee Hooker, Elmore James, and Hadda Brooks. Like Aladdin, they were one of several small labels that sold R&B while the majors were ignoring the music. I was excited to meet the brothers when they showed up in Memphis. Right away I related to one brother in particular: Jules.

I soon learned to love Jules Bihari. He reminded me of Flake

Cartledge. He was more a buddy than a boss. Jules didn't show the prejudice or reserve of many white men of that era. He hated segregation and paid it no mind, crossing the color line like it wasn't there. We'd go to Beale Street, hanging in clubs, listening to music, eating chili, chewing the fat. Jules gave me confidence. After hearing my blues, he said I was an artist with a future. No businessman had told me that before. I was motivated to justify his faith in me, and for the next decade or so I recorded for his company under the Modern or RPM or Kent labels.

Jules had a good feel for black music, but no expertise in the studio. He essentially left it up to me. He felt I could write my songs and tell other musicians the sound I wanted. I did have some ideas. For example, I did a version of Tampa Red's "She's Dynamite" all sped up and rocking. I wanted to be blue, but I wanted to be modern. I wanted my energy to get all over the song. I had good support on all my early efforts; I loved having the Newborn men behind me—Papa Phineas on drums and his boys Junior on piano and Calvin on guitar. Nothing feels as good as family.

I felt good recording over at Sun Studios, owned by Sam Phillips. Jules told Sam to give me time whenever I came up with material. In the early fifties, I'd work there often. Sam served as engineer. A little later, he'd be busy with Jerry Lee Lewis, Carl Perkins, Johnny Cash, and Elvis Presley. I saw all of them, but they didn't have much to say. It wasn't anything personal, but I might feel a little chill between them and me. But Elvis was different. He was friendly. I remember Elvis distinctly because he was handsome and quiet and polite to a fault. Spoke with this thick molasses Southern accent and always called me "sir." I liked that. In the early days, I heard him strictly as a country singer. I liked his voice, though I had no idea he was getting ready to conquer the world. Funny when I think back, but I was in the very delivery room—Sun Studios—where that baby called rock 'n' roll was being born.

I guess I was going through some kind of new birth myself. I was making records and I was playing records on the radio by Dinah Washington and Al Hibbler and Larry Darnell and Little Esther and the Orioles and Milt Buckner and Bull Moose Jackson. It was a good time. I'd see all these discs by all these artists from all these labels—King, Atlantic, National, Imperial, Jubilee, Peacock, Regal, Roost, Swing Time—and think to my-self, *I'm out of the cotton field and in the music field!* I'd think that for a little while, but then—if the temperature was right and my money was low—I still might run over to Arkansas and pick a few hundred pounds.

13

Doing the "Do"

I did it all through the fifties and into the sixties. Actually, I started doing it back in the country in the forties. I'm talking about straightening my hair. Some Caucasians use permanents to curl their hair. Well, we did the opposite. We liked turning kinky to straight. Some folks see great social significance in all this. I ain't sure. To me, people just like changing up their appearance. In the Delta, there were no hair products for blacks, so we invented our own. Took lye—strong lye that's like acid in a battery, lye that'll eat through anything—and mixed it with mashed-up white potatoes. The result was a paste you'd put on your head after greasing your scalp with Vaseline. If it sounds messy, it was. Leave it on for five minutes, wash it out, comb it through, and—*presto!*—your hair's smooth and easy to manage. That's your "do." The trick, of course, was to wash it out after five minutes. If not, your scalp feels like it's on fire. You might also wanna go to bed with a rag on your head to keep the "do" in place.

Reminds me of a routine by Patterson and Jackson. In addition to the musical soundies, Memphis movie theaters had soundies with black comics. Patterson and Jackson were vaudeville dancers and clowns funny enough to make you pee in your pants. They had a "do" bit. When Patterson starts helping Jackson do his "do," you just know something's gonna go wrong. Carefully and patiently, Patterson is putting the Vaseline grease on Jackson's scalp. Now, just as carefully, he's applying the lye, nice and thick, all over. "Just sit there," he says, "and I'll be washing it out in a couple of minutes." They kill a couple of minutes trading jokes. "Getting a little warm up there," says Jackson, pointing to his hair. But Patterson tells another joke. "Funny joke," says Jackson, "but get that stuff out of my hair. It's burning like the devil." Patterson has another joke to tell, Jackson's hurting like hell, and then, all of a sudden, a fire alarm goes off, sirens are blasting, and firemen are rushing 'round yelling how they gotta hook up their hose to the sink and take all the water. Jackson is hysterical as a headless chicken, screaming bloody murder, not knowing what to do, when Patterson points to the toilet. You can see Jackson doesn't want to, but he's got no choice. He sticks his head in the toilet as his hair starts to sizzle and steam starts to rise.

I guess we're all a little preoccupied with appearance. I sure was. I was in an industry where entertainers looked sharp. I wanted to be sharp. Sometimes I'd flip through the pages of *Esquire* and get ideas. Even started wearing Bermuda shorts onstage, which was pretty daring for those days. Began to think of myself as *Esquire*-ish. Began thinking that maybe I could really get somewhere in this business. I'd spin a record by Joe

Morris with Laurie Tate singing "Anytime, Anyplace, Anywhere" and think of the possibilities ahead of me. I'd spin saxist Earl Bostic's "Apollo Theater Jump" and dream of playing the Apollo. Bostic was bad; I loved his sound and was proud to learn he was a college graduate and teacher to boot. Hearing Little Jimmy Scott sing "I'll Close My Eyes" or Ruth Brown doing "I Can Dream, Can't I?", I related. I was dreaming. Working my little circuit. And also recording.

Cut maybe ten tunes, mainly using the local guys. Tunes like "B. B.'s Blues," "She's a Mean Woman," and "She Don't Move Me No More." Maybe the songs say something about the end of my marriage to Martha, or maybe I was just making up stories. Either way, I was getting something like $100 a side, which seemed like good money. I was too uninformed to understand royalties or songwriting credit. Though I wrote words and music for almost all my tunes, someone else's name would appear on the label next to mine. That didn't bother me. Just put me in the studio and let me sing.

When I sang "Three O'Clock Blues," I was thinking of how much I loved Lowell Fulson's version, but how I also wanted to put my own hurting on that beautiful song. For reasons I can't remember, we recorded in an empty room in the YMCA on Lauderdale and Vance. We used two Ampec reel-to-reel tape recorders, and of course it was recorded mono with no editing. Make a mistake and start over. We did it in two takes. Richard Sanders and Billy Duncan were on saxes, Johnny Ace on piano, and Earl Forrest on drums. "Three o'clock in the morning," it goes, "can't even close my eyes . . . well, I can't find my baby, Lord, I just can't be satisfied." I give lots of room to Lucille, who's featured as much as me.

I can feel Lucille coming into her own; she's finding her

soul. At the start of the song, she grabs your attention and she also solos in the middle. At the conclusion, I sing, "Goodbye, everybody, I believe this is the end . . . you can tell my baby to forgive me for my sins." The mood is sad as suicide. To me, it's a pure blues with the only two voices, mine and Lucille's, trading laments. It sounded sincere to me. I know it sounded good to Jules Bihari 'cause he released it as my seventh single. The others didn't go anywhere. This one went to the top.

In early 1952, when I was twenty-six, "Three O'Clock Blues" reached and remained #1 on *Billboard*'s rhythm and blues chart for some three months. That changed my life. I didn't become rich or famous, but, in the world of black music, I became a national name. Just like that, my territory spread beyond Tennessee, Mississippi, Arkansas, and Alabama. It's important to remember that I was entertaining in an all-black world. I wasn't selling to whites, and I wasn't performing for whites. That wouldn't happen for another twenty years.

I said *Billboard* called the chart "rhythm and blues." I took that designation seriously. R&B was the new music I related to, the music of Fats Domino singing "The Fat Man," Eddie "Cleanhead" Vinson singing "I'm Gonna Wind Your Clock," Louis Jordan singing "Saturday Night Fish Fry," and Percy Mayfield singing "Please Send Me Someone to Love." Like all music, it was new music based on old music, but it was my music, the sound that seemed to express the time and temperature of my world. I was a rhythm and blues artist and, in my mind, that's the route I'm still traveling.

I saw the world of black entertainment as more than I could handle on my own. I wanted bookings in places I'd never been, but I needed help. I needed a manager. Mama used to say, "Riley, if you don't know something, ask someone who does."

That someone was Robert Henry. He was a local promoter, a light-skinned black man who owned a pool room and shoe-shine stand. He'd been operating out of Beale Street for years. He had a worldy air and seemed to know the entertainment business.

"Mr. Henry," I said, "I'd like to get somewhere in show business but don't know how. Could you help me?"

He said he could. He said "Three O'Clock Blues" meant I could work shows in big cities. I could perform in big theaters. He said he knew the booking agencies, and they'd find me work 'cause they read the trade magazines and knew about my hit. Hits meant bookings. Bookings meant money. "Please, Mr. Henry," I said. "Book me wherever you can."

With Robert Henry's help, Universal Attractions started booking me out of New York City. They said they didn't want my musicians. They had enough bands. They'd hire me only as a solo, letting me sing with whatever bands were on the same bill. That was risky business and made me insecure, but I would have sung with Spike Jones's rag-tag band if it meant a big-time gig. I apologized to my guys and then let them loose.

Johnny Ace took over the band and put it under his name. I was glad 'cause Johnny had him a couple of nice hits—"My Song" and "Cross My Heart"—right off the bat and was on his way. Johnny had looks, guts, determination, and talent. But don't ever dare Johnny to do something dangerous 'cause the boy would up and do it. Finally that did him in. There are lots of stories of how Johnny killed himself playing Russian roulette after a gig in Houston in 1954. By then he was riding high with "Pledging My Love," his big smash. I don't know the true story; I wasn't there. But I loved his talent and mourned his passing.

* * *

The booking agents wanted me to work the Howard Theater in Washington, D.C., the Royal in Baltimore, and the Apollo in New York. If that went well, they promised the Regal in Chicago. These were the four most prestigious black theaters. Tiny Bradshaw's big band was backing all the artists. Man, I was excited.

I boarded my first plane and flew to Washington. In a mixture of fatigue and fear, I fell asleep and woke up while we were flying over the Potomac River. Seemed like we were about to land in the water. I wanted to warn the captain, but I kept my mouth shut. Got to the theater and discovered I was on the same bill as H. Bomb Ferguson.

Like his name implies, H. Bomb was explosive, the extrovert of extroverts. His idol was Wynonie Harris. H. Bomb was loud and cocky, one of those guys who seemed to know it all. In comparison, I was nervous, shy, and close-mouthed. Even though H. Bomb was from Carolina, he'd been living in New York and acted so slick, he made me feel like a hick.

To make me feel more presentable, Robert Henry had taken me to Paul's Tailoring Shop on Beale Street, where I'd bought a red-and-black shirt with flowers all over it, two custom-made suits—lavender blue and red—and two pairs of shoes—patent leather trimmed in lavender blue and red to match the suits. When I got to Washington, I was showing my new wardrobe to a dude in Tiny Bradshaw's band named Tiny Kennedy. "Goddamn," he said, "you can't wear this shit. I'm from Tennessee and people know you're coming from Tennessee and these clown clothes will give Tennessee a bad name. You'll look like a bumpkin just off the farm." Man, that's all I needed to hear. Tiny took me downtown, where I splurged for a plaid black-and-white dinner jacket, a white-on-white shirt, and a snappy bow tie. I liked the outfit so much, I wore it on the photo for my first album, *Singin' the Blues*. That was lesson #1.

Lesson #2 involved arrangements. I'd brought the six-piece chart on "Three O'Clock Blues" by Bill Harvey. "Won't work," said Tiny Kennedy. "We got eighteen pieces. This is a big band. You need a big-band chart." "Where do I get one?" I asked. "At the liquor store," Tiny answered. "What does that mean?" "Buy some booze for the cats writing the arrangements," Tiny advised. "Let the cats fix you up."

The cats fixed me up. For the price of a few bottles of Scotch, I got me a kickin' arrangement of "Three O'Clock Blues" that let me shine at the Howard Theater. H. Bomb, on the other hand, refused to give the guys anything, so they played in keys that gave him fits. He flopped. That didn't make me happy—I like to see my colleagues do well—but it did teach me a lesson: Treat the cats right.

Tiny Bradshaw treated his cats real right. He was a true showman who came out looking like the Secretary of State. Distinguished and hip at the same time. He had a hit called "The Train Kept Rolling" and he'd been rolling 'round the circuit for so long, fans in all these cities loved his music. His musicians could have been with Count or Duke—that's how good they were—and he was a role model of polished professionalism.

When it came to women, I was anything but polished. I was naive. Easily distracted. During that same Howard gig, I met a girl who took me back to her hotel room and, before sex, started shooting up. I didn't wanna look. I can't even stand vaccinations. "It'll make you feel good," she promised. And I was dumb enough to go along. I let her shoot me up and, within seconds, I got sick as a dog. Went to work that day with my fly open, no socks on my feet, and my mind all muddy.

Ran into Tiny Kennedy, who set me straight. "You the damnedest fool I ever did see," he said. "That shit will kill you. And if it don't kill you, it'll turn you into a raggedy-ass junkie like her. You better check whether you got outta there with your rings and watch." I did check, and she had stolen my watch, which was warning enough for me. Never did another drug again. Later on, if guys in my band were using dope and I found out, I'd fire 'em—just like that.

In Washington and Baltimore, me and the Tiny Bradshaw crew stayed in boarding houses, but in Harlem we stayed at the Theresa Hotel. That was another novelty for a boy off the plantation. The idea of walking around New York City and seeing blacks and whites sitting and walking and talking together was something new. Harlem was wonderful, with its churches and politicians and newspapers and nightclubs. It was a black world, sophisticated beyond anything I'd seen before. And the Apollo Theater, where audiences were so critical and quick to boo, became a second home. The Apollo was good to me. In the course of my career, I'd play there thousands of times. The routine was rough. In between showings of a current movie, you'd play five shows a day, starting at noon and running through midnight. But I would have played fifteen or twenty shows if they'd said so. I would have done anything to stay on the circuit.

Part of what made the circuit fun were comics like Mantan Moreland, Redd Foxx, Pigmeat Markham, Nipsey Russell, and Moms Mabley. When Richard Pryor came along later on, I loved his wit and weird way of seeing things. I loved the combination of music and humor 'cause there's so much humor in music anyway. Onstage and off, they were fabulous characters who cracked me up and kept me loose. When the comics opened the show, the fans were looser, already roaring and ready to appreciate my blues.

It was hard to believe, but soon I was making $1,000 a week. Only a couple of years before, I saw myself as a tractor-driving superstar at $22.50 a week. When I got home to Memphis after this first circuit, I was exhilarated and full of gratitude. So when one of my good buddies needed $100, I loaned it to him. Then something funny happened; he started to avoid me. I wanted to tell him to take his time paying me back, but he wouldn't give me a chance. He ran off before I could say a word. I mentioned this to my manager Robert Henry. "B," said Robert, "when you were each making sixty dollars a week at Newberry Equipment, you might loan him twenty dollars and you'd still have forty dollars to buy your groceries and pay your rent. But a hundred dollars is fifty dollars more than he makes. That kind of loan puts him in another place. People who can't pay you back either feel shame at themselves or resentment at you. If you really like the person, just give him the money. That way the friendship will go on."

My marriage was going on—but just barely. Martha was working as a waitress so she could have her own money. I admired that, but I also knew it was another way we were growing apart. She didn't need me. I had begun my lifelong commitment to the road, a commitment that's serious, solitary, and damaging to the idea of a full-time love. I loved the road, needed the road to achieve my goals, and—come hell or high water—would never get off the road. Fact is, I'm writing this book on the road.

Most marriages can't survive the road. Mine didn't. After eight years, Martha and I divorced. Maybe it would have been different if we had had children—or maybe it would have ended just the same. There was more disappointment than bitterness. I still loved her and cherished her ways. But I couldn't stay home and, as our disagreements increased, I couldn't stay faithful. The road became more than a distraction; it became my life.

It was on the road where I met a white woman who became my lover. It happened in Arkansas. Playing Arkansas was still getting me in gambling trouble. For all the new money I was making, I'd fall into periods of debt. I'd get depressed about my ability to handle money and go to my father, who I saw as the Rock of Gibraltar, for advice. "For all this work I'm doing," I told Daddy, "seems like I'm just living day to day."

"Heard you been gambling. That true?" he asked.

"Yes, sir."

"You make money gambling?"

"No, sir."

"You make money with your music?"

"Yes, sir."

I waited for him to say something else, but Daddy stayed silent. He'd made his point. I listened to him and cut back on my wagers. But loving was something else. With my marriage gone, there was no reason to cut back on my loving.

I met this pretty white woman in Little Rock, Arkansas. We were backstage in the auditorium when this lady with a sweet face and voluptuous body told me how much she enjoyed my music. We talked about music for a long time. She knew lots about rhythm and blues and seemed genuinely pleased to meet me. I didn't see any sexual suggestions at first, but when I mentioned I was going back to New York to work, she said she was going there too. She said she'd love to catch the show.

True to her word, she showed up in New York. I was mighty happy. I invited her to dinner. She accepted, and our musical dialogue continued. New York gave us a feeling of freedom, because we found ourselves walking back to my Harlem hotel. I've made many moves on women, but never forced myself. I couldn't do that if I tried. Don't want anyone who doesn't want me. But this lady did seem to want me, and I sure wanted her, and up in my room we indulged in pleasures that went on and on. We carried on, even back in Little Rock. In those days, that was extremely dangerous. Maybe danger added to the thrill. We'd go to black hotels where the clerks were discreet, but I was still nervous, knowing that, when it came to black-white sex, the South wasn't exactly friendly territory.

I don't believe I discriminated with women. Skin color doesn't matter to me. I've been involved with more black women than any other—all the mothers of my children are black—and love black women with all my heart. I'm thinking of the love I feel for my mother and grandmother. Living in a black world, it was natural that I got involved with black women. As my world expanded, so would my experiences with love. Love means the world to me. Searching for love, like working on the road, has been a full-time occupation. I'm grateful to the women I've loved and feel that I owe them—and my children—an explanation for my behavior.

14

Who Can Explain Love?

mentioned my fifteen children. I mention them again because this is the period—the fifties—when many of my babies were born. This book is dedicated to them. They are my flesh and blood. I have not been a good father, but no father has loved his children more. They know this. They know my schedule, they can reach me whenever they want, and many of them do—vocally and often. I was an absentee father. Sometimes I must seem foreign to my children, the same way my father seemed foreign to me. Like my father, I decided the best thing I could do for my kids was to work and provide. Fortunately, I've been able to do that. Unfortunately, my work was on the road, and that's meant a lifetime of one-nighters. I never stopped moving. But I never stopped loving them or caring for them.

Many of my kids are doing well, while others struggle to find their place in the world. I love them equally and believe in the potential of every one of them. I don't want to discuss their lives or mention their mothers by name. I want to respect their privacy. Because I've decided to tell my story doesn't give me the right to divulge theirs. I just want them to know that my encounters with their mothers were real and right. I was—and still am—a man looking for love who was blessed to find it on many occasions. I don't see these episodes as superficial or sleazy. These were women who understood me, women I tried to understand, and women I wanted to love.

I think of myself walking into a flower garden. Wherever I look, I see beautiful flowers. I want to pick one. And I do. It's not the flower's fault. It's mine. The average woman doesn't come up and say, "I want to go to bed with you." I make my move. I make overtures to women who seem kind and gentle, sympathetic and beautiful in ways beyond what most people can see. There's inner beauty, feminine beauty, what I call motherly beauty. I want a soft shoulder, a soft caress. I didn't think of the consequences of having children.

But when it comes to children, you can't make up for lost time. Kids need their daddy on a daily basis, and that proved impossible. I made a choice. I'm a workaholic. You could say I chased a dream, or you could say I was obsessed with my career. You could say I wanted material comfort for my kids, or you could say I wanted acceptance for myself and my music. It's all true. My decision helped me, but hurt others. I tried to be like my own father. Tried to be there when it counted. Sometimes I made it, sometimes I didn't. I'm sad when I think back at the lives I injured; I'm glad when I see any of my kids, whether they understand me or not. I have thirteen grandchildren—seven in college—and seven great-grandchildren. All of them know their education is something I'm pleased and proud to support. .

Being a soft touch with my kids, though, doesn't relieve the guilt I feel for having missed their upbringing. As they were being born, I was working harder than at any time in my long working life. The fifties was my proving period, a time when I drove up and down and around this country hundreds and hundreds of times. I didn't get sick, I didn't stop, I didn't even think of stopping.

I'm the kind of guy who'd like to live life without confrontations or nasty entanglements. I'd like to tell you that I've smoothly sailed the sea of love, but I haven't. Haven't even come close. I've gone overboard a few times. But I am glad to report that I've never been involved in paternity suits. I was told a long time ago that if you were with a woman, and the woman says the child is yours, then the child is yours. I've had good relationships with the mothers of my children—before, during, and after. When misunderstandings surfaced, I was able to work them out without harsh words.

As my work grew more intense, so did my desire for sexual relief. I loved it. I looked for it. I didn't grab, but I did use all my meager powers of persuasion. I didn't like sleeping alone. I kept working what they called the chitlin circuit, my meat and potatoes for decades, along with the big theaters in the black neighborhoods of urban America. On the national tours, I started making $1,500, $2,000, even $2,500 a week. I bought some jewelry, got a ring with B.B. set in diamonds, made money, lost money on gambling, pawned jewelry, stopped gambling, got the jewelry out of hock, and started all over again. Bought me a white Cadillac and always put up a good front. Daddy used to say, "If a jackass is sitting in church, no one knows he's a jackass till he hee-haws." I tried not to hee-haw. Tried to look sharp, remembering Cousin Bukka's advice: "Dress like you're going to the bank to borrow money."

Took some of the money and bought Daddy a 147-acre farm outside Memphis. When I came home, I still did my program on WDIA, but the road was messing with that. WDIA wanted someone they could count on all the time. Soon I'd stop. But it was hard for us Kings to quit *any* paying gig. Even after he moved to the farm, Daddy kept his job at Firestone. He loved the new place. He cultivated the soil and raised corn and cotton. He drove a tractor around a piece of land he could finally call his own. I had my children and my sisters had children and I suppose I was dreaming how one day we all might live on the farm. As long as there was a King, he or she would have shelter and food. That was my thinking. But it never happened because my thoughts went back to working the road.

"I'm wondering if I'm working too much," I said to Daddy one summer night when I was home for a few days. We went into town to watch the Memphis Chicks. They were a white baseball team, and blacks sat in a separate section. Jackie Robinson and Roy Campanella, our heroes, were already in the majors with the Brooklyn Dodgers. But segregation was still stiff in the South. We had the Negro Leagues, which we loved, but we also followed the Chicks. Night games were exciting. The sky was crowded with stars, the evening warm and pleasant, the green field bathed under the yellow lights. Kids were running around, the smell of popcorn was in the air, and me and Daddy were munching on juicy hot dogs. It was a rare time for us to be alone together. I was tired from playing sixty gigs on sixty consecutive nights in sixty different cities. "Work too much?" asked Daddy. "I don't know what that means. How can a man work too much?"

And for the rest of the game, other than cursing out the umpire, my father didn't say another word.

Some of the songs I was recording may have reflected my thoughts. "My Own Fault" said one of the titles that might have referred to my marriage. "You Didn't Want Me" said another. I mainly wrote blues, but I also wrote blues ballads like "Story from My Heart and Soul" and "You Know I Love You." "You Know I Love You" was very big for me. Biggest thing after "Three O'Clock Blues." I recorded it at Tuff Green's house, where we covered the walls with quilts and blankets to soften the sound. We had five mikes for five musicians. The mikes ran into a single control board, meaning that if anybody screwed up, everybody screwed up.

I worked on my songs, sometimes on the road, often in the silence of my head. I didn't have Percy Mayfield's gift for poetry or Louis Jordan's wonderful wit. I can't write fancy. My stuff is simple. In one form or another, I'm usually dealing with the tug-of-war between men and women. My aim is to express the longing in my soul and the joy in my heart. If I do that, I feel fulfilled. To perform honestly, I need to believe the stories I'm singing.

My audience needs to believe me as well. Some said I was developing a stage presence. I took that as a compliment without being sure what it meant. I got two left feet and could never move like Rufus Thomas or James Brown. I couldn't do the splits or play behind my head like T-Bone. To get me out on the dance floor, you'd need to pour whiskey down my throat and watch me make a fool of myself. I couldn't move like my friend Eddie Jones, who called himself Guitar Slim and had a big hit with "The Things That I Used to Do." Slim would attach a long cable to his guitar and prowl through the audience, even roam out in the street. He'd duckwalk along the bar and do Olympic-quality gymnastics. He'd also wear crazy-colored clothes and dye his hair and give you a helluva show for your money. Slim was a poor boy like me, trying to make his way. Beyond the fireworks, though, he was a killer musician. If you were a guitarist looking for a cutting contest, you wouldn't wanna mess with Slim.

In contrast, my show was straight-ahead. I had no choice but to concentrate on music. My technique of bending strings and trilling notes was giving me an approximation of that steel pedal sound that haunted my musical dreams. Lucille was singing the blues better than me. By now I was carrying another Lucille, an ES-5, an electric Spanish, the only hollow-body Gibson electric with three built-in pickups. My previous Lucille had been stolen in Brooklyn when I left her in the trunk of my car. Thought she'd be safe there. Goes to show how much I knew about Brooklyn.

My wife Martha used to call me ol' lemon face because of my facial contortions when I play Lucille. I squeeze my eyes and open my mouth, raise my eyebrows, cock my head, and God knows what else. I look like I'm in torture when, in truth, I'm in ecstasy. I don't do it for show. Every fiber of my being is tingling. Notes are passing through me and I'm feeling something down in my gut.

My gut was telling me that the big-city blues based on my country childhood was a true-life portrait of my past, present, and future. The older I got, the more I could see the majesty of the blues. The blues reminds me of the Pepticon I used to advertise, a tonic good for whatever ails you. The blues is the source. I still get irritated when I hear folks call the blues gloomy. The fact is that the blues contains all the basic feelings of human beings: pain, happiness, fear, courage, confusion, desire . . . everything. Complicated feelings told in simple stories. That's the genius of blues.

Dizzy Gillespie was a genius of jazz. Being out on the road, I got to meet the great musicians of the day. Given my keep-to-myself nature, though, they were mostly passing acquaintances. Dizzy was different. He was a country kid from South Carolina and the least pretentious man I've ever met. Naturally I was in awe of his reputation and talent. He'd practically invented bebop, was a brilliant writer and arranger, and had led a big band whose sound was revolutionary. Dizzy understood chordings and harmonics in ways that went over my head. A trumpeter like Bobby Hackett had more influence over me. Bobby caressed the melody like the melody was a lovely woman. I loved the mood music records he made with Jackie Gleason's orchestra. Hackett's approach was soft and romantic and filled with feeling. Dizzy also expressed strong feelings; he was a frantic and funny dude who always made me feel good.

I first got to know him in Houston when he was in a traveling show with Nat Cole, Stan Kenton, and Sarah Vaughan. Nat was the headliner, and Diz was with Charlie "Bird" Parker. They were playing the downtown auditorium. I was playing a small venue with a blues package. We all stayed at the same hotel. Me and Diz hit it off. He told me he liked my "Three O'Clock Blues," and that made me feel like a million bucks. We spent hours talkin' 'bout life back on the farm. Turned out he had somewhere to go before the gig and was worried about

Bird getting to the auditorium. Well, I had a car and offered to give Bird a ride. I was honored.

Charlie Parker was a handsome man who spoke like a professor and smiled like a saint. Naturally I knew he wasn't; I'd heard the stories about drugs, but I didn't see any drugs, not that day. Bird was clear-eyed and well-mannered and treated me with so much respect, I felt humble. Sitting next to me, I told him how I'd peeped in on him at the Jones Night Spot in Indianola when he was with Jay McShann. He smiled and reminisced about Walter Brown. "I'm a blues player, B," said Bird. "We're all blues players. It's just that we hear blues in different ways. The day we get away from blues is the day we'll stop making sense." That made all the sense in the world to me. And it was coming from the man seen by modern jazz musicians as the messiah.

Back in Memphis, Bill Harvey was our messiah. I looked to him to save me from the traveling shows where I sang in front of strange bands. Those shows weren't all bad; I liked meeting Fats Domino and sharing a bill with Ray Charles. We were put on packages promoted by Ralph Weinberg that left New York, stormed the South, toured Texas, shot up into Oklahoma, pushed into the Midwest, and wound up in Cleveland some eighty-two dates after we started. Not a night off. I liked that; I liked the exposure and I liked the money. What I didn't like, though, was that those tours were starting to dry up. I also didn't like the uneven quality of the backup bands that varied from good to lousy.

Bill Harvey's bands were always good. And it was good that I had a couple of other nice-sized hits—"Woke Up This Morning," "Please Love Me," "Neighborhood Affair"—to help establish my consistency in the R&B market. I thought of going on my own, and when Bill mentioned his connections with business folk in Texas, I listened. I wanted more work, and I wanted to reverse the curve that had my fee drop from $800 a night to $400. I wasn't sure why the booking agency kept trimming me back. I felt like I had no control.

Bill Harvey put me in touch with Maurice Merritt, an agent, and Evelyn Johnson, who worked at the Buffalo Booking Agency, owned by Don Robey, who also ran Duke and Peacock Records. They operated out of Houston. Maurice said, "Let Evelyn book you and let me manage you and I'll advance you some money to cover transportation. That way you can tour exclusively with Bill Harvey's band." For a down payment on a new Cadillac and two new station wagons to carry the band— somewhere between $2,000 and $3,000—I switched management.

Robert Henry was against the Texas connection. He urged me to wait, promising things would get better. But I knew Robert owned his pool hall and other businesses. He wasn't as hungry as me. He also argued that it was more prestigious to work with a New York agency. But I didn't care about the prestige; I wanted gigs. Besides, Robert wasn't willing to reach in his own pocket like Maurice. Maurice seemed to have the bigger picture in mind. He knew I wanted a band I could count on, and Evelyn knew I'd grab all the work she could find.

For a while, it did work. I knew it wasn't the best deal in the world, but it pushed me forward—at least a little. I was still taping my program on WDIA when I was in town. The station, though, was tired of that and, within a few months, my deejay career would end. My new career as a self-contained package had begun. Bill Harvey was masterful. He put together a seven-piece group and we went out, in '53 and '54, as B. B. King featuring the Bill Harvey Band. All the guys were showmen, especially Fred Ford, who played sax and moved onstage with a beautiful combination of grit and grace. We had a review, something like Johnny Otis's. We had a girl singer, Benita Cole, and two guy singers, Paul Monday and Harold Connor. Paul, who also played piano, was a more sophisticated blues vocalist than me, and Harold sang the beautiful ballads of the day like "Prisoner of Love." The show had style. I probably had less than anyone; I was the flat-footed no-nonsense bluesman. But because of my hits, I was the main attraction.

We took our little review wherever Evelyn Johnson could book us. There were tiny clubs and big barns, nice black theaters and nasty roadhouses. The circuit wasn't as organized as today's schedules. That meant we might get up on a Monday in L.A. and drive straight through to New York City, alternating drivers, not stopping for nothing except bodily functions, watch the sunset, watch the sunrise, keep on keeping on till we found ourselves driving down 125th Street in Harlem.

Most of our work, though, was in the South, especially Texas. Texas has more juke joints than rattlesnakes. You can gig in Texas for months on end. There were times when I thought we'd never leave Texas. We drained the South dry— Louisiana, Alabama, Mississippi, Georgia. In the South, of course, blacks couldn't stay in hotels or motels, so people put us up. That was pleasant or uncomfortable, depending on the hosts. Buying food on the road was a hassle. Not everyone would serve you. Some of the dudes in the band would get mad and cause a scene. I held the anger and pain inside and moved on. Didn't have time for trouble.

Often, without room or board, we'd say the hell with it and sleep in the car, which meant sore backs and sore necks until that night's blues blew away the pain and I was back in my Cadillac and the cats were in the station wagons, running up and down the two-lane highways as Harry Truman was retiring to Missouri and Ike was heading for Washington. I hoped I was heading for easy street, but easy street wasn't part of my destiny. For a bluesman—least the ones I know—nothing comes easy.

15

Lousy Leader

Maybe I'm too tough on myself, but I wasn't cut out to lead. I'm better at taking orders than giving them. I actually like taking orders. Being told what to do takes the pressure off me. As a farmer, I was conditioned to follow instructions. I never learned to plan. Great leaders are planners. I'm a dreamer. Let me fool with my music or watch a movie. Let me get lost in a soap opera or make up a song about some lonely guy. Better yet, just tell *me* what to do. If you assign me a task, chances are I'll get it done—and on time. Directing doesn't come naturally. But I did it. Been doing it, in fact, for the past forty years.

Even though Bill Harvey was a fabulous musician who could accommodate any style, he wasn't the greatest leader either. Drinking muddied his mind and made him sick. After a tough year of touring with his band behind me, the old pattern resurfaced. Gigs dwindled and money faded. I fell into another rut. I felt myself moving horizontally, while I wanted to go up. Had some nice songs out there like "She's Dynamite" and "B. B.'s Blues" and "You Upset Me Baby" that said, "I've tried to describe her, it's hard to start, I better stop now 'cause I got a weak heart. Like being hit by a falling tree, woman, what you do to me . . . you upsets me, baby." These songs were all familiar to the people who liked B. B. King. They weren't smashes like "Three O'Clock Blues," but they were respectable sellers. Seems like "respectable," though, wasn't getting me anywhere. "Respectable" meant the grind would never end. I didn't want "respectable"; I wanted "fantastic" or "spectacular." I wanted to make a change.

Went home to Memphis. Gave up everything: the Cadillac, the station wagons, the tour, the review, the whole thing. Bill Harvey kept the transportation and his band. Maurice Merritt was mad. I didn't care. Had an idea in my head. Big idea. Kept it to myself 'cause Daddy once said, "If you don't say what's on your mind, people won't know." Let it stew for a couple of weeks. I knew it was risky, but it seemed right. What if I took over the whole shooting match? What if I formed a real big band under my own name, got my own transportation—my own bus—and tried going out again, only on a bigger scale? Would that work?

"Sure," said Evelyn Johnson. She was the one I was counting on most. She was the gal booking me. I couldn't count on royalties; for the most part, royalties didn't come. Didn't have the legal sophistication to make them come and didn't have the disposition to up and quit Modern because no other label seemed to be paying my colleagues any royalties either. But once Evelyn heard the idea, she kept pushing me, kept saying how I had enough hot records to put together a bigger show and make bigger money.

I liked the idea of independence. The idea of my own big band was thrilling. I could see how, like the bands of Tiny Bradshaw or Lucky Millinder, mine could be the backbone of a show including other artists. That would mean more work. My own bus would mean status. I associated those things with the entertainers I idolized. Count Basie always had his own bus. So did Duke. In the R&B field, we all took note when Percy Mayfield rolled into Memphis with his name written all over the side of a long bus. That said prestige and permanence. Meant someone believed in you enough to loan you the bread to buy a big vehicle. Maybe it goes back to my love of tractors, but to me a big vehicle represents success. I loved the cylinders, gearbox, tires, seats and windows and luggage bins, and especially the sound of that big engine roaring down the highway. Man, I wanted a bus.

I found a CPA. Black dude named Turner. Good with numbers. Mr. Turner projected that, with enough work, we'd clear $25,000 our first year. Proved it to me on paper. I was an easy sell. "But, Mr. Turner," I said, "I need five thousand dollars for the bus and another five thousand to operate it." "Leave it to me, B. I got connections." Mr. Turner had pull with the white banks. He talked their talk. He got me a credit line and I got me a driver called Cato Walker who found a big ol' used Aero coach. Cato, a fine mechanic, was devoted to his family but ready to leave Memphis. He became my friend for life. His brother James, a bass player nicknamed Shinny, had already been my road manager and, along with my valet Sleepy, was also eager to come along. For years they'd be my solid support, my right-hand men. So would Norman Matthews, who's still with me today, and Bebop Edwards, my man for a quarter-century. From the get-go, I was blessed with devoted employees. I tried my best to return that devotion.

But the question is still there: Why would a guy who sees himself as a lousy leader decide to lead a band? Why would I go against my nature?

Forty years ago, at age thirty, I didn't know myself like I do now. I knew I didn't have the qualities of someone like Booker Baggett, foreman at Mr. Johnson's farm. Booker had the quiet strength to lead a platoon into hell. I knew I was shy about telling people what to do, but I figured I could learn on the job. It was my responsibility to learn. I felt obliged to care for my band with the same conscientiousness that Flake Cartledge or Johnson Barrett had cared for me. I also had no choice; if I wanted a better life, I had to take charge. Couldn't go back. I heard the Fates telling me, "B, you've reached this plateau. To reach the next one, you're gonna have to do it yourself." The voice of the Fates was louder than the voice of my doubts. I formed a band.

I've had a band ever since. In my prejudiced opinion, the B. B. King bands have been good, giving me the snap I need, playing a mix of jazz and blues that sets the right tone for my show. The horns give me the harmonies I first heard in church, and the rhythm section locks me into grooves that satisfy my soul. My bands have also instructed me. Dozens of musicians, many of them far better than me, have passed through.

Some, like George Coleman, were brilliant beboppers. George's ideas flowed; he had a superb knowledge of music and could play anything he heard. Eventually, he'd join Miles Davis. With me, George would grow restless and urge me to learn chord changes on modern jazz. I went along, and my dumb fingers did pretty good. Learned songs like "How High the Moon" and "Body and Soul." Listening to Barney Kessel and Herb Ellis and Johnny Smith as much as I did, I understood jazz phrasing and could adopt the approach—to a degree. I incorporated some jazz things into the show. But they were more Basie-based and blues-based than bebop. Blues was my bread and butter. I knew why the George Colemans of the world wanted me to expand. I respected their musicianship and appreciated their encouragement. But because of the audience I wanted to please and the constitution of my own musical mind, I stuck to selling blues—then and now.

The bus was a trip. We called it Big Red. Smack in the middle of the fifties, I headed out to conquer the world. I was determined to snatch me a piece of that American dream. Figured I finally had my act together. I had my band. Used Earl Forrest and Ted Curry on drums. Always liked two drummers. Still use two today. Can't have too much rock-steady rhythm. Jerry Smith played bass and Millard Lee was the piano player. Millard Lee was the oldest guy in the band, so we called him Mother. He called me Black Bitch, his term of endearment. "You know better than that, Black Bitch," he'd say to me. I could confide in Mother, tell him things I couldn't tell my own father.

Mother was a great musician; he was the one who told me about this guy who chorded the guitar like an orchestra. Talked about him like he was the Second Coming. Called him Wes Montgomery. A few years later, when I saw Wes in person, I heard how right Mother had been. Mother was our teacher. He taught me to mimic the ladies by putting my hand on my hip and shaking my backside while singing in falsetto. Became part of my show.

Evelyn Young was a lady who blew alto. Evelyn was fierce. We called her Mama Nuts and she could flat-out play anything. A lot of the younger saxists in Memphis who went on to stardom, musicians like Hank Crawford, will tell you Evelyn shaped their style. Floyd Newman, Dickie Boy Lillie, and Lawrence Birdine also played sax.

Kenny Sands and Calvin Owens blew trumpet. Off and on, Calvin stayed with me for decades. He was part of the Houston connection and turned into one of the best arrangers around. He's living in Belgium today and has the respect of all the master musicians. Calvin's a master himself.

Meanwhile, back in the recording studio, I was introduced to another master. His name was Maxwell Davis; he's the man responsible for my best work. Maxwell was an arranger-producer who understood me inside and out. He had worked with many of the R&B stars on Modern and served as the Biharis' main music man. He'd made great records with Roy Hawkins, Little Willie Littlefield, and Smokey Hogg. He had experience, and his musical education gave him wide flexibility in the studio. The man could write, think, and adapt. He also blew a mean tenor sax and had a hit of his own called "Slow Walk." Maxwell was another Luther Henson—a loving teacher.

Maxwell became a dear friend. He looked like Nat Cole and dressed just as sharp. He was the only arranger who could put on record 95 percent of everything I was hearing in my head. Maxwell had a sound—lean, clean, the perfect complement to my blues. I'd come in from the road with a tape of something I was writing, and within minutes Maxwell would punch out a chart that expressed the soul of the song. He amazed me. He always left room for Lucille, understanding so well how she and I worked together. He wrote a chart of "Every Day I Have the Blues" with a crisp and relaxed sound I'd never heard before. I liked it so well, I made it my theme.

"Every Day" has a noble history. Memphis Slim wrote it and Lowell Fulson, one of the sleeping giants of the blues, recorded it. Joe Williams also recorded it with King Kolax's band. Then I came along and did my version. But the version of versions, the one that put us all to shame and will never be topped, was when Joe Williams joined Count Basie and sang it over Ernie Wilkins's majestic arrangement.

Maxwell Davis didn't write majestically; he wrote naturally, which was my bag. He created an atmosphere that let me relax. When I sang, "What can I do? I just sing the blues . . . 'cause that's the only thing I know to do," Maxwell set it in a tempo that fit me fine. Many of the songs of my Maxwell Davis era have survived. He took my "Sweet Little Angel" and helped me spread her wings. "Got me a sweet little angel," I sang, "I love the way she spreads her wings . . . when she spread her wings around me, I get joy and everything." Maxwell understood joyful blues as well as down-in-the-dumps blues. Some of the things I wrote were a little less poetic than "Angel." "I made a fine beautician" went one song, "in a very fine condition, she was long and lean and you know what that means" are lines that don't rival Shakespeare. But "Sweet Sixteen" is something I still sing. "When I first met you, baby, you were just sweet sixteen . . . you just left your home, woman . . . the sweetest thing I'd ever seen."

I did see a sweet thing, no older than sixteen, back down in the Delta. Her name was Sue Carol Hall and her mama had bought an old nightclub and renamed it Club Ebony. Sue's father was white and Jewish; she was a bright-eyed, light-skinned beauty with a beautiful body and an inquisitive mind. When I'd play the Ebony, Sue would show up, telling me how she liked my music and how she planned to go to college and improve her lot in life. I liked that talk. I liked her mom and I liked coming home to play for folks and family from my earliest memories. When I went away from Indianola, Sue stayed on my mind.

When music wasn't on my mind, women were. When it came to women, I still had some lessons to learn. I learned one of the scariest lessons in Columbus, Georgia. Thinking back, chills run up and down my spine.

I'm at the club, the gig's over, and I'm feeling good. Maybe had a drink or two. Hanging out in my dressing room with Sleepy and Shinny, who introduce me to some ladies who tell me how much they liked the show. Thanks. One lady is looking like she *really* liked the show. "Oh, I just loved it, B. B.," she says. "I've always loved your music." I love the way she looks. In my mind, I call her Miss Fine. Fabulous figure with generous curves in all the places that please me most. Sweet disposition and come-hither smile. Well, I'm ready to come hither. So when Sleepy whispers she's separated from her husband who's overseas in the service, I see no reason not to join Sleepy and his lady friend and accept Miss Fine's invitation to see her home.

I see more than her home. I see her bedroom and her incredible body. I see hours of fantastic lovemaking that leaves me exhausted and free to dream in peaceful tranquillity. But in the middle of the dream, I hear a commotion. Voices. Voices outside the dream, real-life voices coming from the next room. Two guys talking. Sleepy and another dude. The other dude is saying, "Just flew home from Europe and wanted to surprise my old lady. Yeah, man, I served as an MP." MP! I'm thinking .45s and bullets piercing my brain. My heart's leaping out my chest; I'm frantic, thinking faster than I've ever thought in my life.

I see the bedroom has two doors. Behind one door is the voice of the man who wouldn't be thrilled seeing me in bed with his wife. Behind the other is the kitchen. While the men keep talking, I reach under the bed, grab my boxer shorts, slip 'em on, and gently turn the knob of the kitchen door. The knob creaks like something out of a horror movie. When I finally get it turned and open the door, staring me in the face is a dog as big as a small horse. He's doing a low growl, showing his fangs, and seems to be saying: *Fool, you ain't getting past me.* I say, "Me and you, we gonna fight each other 'cause I ain't fighting the dude with the .45." Must be fear, but I leap over the dog and before he has chance to get me, I'm out the back door, into the yard, where a fence stands between me and freedom. Jump the fence and find myself running down the street in my boxer shorts. Running like a man possessed. My run is interrupted by the sight of spinning cherry-tops. Cop car catches up to me. Two cops inside. "Where you coming from?" first cop wants to know. "That house back there," I say. "Don't you know it's against the law to be out here in your drawers?" asks the second cop. "I know," I say. "Leave him alone," says the first cop, who gives me a ride back to where I'm staying. I'm sighing, I'm saved, I'm grateful to God.

Next day Sleepy doesn't get back till late afternoon. All he can do is laugh at me. All I can do is swear I'll never go to a lady's house again. The rule I adopt is simple: Come to my home or my hotel or don't come at all.

In 1956, while the band rode in Big Red, I bought a pink Eldorado with whitewalls and big fins. Hooked up an antenna and put a TV in the back, which was unheard of at that time.

I liked my musicians and I think they liked me. I paid good and never had trouble finding good players. I was an easy guy to work for. I didn't go for any drugs, but I was a pretty liberal leader. It took a lot for me to fire anyone, though we had some rules on the bus. Don't take a lady between cities if you're gonna misuse her or put her out. That happened a couple of times and I wound up paying her ticket home. If two dudes get in a fight, that's fine with me, long as I don't know about it. Make sure your suit's clean. Don't miss rehearsals. Don't leave the bus with a do-rag on your head. And, for God's sake, don't mess with Mama Nuts. Just leave the woman alone.

For the most part, I left the guys alone. Rode in my Caddie and slept or watched the world go by. I've lived most of my life on the road in silence. Silence does me good. Silence allows me to settle down and feel the rhythm of the road. For me, the road is like breathing. It's always there, it never stops, it just is. In 1956, the booking agency gave me a gold ring for doing 342 one-night stands. Other years I did even more. Since the mid-fifties when I went out on my own, I've missed a total of 18 gigs, usually because of bad weather. For over forty years, I averaged some 330 shows a year. In the past five years, I've cut it down to 250. Someone said there's no one in show business who's worked more one-nighters or covered more miles. If that's the case, I'm proud. I've done it 'cause I haven't known what else to do. You don't hear my records much on the radio, so I've had to go to the people through live performance.

Living on the road makes you either mean or patient, depending on your temperament. I hope it's made me more patient. I've put up with more humiliation than I care to remember. Cops like to mess with black men in Cadillacs. The cops in Georgia and Florida got a kick out of stopping me for no reason, wanting to know where and how and why I got a car like this. When I said, "I earned it," they said, "Well, you were speeding" before hauling my ass down to another judge to pay another fine. Those were the times and conditions.

Other times were dangerous due to unforeseen forces. Once me and my man Norman Matthews were staying at a boarding house in Macon, Georgia, owned by a black man who worked as a skycap. Nice dude with one leg shorter than the other. Morning after the gig, we're packing to head out when we hear shooting. Me and Norman hit the floor. When the shooting stops, we run into the living room to find the skycap slumped against the wall, covered in blood and urine. Suspecting something, he had doubled back from work to find his wife with another man. That other man shot and killed him. But before me and Norman have time to call an ambulance, here comes the skycap's brother, hungry for revenge. He's got a gun and he starts shooting the man who shot his brother and me and Norman hit the floor again just as the cops arrive shooting at anyone who's moving. We ain't moving. We don't move for another half hour when the dead skycap is finally dragged away and the cops arrest everyone in the room but us. Then on to the next gig.

You see strange things on the road. A car is turned over on the highway, and a white family—a man, his wife, and kids—are trapped underneath. We stop Big Red and rush out to help them. Everyone pitches in. We carefully flip the car and take out everyone but the wife. She's trapped in a way where we can't move her. Another car stops and two white men get out. They look at us suspiciously. "What are you doing to these people?" they ask. We try to explain, but they don't believe us. They call an ambulance to free the woman, and when the woman is freed, everyone is still looking at us like we're perverts or thieves. All 'cause of color. No one can believe we're just people helping other people. Those are things that break my heart.

Other things heal my heart. Down in Florida, we're roaring down the highway when we see a car pulled over to the side of the road. The hood's up and a black man is trying to fix the engine. We stop and see if he wants help. "Can't get it started," he says. He's going to Miami, and so are we, so we give him a ride. He's a salesman selling hair products. Fifteen years later, he calls my manager to invite me on a TV show he's producing. Turns out he's Mr. Johnson of Johnson Hair Products. He went on to head the biggest manufacturing company of black hair products in the world.

Out on the road, I was still concerned about my own hair. The days of the homemade perms were behind me. Certain barber shops in certain locales did beautiful do's. We also called it gassing your hair or wearing a conk. In New York, I'd go to Sugar Ray Robinson's. He had a slick shop in Harlem where I might run into Billy Eckstine or Nat Cole. When they did your hair, your head looked real good. I'd walk out of there feeling like a million bucks. There was also Nat's Barber Shop in Miami and the Crystal White in Houston. We'd have someone on the bus who could do a do, but if you wanted those pretty finger waves, you'd go to a professional shop.

Always wanted to look good. Wanted to make a positive flashy impression. I remember one night, though, when the only impression made was my ass pressing the floor. Happened in Austin, Texas. After the show, I'm still onstage signing autographs. Got this policy I've honored for forty-five years: I'll sign any autograph for any fan. I see my fans as my bosses—

they pay my way—and I'll never do anything to hurt their feelings. On this night, one of the ladies wanting an autograph is especially pretty, so I get up off my chair and lean over to hand her the slip of paper. My mistake is not looking before I sit back down. A dude has intentionally moved the stool. I fall flat on my booty, my legs raised in the air like a plucked chicken. I'm pissed. I say a few words to the dude, who's now surrounded by his cronies. Suddenly I'm surrounded by my band, led by Millard Lee. Mother's as treacherous as he is talented. He's sunshine one minute and Hurricane Sally the next. We keep a few Winchester rifles on the bus, and sure enough Mother's aiming one at the guy who moved my chair. Then someone has a gun on Mother, and before I know it guns are pointing every which way. Me, I don't have no gun. Don't know if I'm more mad than scared, but I just stand there till the guns are slowly lowered and we make our way to Big Red. Before we can pull away, though, gunshots ring out. I hit the floor, but some of my boys are returning the fire. It's the Wild, Wild West Show. Next day the papers write it up big, making us sound like gangsters. Fortunately, no one was hurt, and I just write it off as one of those terrible times on the road.

The road was one challenge. Selling records was another. Both challenges could be frustrating. Unexpected twists and turns could throw me off-track. I was still trying to move in one direction—up—when the facts said I was actually moving in another—sideways. Challenging my world even more were these explosions in American music. I was living through a revolution while trying to understand what the hell was happening. Everything was changing—and changing fast.

16

Where Was I When Rhythm and Blues Became Rock 'n' Roll?

was working. That's the answer to almost any question about where I was at almost any time. Working. Working Seattle or Amarillo or Dayton or Dallas or Des Moines. I was singing for my supper, either heading to L.A. to cut a record or just leaving L.A. I'd cut seven or eight sides every time I'd get to L.A. And do it fast—four, five songs a session, maybe more. I'd bring songs and arrangement ideas to Maxwell Davis, who'd write the charts that let Lucille soar. That made me happy. My blues and blues ballads—"Sneakin' Around," "Early Every Morning"— were moving in the same direction: straight ahead. "Looking at my future," I'd sing, "forgettin' 'bout my past . . . well, I'm so glad trouble don't always last . . . have fun while you can, fate's an awful thing, you can't tell what's gonna happen, that's the reason I love to sing."

Tried to remain optimistic, though the signs around me made it difficult. See, I was living through a revolution that seemed to have everything and nothing to do with me. I'm talking about the explosion of rock 'n' roll, which was really rhythm and blues written and performed for white teenagers. White teenagers were the new market. They had the money and the rebellious attitude. They didn't care that their parents looked down on black music; they liked it, they wanted to dance to its rhythms and taste its sexy flavor. These teenagers, God bless 'em, represented a new and hipper generation of fans. Trouble was, none of them were fans of mine.

Didn't complain then and ain't complaining now. I liked the revolution of rock 'n' roll. In some ways, it felt like an acceptance of the beauty of black music. The roots of rock 'n' roll went back to my roots, the Mississippi Delta. It was born of the blues. Rock 'n' roll was making young people happy. I understood it, but couldn't embrace it. I lacked the flash of other black entertainers like Little Richard, Chuck Berry, or Bo Diddley. I missed the boat.

When Little Richard sang "Tutti-Frutti," "Long Tall Sally," or "Slippin' and Slidin'," he was lighthearted and funny and filled with the fire of youth. My audiences were always my age or older. And I was thirty-one years old. If I could have written witty lyrics with teens in mind like Chuck Berry's "Maybellene" or "Roll Over Beethoven," I might have done it. But I lacked that skill. I liked the Bo Diddley shuffle; it reminded me of something we used to do in grade school. It was good for Bo, but it wasn't for me; it didn't fill my soul. When Fats Domino did "Ain't That a Shame" or "Blueberry Hill," he hit a chord with the public I never found. I had hood hits, successes in black neighborhoods only.

Even true bluesmen like Joe Turner and Jimmy Reed had considerable crossover hits. Joe had "Shake, Rattle, and Roll" and "Flip Flop and Fly" and Jimmy had "Honest I Do" and "Big Boss Man." Maybe it was the sound of their voices, maybe the rhythm underneath, but something about Joe and Jimmy's music turned on teenagers.

I think of Ray Charles. I knew Ray in the forties when he was singing like Charles Brown and Nat Cole. I knew him when he played piano for Lowell Fulson, when he had R&B hits on Swing Time like "Baby, Let Me Hold Your Hand." Ray's a perfectionist and one of the best musicians I've ever known. He went to Atlantic Records and combined gospel and rhythm and blues, something no one had done before—least not Ray's way. He was a genius for doing that. I couldn't do it—I was brought up to separate church and state—but I appreciated Ray's contribution. When he sang "Drown in My Own Tears" and "The Right Time," his voice went all the way through me; I felt it in my gut. When he sang "What'd I Say," he found him a big white audience, and I was glad for him. I wished I could have done the same. But my songs weren't that clever or sexy. I lacked a hook. I didn't have Little Richard's pompadour or Chuck Berry's duckwalk. All I had was Lucille, who, like me, was pretty much married to the blues.

I say "pretty much" because I did try to adapt. I've never been a purist. If someone brought me a song that sounded rock 'n' rollish but still fit my style, I'd give it a try. Only once did I sing a song I hated. It came from a friend of the Biharis and was called "Bim Bam Boom." I did it, but if I listen to it today, I cringe. Nobody liked it, nobody bought it, and I wish I'd stuck to my guns and refused to sing the thing.

Naturally the Biharis wanted me to jump on the bandwagon of crossover success. I made certain concessions. I didn't mind singing pop-style ballads like "You Can't Fool My Heart" and

"On My Word of Honor," a beautiful song recorded by Tony Bennett. I even tried my hand at writing pop ballads like "I Love You So" and "My Reward," dreaming of big financial rewards. I liked "The Great Pretender" and "Unchained Melody" and thought a song like "I Am" might bring me a mainstream audience. It didn't.

I could complain that the Biharis didn't know how to sell a black artist to white America, but that would be passing the buck. Besides, I don't believe that to be true. If I'd been Little Richard, they could have sold me. But I was who I was.

The rock 'n' roll revolution rolled on without me. The more the revolution developed, the more I realized I'd have to keep on keeping on with the same B. B. King show. I just wasn't going to be a rock 'n' roll star. I wasn't even being "covered" by the white stars, like Pat Boone singing Fats Domino's "Ain't That a Shame" or Georgia Gibbs singing Etta James's "Dance with Me Henry." I realized that Bill Haley and His Comets were a fifties' cover version of Louis Jordan's great jump bands from the forties. Some black stars resented those covers. Some said the whites were stealing our thunder. But I didn't buy that argument.

I saw rock 'n' roll as breaking down some prejudices against blacks and black music. If some Southerners could have segregated the airwaves, they would have. But the beautiful part is that airwaves are free. Randy's Record Shop was one of the forces behind that freedom. Randy Wood was a white guy in Gallatin, Tennessee, with a mail-order business tied into black music. Every night from ten till midnight, you'd hear deejays like Gene Nobles on WLAC out of Nashville talkin' 'bout Randy's Record Shop as the place to buy R&B records. On a clear night, you could hear WLAC all over North America. Can't tell you how many white people have told me they got hip to black music 'cause of Randy's.

White kids hearing black music on the radio liked it 'cause it sounded good; it felt good. The racists couldn't legislate musical taste. And along with the music, these white kids were hearing and feeling the souls of black people. They were getting to know us and like us and appreciate our talent.

So I was a man on the inside and the outside at the same time. I was included on rock 'n' roll shows—I toured with Fats and Ray and Sam Cooke and nearly all the big names—but I was always the bluesman. I kept my distance. I didn't feel a part of the movement. I was just doing all I could to keep my career alive.

More than anyone, the guy who kicked the revolution into high gear was Elvis. When I went home to Memphis in 1956, Elvis had gone through the roof. He'd switched over from Sun Records to RCA and scored with "Heartbreak Hotel," "Don't Be Cruel," and "Hound Dog." I was a little surprised. I remembered him singing country-style. I knew he liked blues 'cause he cut Big Boy Crudup's "That's All Right," but this new stuff was different. The new stuff was R&B sung by a good-looking white boy.

I liked the new stuff, and I liked Elvis. I saw him as a fellow Mississippian. I was impressed by his sincerity. When he came to the Goodwill Revue, a yearly benefit for needy black kids sponsored by WDIA, he did himself proud. The Goodwill Revues were important. The entire black community turned out. All the deejays carried on, putting on skits and presenting good music. In the early days of the revue, the program would start with gospel, followed by R&B. But when the gospel part was over, the ministers would escort the church crowd out. So Mr.

Ferguson, the station owner, turned it around so that R&B was first and the gospel crowd had to stay for the whole show. That made everyone happy, including the gospel crowd, who loved R&B.

When Elvis appeared that year, he was already a big, big star. Remember, this was the fifties, so for a young white boy to show up at an all-black function took guts. I believe he was showing his roots. And he seemed proud of those roots. After the show, he made a point of posing for pictures with me, treating me like royalty. He'd tell people I was one of his influences. I doubt whether that's true, but I liked hearing Elvis give Memphis credit for his musical upbringing.

I hold no grudges. Elvis didn't steal any music from anyone. He just had his own interpretation of the music he'd grown up on. Same was true for me; the same's true for everyone. I think Elvis had integrity. I've heard blacks ask, "Why couldn't the first big rock star be black, since rock comes from black music?" The commonsense reason is in the numbers. Blacks are a small minority. The white majority, whether in movies or music, want their heroes and heroines to look like them. That's understandable. Sure, there are exceptions, but few. We blacks want our own heroes and heroines too. Back then, we had Dorothy Dandridge and Harry Belafonte. Now we have Whitney Houston and Denzel Washington. Blacks might invent a new style, but chances are, only the white artists' adaptation of that style will result in mass-market success.

My own success started to shrink. I could work. I could always work. But my work was restricted to the black theaters and roadhouses and nightclubs—some funky, some fancy. I stayed on the same circuit, played the same joints, plugging ahead as best as I could. I didn't envy my cohorts. I was glad Ray Charles was playing the Newport Jazz Festival, but I also wish they had invited me.

I wish I hadn't played a gig in Milwaukee where the promoter let in people who had Louis Jordan tickets from the week before when Louis's show was canceled 'cause of bad weather. I was supposed to get 40 percent of the proceeds. We sold out—six hundred people came to see us—but I got only paid for two hundred tickets. The other four hundred fans had Louis Jordan tickets.

After the show, I went back to see the promoter, a black dude in a cowboy hat. He was leaning back in a chair, smoking a cigar, his feet up on his desk. I remember him wearing big cowboy boots. Two big burly guys were standing by his side. A pistol was sitting in the middle of the desk. I was concerned about the gun, but more concerned about my money.

"Hey, man," I said, "why penalize me for something I had nothing to do with?"

"I gotta make up my money from the cancellation," said the promoter.

"Not at my expense, you don't. You owe me money on four hundred tickets."

I stood my ground. He kept chewing on that cigar and said, "Tell you what. I'll pay you on two hundred more tickets, but that's it. I don't wanna hear any more griping out of you."

I looked at the man, I looked at the pistol, I looked at the man again. He offered me a wad of money. I took it, counted it—there wasn't much there—and, just before leaving, I looked back at the dude and said, "You're a son of a bitch, and I hope you die with your boots on."

I surprised myself. I don't usually say things like that. And four months later, when he fell dead of a heart attack, I felt terrible.

I hit another low point heading for a gig in Montgomery, Alabama. The bus broke down in a rainstorm. I called the promoter and said we were running late. I gave him the option of canceling. "No way," he assured me. "We got a house full of people who ain't leaving till you get here." We found a mechanic, got the bus fixed, and drove like hell, arriving only forty-five minutes late.

"You can forget it," said the promoter. "You're too late."

"But I called you and told you we were running behind."

"Sorry," he said, "I can't pay you."

I heard the crowd clapping and calling my name so loud that I decided to go on anyway. Didn't wanna disappoint the fans. We put our frustration into the music and played hard. That was a period when I had a beefed-up sax and brass section and the band was extra-strong. The fans were dancing and screaming and going crazy while my mind was still going a little crazy for the money we weren't getting. In the middle of the show, I took the mike and said, "Ladies and gentlemen, you've been so beautiful and we love playing for you. We love playing for you so much, we're doing it for free. Seems the promoter has decided not to pay us. Well, I figure if he ain't paying us, why should you pay him? So I'd recommend you request a refund while we jump into our next number."

Now the fans are storming the ticket booth and demanding their money back. By the time our show's over, the promoter is forced into refunds—either that or risk serious property damage. Like me, the fans have a free night, leaving me with the feeling that some justice prevailed.

The road could provide another kind of diversion. I remember being in New York, playing the Apollo, when after the show I got the yen to go hear some good jazz. Went by Birdland. I loved Birdland 'cause I might catch Basie or Sarah Vaughan or Oscar Peterson. I loved sitting in a back booth, sipping a little something and grooving on the mellow music. Some nights I'd go in there and it'd be so crowded that I couldn't get a table. That's what it was like the night I went to see Miles Davis.

Miles has his hot quintet with John Coltrane, Red Garland, Philly Joe Jones, and Paul Chambers. They call Birdland the Jazz Corner of the World, and tonight it feels like the whole jazz world is out in force. The joint's so jammed, I have to stand behind a rope with a big crowd of people. Inside I see some celebrities, but I'm not pushy and I don't think anyone knows who I am anyway. Looks like a sophisticated New York crowd. But I'm happy just to be there 'cause Miles is on his game. He's playing all the pretty standards—"When I Fall in Love," "It Never Entered My Mind"—and gorgeous jazz lines like "Green Dolphin Street." Him and his rhythm section have a beautiful flow going and Coltrane is exploding with ideas. If Trane says a lot with a lot of notes, Miles says even more with less notes. Miles uses silence better than anyone. I love how he spaces between phrases, how he moans low into his mute. They call him the Prince of Darkness, but I call him King of Cool. Miles is a master.

After the first set, I'm in the men's room, standing at the urinal, Miles's version of " 'Round Midnight" still ringing in my ears, when I hear this voice behind me talking to someone else. The voice is low and gravelly and sounds like sandpaper. I know the voice belongs to Miles, but I ain't about to turn around. "Motherfucking blues-singing B. B. King," says Miles.

"Yeah, that's one cat who plays his ass off. Nigger can blow some nasty blues."

That's about the nicest compliment I ever received—and the way I met Miles Dewey Davis.

We became buddies, and I loved how he loved my blues. From then on, if we were playing in the same city, we'd try and see each other. That happened over the course of thirty-five years. We didn't discuss intimate stuff. We mainly spoke musician to musician. For example, just after I met Miles, Coltrane was playing solos that could last a half hour. Miles didn't like that. Miles told me how he asked Trane to cut the solos short. "I've tried," said Trane, "but these ideas keep coming, and I don't know how to stop." "Try taking the fuckin' horn out of your mouth," Miles told Trane.

He'd get annoyed when I'd introduce him at my gigs, but soon I got to know him well enough where I didn't care. Once, in Detroit, he caught me at the Twenty Grand, a club where there were usually a good number of whites in the audience, something highly unusual for me. At the break, I said, "Ladies and gentlemen, I'd like to acknowledge one of the greatest jazz musicians in the world, Mr. Miles Davis."

Pissed, Miles got up and, in that hoarse voice of his, complained, "Motherfucker, I didn't come by to be introduced. I just wanna listen to your ass."

"Then sit your ass down," I said, "and enjoy the compliment 'cause this is my show and you're my man and I'll damn well introduce you if I wanna." Everyone cheered as Miles flashed a rare smile. I got his goat.

Years later, we'd share bills together at the Beacon Theater and Lincoln Center and even talked of doing an album. That would have been heaven. But it wasn't meant to be. Miles left too soon. He left me with something, though, I'll never forget.

We were playing a festival in Spain in the eighties. I was singing one of my ballads, "You Know I Love You." In the middle, there's a space for an instrumental solo. I spotted Miles in the wings. He came onstage, borrowed a trumpet from my man Eddie Rowe, put in his own mouthpiece and, right on cue, played that song with so much tenderness and loving feeling my eyes filled with tears.

That's the memory of Miles I keep in my heart.

During that time me and Miles first met at Birdland, my road trips were getting tougher. As rock 'n' roll created a bigger market for R&B artists making the transition to a younger audience, my audience, like me, kept aging. And so did Big Red, my bus. Maintaining that vehicle wasn't cheap, but I kept her going until sometime in 1958 when the bus burned up in an accident that nearly drove me out of business. It was a helluva thing.

I wasn't on the bus. I was going to join the band that night in Texas. It happened on a Saturday afternoon. Millard Lee was driving. A car started to pass him as they entered a narrow bridge outside Dallas. A butane truck was barreling down in the opposite direction, heading toward Big Red and the passing car. The car couldn't get past Big Red in time. When Mother maneuvered to the right to avoid being clipped by the passing car, Big Red bounced off the bridge wall and wound up colliding with the speeding truck. Head-on. Fiery crash from hell. Fire everywhere. My dudes were able to climb out the back of the bus—none of them were hurt—but the truck driver and his passenger died of burns.

I heard about it by phone and rushed there as soon as I could. But there was nothing to do. I was sickened by the scene—the two dead men, the bus and truck burned like someone had torched them. The deaths were the worst part. But it turned out the tragedy had still another chapter. On Friday, the day before the crash, I'd been told that the government had suspended my insurance company from doing business because of shady practices. That left my bus uninsured. I figured I'd get new insurance on Monday. I didn't figure on getting wiped out on Saturday.

Without insurance, my liability was huge. I got a good lawyer, but even a good lawyer couldn't save me from having to cough up a quarter-million dollars. For me, that was a fortune. It was also the beginning of my IRS blues. Instead of paying unemployment taxes, I had to use my $10,000 savings as the down payment on a new Skyliner bus worth $27,000. That put me in a hole that would take a dozen years to climb out of. As my debt grew greater, the IRS grew meaner. They put the clamps on me, showing up at gigs to take the kitty. Seems like I was making less and spending more. For nearly a year, I was working like a dog and never getting more than $75 a week. That's all the IRS allowed me. My band always got paid—I wouldn't mess with my men's money—but my finances were in ruins. Remember what I told you about being a lousy leader? Well, it was all coming true. Man, this boy was down.

Blues all around me.

17

"The Eagle Stirreth Her Nest"

As a kid, I was a regular churchgoer. I felt the spirit of God in gospel music and dreamt of being a gospel man myself. When my life started moving in a different direction, I missed church but never left it, not in my heart. Living on the road meant I didn't have a church of my own. Saturday was always the big night—and the late night—and getting to church Sunday morning was next to impossible. I was usually sleeping in the backseat of the car as we moved on to another city. The road can get you down, and though I believe I have a positive spirit, I was suffering serious heartache. I knew I needed church.

I found it in the sermons of a man I consider my main minister. I'm talkin' 'bout Reverend C. L. Franklin of the New Bethel Baptist Church of Detroit, Michigan. The man could preach. Whenever I was in Detroit, I'd make it a point to get myself up on Sunday morning to hear him. He inspired me. He also traveled with a gospel show, sometimes featuring his young daughter Aretha. I'd catch him whenever I could and was proud to call him my friend.

Later, when cassettes came out, I bought me a bunch of his sermons on tape and listened to them on the road. He spoke simply and beautifully, telling stories in hypnotic cadences that called forth the power of Scripture. He gave examples I could understand. His sermons were musical, moving with the rhythms of his emotions, building to a climax, and leaving you renewed. He also injected strong messages about racial pride. Listening to Reverend Franklin's messages was like listening to a good song. You felt better afterward; you felt hope.

As I trudged along my highway, I sure enough needed hope. I remember listening to Reverend Franklin's famous sermon *The Eagle Stirreth Her Nest*. He explained how God stirs the nest of history. He also stirs the nest of our personal history. He challenges us, like he challenged Daniel in the lion's den. Reverend Franklin would remind me that God's angels made the lions lie down like lambs. Like an eagle, God is swift and strong in healing our hearts. I could understand God stirring the nest of the circumstances of my life. I was being challenged, tested to see the extent of my faith.

That faith was reinforced by the power of gospel music. I loved listening to Mahalia Jackson and Clara Ward and Albertina Walker and the Soul Stirrers with Sam Cooke singing lead. I loved the sound of James Cleveland's voice and his songs like "Peace Be Still." These were artists who nourished my soul. But for messages delivered with fiery poetry and stirring symbols, no one excited my spirit like Reverend C. L. Franklin.

My sexual spirit was just as excitable, but by 1958 I was

starting to feel the need to settle down, as I had once tried to settle down with my first wife, Martha. Maybe it was the financial difficulties I was facing, or the fact that my career felt stalled. Maybe it was the monotony of the road. Anyway, I was doing what I've been doing my whole life—what most of us are doing—looking for love. When I went back to Mississippi, maybe I felt closer to the love I had lost with my mother, or maybe I just plain liked being home.

Memphis was a little less home for me 'cause Daddy was moving away. He'd been fighting with his neighbor, who claimed the fertilizer from Daddy's cotton field was getting into his pond. They couldn't resolve the dispute and Daddy, being Daddy, just up and left, moving to Gardena, California, outside L.A. I wish I could have seen my father more. I also wish I could have heard him say he was proud of me. Friends like Norman Matthews would tell me, "Man, your daddy's always bragging on you, B." He'd tell others, but not me. That was my father.

My mother stayed in the memory of my heart as a missing link. Sometimes I would pray to God to show me a sign of her afterlife, something to let me know her spirit was around me. But a sign never came, and that's one of the reasons I have doubts about life after death. Other times I envision my mother living on a star, looking down at me and smiling because, for better or worse, I'm trying to do my job. I wish my faith were as strong as a sermon by Reverend Franklin or a hymn by Mahalia Jackson. I wish the pain in my heart that came from missing my mother would subside. But it didn't, and it doesn't, and her lost love remains forever lost.

I found love back down in the Delta. I was in Indianola, playing the Club Ebony, with all the musical ghosts of my childhood surrounding me on the bandstand. Couldn't play that club without thinking of all those nights I spent peeping in on Count Basie or Sonny Boy. Around this same time, I had just recorded "I Want to Get Married," a song that said, "No woman will hear my plea, can't get no woman to walk down the aisle with me." Like most of my blues, the story was half-fact, half-fiction, but as I looked at the hometown crowd filled with family, friends, and fans, I noticed Sue Hall. Good God Almighty, she was pretty. There was something about her—a bouncy charm and spirit—I could never resist. She was eighteen, and I was thirty-three, and all during that gig we stayed together as friends. She told me she had a baby son and I told her 'bout some of my kids and she said she liked me very much and I knew I liked her. Didn't take long for like to turn to love.

Sue was different than any woman I'd known. She had a modern outlook. Like her mama, she had a good head for business and wasn't afraid to show her ambition. She asked me about my business practices and saw I was a lousy manager. I was loose with my money, often forgetting to keep receipts and always behind on my taxes. "B," she'd say, "your musicians love you because you pay them well and treat them good. But until you treat the IRS just as good, you'll stay in trouble."

No woman had ever been so blunt with me. Part of me was attracted to a female with keen business sense, but part of me felt like it was my concern and mine alone. Sue had more than sense, though; she had sweetness and a soulful beauty that kept me coming back. Maybe I could still have a normal family and find happiness with one woman. I asked Sue to marry me.

She said yes, but always made it clear she wouldn't be a wait-at-home woman. She wanted to come on the road with me. That was new. And a little intimidating. The road, after all, was my private territory, where I'd always done what I wanted. The road was my turf. "But if you're living on the road," said Sue, "and I'm waiting at home, it'll never work. I want to be your wife and be with you wherever you are. I love you, B."

Felt so good to hear a woman say that. Felt so good to be able to satisfy a woman as sensuous and smart as Sue. I was thrilled she accepted my proposal. If there was one man I wanted to marry me, though, it was my favorite preacher: C. L. Franklin. And that's what happened.

In June of 1958, Sue and I went to Detroit and got married in the Gotham Hotel. It was a private ceremony with just a couple of witnesses and Reverend Franklin officiating. My fabulous drummer Sonny Freeman was there by my side. I'd met Sonny through the Houston booking agency. He'd be my mainstay for seventeen years. When my tax troubles continued and I formed a corporation using another name to straighten my business, I called my band Sonny Freeman and the Unusuals. That's how much Sonny meant to me.

I liked being married. For a short while, we got a place in Memphis, where Sue studied at the Henderson Business College. That gave us both a feeling of being grounded. We were close to home. But Sue was just as adventuresome as me— maybe more so—and in less than a year decided she'd rather live around Los Angeles. Sounded good to me. I'd never been headquartered outside the South, and Southern California seemed right. I liked warm weather and being close to the big recording studios. The move couldn't hurt my career, and maybe it would give it a boost.

The boost didn't come, but the house in South Pasadena was pretty and the weather was mild and Daddy was close by and Sue was a loving wife. I was crazy about the lady. But I was never crazy about her accompanying me on the road. Sometimes I'd talk her out of those road trips, and sometimes I couldn't. It was an off-and-on thing. Wasn't always smooth. I can't blame Sue, though. It was my hangup and the tough times I was living through. I'll give you a couple of examples.

I was playing a job in Ocala, Florida, on the same bill with Buddy Johnson's great band, when someone said the cops had hauled Sue off to the police station. "What for?" I wanted to know. "Said no white woman had any business being in a black club." Naturally I rushed down there. Sue was explaining that she wasn't white and that she was my wife, but they wanted papers. Who the hell carrries a wedding certificate around in the glove compartment? So we stood there, trying to be reasonable with unreasonable people, fighting back the urge to curse and scream and smash someone's head. Finally they released her for having done nothing but be herself.

On our move from Memphis to California, we were driving through Texas—me, Sue, and Sue's son Timothy, who I regarded as a son of my own. I saw a cop trailing me, so I was careful not to speed. Trails me for several miles. Finally pulls me over. Here we go. He slowly—very slowly—walks up to the car. Takes forever. Doesn't say anything at first. Just looks over Sue and Timothy, then looks at me, then looks back at me. I know what the dude's thinking.

"Something wrong, officer?" I ask, containing my anger.

"Been a kidnapping 'round here," he says. "We're stopping suspicious cars."

"This is my wife and my son," I said.

"What's your name, girl?" he asked.

"Sue."

"You okay with this guy?"

"He's my husband."

Her husband was mad enough to chew glass, but all I wanted was to get outta there.

"You drive on, boy," he said to me. "Just be careful."

I drove on, all right, but inside I felt so little. There's nothing I could do, no complaint I could file. To go crazy would be a waste of time. But sometimes small incidents like this—and I've experienced dozens—hurt you most 'cause you don't realize the damage. You hold it in. You feel empty, like someone reached in and pulled out your guts. You feel hurt and dirty. You feel like you're less than a person. You feel that your wife has been disrespected, your dignity has been marred, your manhood has been challenged, and yet you're powerless. If you're a militant, I suppose you could pull out a gun and shoot the cop—and ultimately get shot yourself. If you're a practical, peaceable man like me, you absorb the blow and get ready for the next one. Because you can bet your sweet ass the next one's on its way.

Funny, but at times like that, when I understood how the politics of race was hurting me, I'd think of personal hurts. My mind would go back to the time when, after Mama died, my cousin asked me, "Where's your dinner?" as he ate his, knowing there was no dinner for me back in my empty cabin. Maybe it's being oversensitive, but it's part of my character. The hurt can come from a cop or a cousin—it doesn't matter—because the hurt lingers on, like a virus that never dies.

Sometimes it's hard for me to draw differences between political and personal pain. The two get mixed together, es-pecially on issues like skin color. When the civil rights movement began, I understood exactly where Martin Luther King was coming from. He wasn't a close friend, but I knew him and respected him greatly. I don't have his education or knowledge of history, but I do have knowledge of the South and the South's racist ways. I saw Dr. King's nonviolent resistance as the only solution.

The point hit home when, down in Birmingham, we'd both been staying at the Gaston Motel. Dr. King had left, but his enemies thought he was still there. We were still there when they bombed the place. The bomb rocked my room, but didn't do any bodily harm. The force of the explosion, though, reminded me of the seriousness of hatred. People were willing, even eager, to kill. Their warped way of thinking led to violence. I saw that people were going to die. Before it was over, I'd lose friends in the movement. I can't say I was much of a marcher, but I did what I could. I ran benefits for Dr. King, gave money, supported our cause. He knew he could count on me, and we—the right-thinking people in the country—knew we could count on him.

I like to think I'm a person people can count on. In the rhythm and blues field, many artists from the early days would freelance from one label to another. They might record under an assumed name and work for two or three labels at once—whoever paid them cash on the line. I hardly blamed them. The labels might stick the name of a phony writer on your song and never give you royalties. For example, I kept seeing the composer credits on my songs listed as "King and Ling." Well, I never did meet no one named Ling. Who the hell was Ling? The labels weren't exactly famous for being honorable, so you could understand why artists learned to sneak around the system.

But I see myself as a square. I see myself as a loyal dog. I like working for one person at a time, and I'm not comfortable sneaking on anyone who's paying me money. If you don't count those first few records I made for Jim Bulleit, I've recorded for only two companies in forty-six years. I stuck with the Biharis all during the fifties, and I believe I was their best seller. I already told you I wasn't no Little Richard or Chuck Berry, but my sales in the mom-and-pop black record shops were always good. My fans might have been getting older, but they were loyal. They came to my live shows and they bought my records. With Maxwell Davis producing, those records had a consistency that gave me pleasure. The sound was clean and my blues mirrored me. I kept having little R&B hits like "Please Accept My Love" and "Got a Right to Love My Baby."

By the end of the fifties, though, the Biharis' products didn't look good. When I went into the record stores and looked at everyone else's stuff—Ray Charles or Joe Turner—they'd have liner notes and beautiful photographs on the cover. The albums would cost $3.99. But the Biharis' labels—RPM, Modern, Kent, and Crown—would be thrown in the cut-out bin. You could buy practically any B. B. King album for 99 cents. And on the reverse side there weren't any liner notes, just a listing of all the other Bihari products. I thought I was being undervalued and undersold.

I never asked for more than $3,000 or $4,000 for an album advance. But now I wanted more. I asked for $5,000. The Biharis refused. That hurt me, so when Chess Records of Chicago approached me, I listened. Starting in the forties, Chess had recorded many great artists like Muddy Waters, Howlin' Wolf, Chuck Berry, and Etta James. My contract with the Biharis was due to expire in less than a month, and Chess said they'd pay me $5,000 and also cover the cost of a session I wanted to make in a super-simple manner. Wanted just drums, bass, and piano behind me and Lucille. Wanted to stay with the basics and sing stuff like "Driving Wheel," "Catfish Blues," "My Own Fault," and "Walkin' Dr. Bill." Turned out to my liking; in fact, it's one of my favorite records. The Biharis must have liked it too, 'cause when they heard about it, they offered to pay the $5,000 if I'd stay with them. I stayed, and they issued the album as *My Kind of Blues*.

Even though we tried to stay together, something was still separating me and the Biharis. I could see I wasn't getting anywhere. I remember going for advice from one of my idols, Louis Jordan. He honored me by inviting me to his home in Phoenix. I was crazy about Louis. He spoke to me like a son, and he listened as I told him my concerns about my record company. I wanted to be loyal, but I wanted a bigger audience. I wanted to be accepted by more people.

"I understand what you're saying, B," Louis said. Then he showed me a royalty check for $160,000. I'd never seen a check that big before. For years, he'd recorded for Decca, a big company. "The bigger the company," he explained, "the better your chance of getting those royalty checks. The big companies are more accountable than the small ones. Remember, B—it's a business. Ain't nothing but a business."

His words stuck. One decade was ending and another beginning. I didn't want the sixties to be like the fifties. I wanted something better and bigger. I needed to manage myself where

I could make some progress. I wanted to go higher. Since I'd been paying some serious dues, I figured my dues-paying days might be coming to a close. I figured wrong. Hard times were still ahead.

18

Forget Regrets

Don't believe in regrets. They ain't nothing but a way to stay down. I wanna be happy. I don't wanna sit around complaining about the long, hard road to success. I wanna be grateful for whatever success I have. Every night I wanna get out there and entertain the people as best I can. Let Lucille sing her heart out. Let me sing from my soul and give the paying customers their money's worth. Let me put on a good show. Let me take whatever the promoter can pay and thank the man. Let me treat my musicians right, keep 'em working, make sure they're as comfortable as I can afford. Let me stay positive.

That's how I was thinking at the start of the sixties. It might have been rough, but I was surviving. I could still work 340 nights a year—and I did. I wasn't walking behind the mule or driving a tractor. I was out there giving it my all. Even if I hadn't been making music, I would have still been loving and listening to music. I loved listening to Ella Fitzgerald singing all the great songs of Cole Porter and George Gershwin. Same went for Sarah Vaughan. And double that for Frank Sinatra.

I'd been a Frank Sinatra fan since the forties when he sang with Tommy Dorsey. I'm a Sinatra nut. No one sings a ballad with more tenderness. I practically put that *In the Wee Small Hours of the Morning* album under my pillow every night when I went to sleep. And when Sinatra wants to swing, no one swings any harder. No one phrases any hipper. With those Nelson Riddle and Billy May charts, with the Count Basie band in Vegas, Sinatra was the slickest singer around. You could hear all the hurt and happiness in his voice; you could appreciate how he put his life experience into his songs. He always sang the truth.

If I felt a little down, dragging six hundred miles from one city to the next, I'd listen to guys like Les Paul to pick me up. Les Paul invented the solid-body electric guitar, as opposed to the hollow body. The solid-body became *the* guitar of the modern era. It's the kind of guitar most of us are playing today. He also invented overdubbing, where he recorded several tracks of the same voice or instrument playing different parts. Him and his wife Mary Ford turned "How High the Moon" and "The World Is Waiting for the Sunrise" into classics. What I liked most about Les were his innovations. He took the instrument as seriously as a scientific experiment; he never stopped trying to expand the possibilities of the guitar. That inspired a lot of musicians, including me, reminding us of the instrument's beauty. Practically everyone playing guitar—at least in the field of blues and rock—owes Les Paul a debt of gratitude.

I'm still grateful for something my wife Sue did for me. It happened during the sixties when I was looking for inspiration.

Sue sensed this. On one of those rare nights when I found myself home in South Pasadena, she told me she had a surprise. Fine. What was it? "You'll have to get in the car to find out," she said. I was tired; I didn't wanna get in the car and go out. Sue insisted. She suggested I put on a coat and tie. Man, I was cranky and didn't wanna get dressed, but I did. What next? "We're driving to the Dorothy Chandler Pavilion," she said. What for? "A concert." What concert? "You'll see." Driving into smoggy downtown L.A., my bad mood wouldn't lift. If it was music we were going to hear, I could stay home and hear it on the phonograph. Didn't need to go to no concert.

Yes, I did. Because this concert was different than any concert I'd ever heard. There was just one small man sitting on a chair playing an acoustic guitar. His name was Andres Segovia. For nearly three hours, I was transported. Never heard the instrument played like that before. Can't tell you the names of his selections, but I believe there were pieces by Bach, Spanish songs, and other classical melodies that made my ears so happy, I was ready to weep for joy. Segovia had an incredibly delicate and tender touch. The audience was so quiet, you could hear a pin drop. I loved the respect everyone gave the man. Everyone was hanging on his every note. And every note was the right note, notes falling down like gentle rain. Over three decades later, I still carry the magic of that concert in my head. I still love Sue for allowing me to hear the master play like an angel.

I think of music—pop songs, symphonies, blues—as angels. Music has been my guardian angel. When portable equipment started coming up, I started carrying records and tapes in the car and bus. I found energy and hope in other people's music. It's the music that kept me going. Musicians like Mickey

Baker, a great guitarist who teamed up with Sylvia and sang "Love Is Strange," continued to teach me. Mickey was a studio ace who played with everyone; he also had an instruction book I loved to study.

Mainly I'd listen to blues and jazz, music of my deepest heart, but I also started listening to flamenco guitarists, who had a blues feeling of their own. I'd listen to anything that lifted my spirit. At the start of the sixties, I also decided my music needed more spirit and a different presentation, at least on record. I didn't renew my contract with the Biharis and instead signed with ABC Records. I was glad that one of my last albums for my old label was gospel, something I'd been wanting to do for a long while. When I sang "Precious Lord" and "Jesus Gave Me Water" with the Southern California Community Choir, it took me back to the beginning and made me feel whole.

It made me feel strange to be with a new label after so many years. ABC was big and I worried whether it would be impersonal. It wasn't. Besides, I liked how they marketed black music. They'd just brought Ray Charles over from Atlantic, and Ray was crossing over with "Georgia on My Mind," "Ruby," and "Hit the Road Jack." ABC also had Lloyd Price with "Stagger Lee" and "Personality" and the Impressions with "Gypsy Woman" and "It's All Right." Fats Domino was about to switch from Imperial to ABC, and it was Fats who set me straight.

Fats is down-to-earth. He gave me good advice. "You need a good company with good distribution," he said. "You don't want a company that'll put you on the shelf." Fats also had advice about performing. "Keep your standards up," he said. "Certain things you gotta avoid, like fooling with women you really don't know anything about." Not everyone could talk to me like this, but coming from Fats I took it to heart.

It was a different world at ABC. Recording techniques were more sophisticated. Soon I'd be able to "punch in" my vocals and solos—that is, splice together bits and pieces, as opposed to playing it all the way through. That gave me more confidence. Didn't worry so much about making mistakes 'cause mistakes could be fixed. Basically, though, it didn't change much else, since I still record a song in relatively few takes.

I was hoping to sell a few more records. With the Biharis, 100,000 copies was a hit. For ABC, 100,000 was normal. With the Biharis, I was more or less in control. I did what I wanted. With ABC, we had meetings. There were supervisors. I wasn't exactly told what to do, but I was being led. I didn't mind. Fact is, I kinda liked it.

I liked that they let me keep Maxwell Davis as my main arranger. They also had a good producer called Sid Feller who understood our style. We used great pianists like Lloyd Glenn and cut sides like "I'm Gonna Sit in till You Give in" and "Blues at Midnight." They put money in the charts and hired the best musicians around. I also teamed up with a lyricist, something new for me, and with Fats Washington wrote "My Baby's Comin' Home" and "Slowly Losing My Mind." I was starting to feel a new zip in my music and couldn't help but be encouraged. Maybe I'd start selling better.

Well, the sales were okay, but not spectacular. As the sixties rolled on, something spectacular *was* happening in black music, something I appreciated, but something that, once again, left me out in the cold. They called it soul music.

To me, soul music is nothing but a continuation of rhythm and blues. It's popular black music with a strong gospel and blues base. James Brown is soul music. Jackie Wilson is soul music. Solomon Burke is soul. So was the music coming out of

Detroit. When it looked as though British groups like the Beatles were taking over the American pop charts, it was Motown who gave the English a run for their money. Some said Motown was watered-down R&B, but I loved Marvin Gaye singing "Can I Get a Witness?" Sounded like church to me. I liked Smokey Robinson and Little Stevie Wonder and Martha Reeves and the Vandellas. I liked them all.

As the decade went on and the civil rights movement spread, the music became tougher and prouder. Made me proud. To me, soul was beautiful music with its Southern roots showing strong. What Ray Charles had started by mixing church and blues, Aretha Franklin would soon carry on. Aretha carried on like no one else. Since the days when I heard her as a little girl singing in her daddy's church, her voice had stirred my soul. Now they called her the Queen, and they say she reigned over the Golden Age of Soul. That was all right with me.

In Memphis, Stax/Volt Records had singers like Otis Redding and Sam and Dave and my old friend Rufus Thomas—who today is seventy-nine years old and still dances like he's sixteen—and Rufus's beautiful daughter Carla. Memphis proved that it was still the center of Southern soul. Just as Memphis nurtured me, Memphis nurtured other generations of eager artists and writers. I'm thinking of Isaac Hayes and Dave Porter.

The sixties were filled with beautiful soul because black people were more vocal about the respect we wanted and the good feeling we had about ourselves. The politics seeped into the music, and the politics were about life-affirming change. I liked all that.

But I didn't like being booed. That cut me to the quick.

Most critics would probably say that B. B. King has soul, but B. B. King wasn't really part of the soul movement. Sure, I played bills with Marvin Gaye and Jackie Wilson and just about everyone else you can name—dozens of bills all over the country—but I was the outsider, the bluesman, just like I'd been the outside bluesman in the rock 'n' roll shows of the fifties. I still felt like a sheep among cows. Marvin and Jackie didn't see me that way—the artists always treated me with respect—but on this particular night in this particular city, the audience booed me bad. I cried.

Never had been booed before. Didn't know what it felt like until the boos hit me in the face. Coming from my own people—especially coming from young people—made it worse.

About the time I switched labels, I also switched from the Buffalo Booking Agency to the Milt Shaw Agency out of New York. Thought that would make things better. Shaw represented crossover artists like Ray Charles. Shaw would book me and use my band to back up a soul star revue. I wouldn't get the top money the stars got—they had the hits—but I thought the exposure to a younger audience would do me good. I usually opened the show.

I realized the kids were anxious to hear Sam Cooke sing "Twistin' the Night Away" or Jackie Wilson sing "Doggin' Around." I knew Jackie could dance up a storm. He was an explosive performer; I was not. I understood impatience and I understood youth. At thirty-five or thirty-six, I still saw myself as young. Young people want instant gratification. I knew I didn't have Sam's good looks or Jackie's dance moves, but I was going to give 'em a taste of the in-your-face blues and give it to 'em good. I'd do a short set, I wouldn't overstay my welcome, and I'd sing "Rock Me Baby," which is, after all, about rocking your baby all night long. It was my sexiest song.

But the minute the emcee said, "Ladies and gentlemen,

here's the blues singer, Mr. B. B. King," the boos started and my head started reeling. I was shocked, hurt, and confused. So many thoughts ran through my mind. For a flash, I saw myself as I thought they saw me: some ol' bluesman from Mississippi with torn overalls and a corncob pipe in my mouth. But I was dressed sharp and I thought of my blues as up-to-date, and they didn't know me, except maybe they heard their parents playing my records and maybe that's why they were booing 'cause they were rebelling against something they saw as old and tired—a music and a way of life they associated with an older generation they wanted to get away from. But understanding them didn't make the pain go away. I was still standing there, stung, angry, convinced no one understood me or my feelings. I was a hurt guy.

Picked up Lucille, though, and went into my blues. Changed my program around to start with "Sweet Sixteen." Sang that song harder than I'd ever sung it before or since. I worked those blues; man, I was singing real-life pain. When I got to the part that says, "Treat me mean, but I'll keep on loving you just the same . . . one of these days, baby, you'll give a lot of money to hear someone call my name," I couldn't stop the tears from running down my face. And when I stopped singing, the tears kept coming, but instead of boos, I heard cheers. In my own little way, I made my point. I got to those kids. At least for the moment.

For a large part of the sixties, I fell between the cracks of fashion. Black music fans have always been fashion-conscious when it comes to music. We like the latest thing. And the latest thing is usually cool. When I was coming up, T-Bone Walker was the latest cool thing. I wanted to play like him, not like Robert Johnson. In the sixties, Chubby Checker or the

Isley Brothers were the latest thing. But because I couldn't twist and shout, I was seen as a dinosaur. I've told you how I've always been interested in progress. In that sense, I'm no different than my own people. We want to get ahead. But in pushing ahead, sometimes we resent the old forms of music. They represent a time we'd rather forget, a period of history where we suffered shame and humiliation. Makes no difference that the blues is an expression of anger *against* shame or humiliation. In the minds of many young blacks, the blues stood for a time and place they'd outgrown.

Now white critics are always "rediscovering" the pure blues. I put "rediscovering" in quotes because I've never understood how you can rediscover something that's never gone away. There was a movement in the fifties and sixties where serious scholars were finding old bluesmen who played in the Robert Johnson style. Dozens of articles and books were written. Usually bluesmen like me and my buddy Bobby Bland were left out. We were seen as corrupting the true blues. Because we used horn bands behind us and stressed the soaring electric guitar, we were looked at as impure. I didn't argue 'cause of something we'd say down South: "If you ain't feeding me, I ain't listenin' to you." Funny, though, because while young black fans were thinking we were too old-fashioned, white scholars were thinking we were too modern.

Well, it wasn't funny on payday. My audience—black blues lovers like myself—was definitely shrinking. I kept my band together, and I kept working the chitlin circuit. But how much longer could I go on playing those gigs? I worried that one day soon even the chitlin circuit would burn out on me. But it's a big country, and it's a big circuit, and if I was willing to keep playing those roadhouses in Alabama and those clubs in Oak-

land, I'd get back to the Apollo in Harlem and the Howard in
D.C. and feel a little bit better before going back down to Mississippi and the Longhorn Ballroom in Dallas that had hillbilly
music one night and blues the next and on and on and on—
tonight New Orleans, tomorrow Biloxi—until the road was so
much a part of my soul that I can't imagine life without riding
the highway, night after night, week after week, like a recurring
dream or an ease-your-mind drug, the rhythm of the road rocking me to sleep, making me feel like I'm moving on and going
where I need to go, even though I've been there a million times
before and will be there a million times again.

It's monotonous but steady. In a strange way, it's secure.
Moving on means I'm never where I am; I'm always leaving the
past and heading into the future. The present is a blur. Monotony ends only on the bandstand when my blues get hot or, if
I'm lucky, after the show with a beautiful lady whose loveliness
extends all the way to the privacy of my hotel bedroom, where,
at least for a few hours, the mean ol' world disappears and I'm
feeling nothing but sweetness and bliss.

19

"Did You Read What John Lennon Said?"

I wasn't exactly sure who John Lennon was. In the early sixties, I was only starting to learn about the Beatles. Later on, I knew their names, but in the beginning they were just these English boys with long hair and a rock 'n' roll beat that drove the girls crazy. I could see—anybody could see—they were a huge hit. Once they arrived in America, their popularity spread and soon the whole world was talking about them. Friend of mine happened to read an interview with John.

"Did you read what John Lennon said about you, B?"

"No. What'd he say?"

"He wished he could play guitar like B. B. King."

Hey, that was a nice thing to say. I listened a little closer to the Beatles' music, though I still couldn't hear any of my influence. But the idea that he mentioned me, and the fact that millions of kids listened to him, may have made a difference. I heard about other English groups, like John Mayall's Bluesbreakers, and felt the blues might be coming back in a new way. John Mayall could play the blues and so could a kid who played with him called Eric Clapton. Eric was always saying good things about me in the press, so I knew I mattered to some young musicians. That gave me hope.

Other incidents got me depressed. I was in Chicago, playing a big venue with some jazz acts, artists I admired tremendously. In a big booming voice, the emcee said, "Ladies and gentlemen, we take pleasure in presenting one of the world's great singers, the Divine Miss Sarah Vaughan." Sarah came out and killed. Then he said, "Ladies and gentlemen, we take pleasure in presenting one of the finest jazz singers, the incomparable Joe Williams." And Joe came out and killed. But when it came time for me, the same dude said, "Okay, folks, time to pull out your chitlins and collard greens, your pig feet and your watermelons, 'cause here's B. B. King."

I hated hearing that. It made me feel terrible, but I came out and played my set. Didn't say a word till afterward. Pulled the emcee aside and said, "Look, man, I eat chitlins and collard greens and I love 'em, but I don't want my table set onstage before I come out here."

"What you mean?" asked the dude. He took offense. He saw I was pissed.

"I mean you introduced those other artists one way," I said, "and you introduced me another. Next time just say, 'Here's B. B. King.' That's all you got to do."

He got the message.

To me, his message was that the blues was less than jazz. No one loves jazz more than me, but no one should pit one against the other. It's like pitting brother against brother, or father against son. I've often said being a blues singer is like being black twice. I could understand why it was that way when I was a kid, but by the sixties we should have been past that. I'm afraid we weren't. While the civil rights movement was fighting for the respect of black people, I felt I was still fighting for the respect of the blues. Discrimination can come from places you'd never expect.

The road almost killed me more than once. I've been in dozens of car accidents, and some of them involved more than people. On a lonely road outside Tulsa, I was speeding through the night, going maybe ninety, when suddenly a mule stepped in the road. I braked, but couldn't avoid him. He fell over and I felt terrible. Thought I'd killed him. Thought of all the mules I'd worked with, how mules had always helped me. I ran out, trying to figure a way to get the animal to a vet, when the mule picked himself up and ran like hell, relieving my heart.

Another time in Memphis, a little dog dashed in front of my Ford. I couldn't stop in time. A man and a boy who'd been playing with the dog rushed over, but no one could do a thing. The dog was dead. They didn't blame me—they saw how the dog took off without warning—but I blamed myself. I still do. I figure if I'd been going slower, I might have been able to stop in time. I still see the lifeless dog out there on the street.

I came close to losing my own life on the way to a Sam Cooke show, a year or two before Sam was killed. I was being driven from New Orleans to Dallas in a Ford van. It was a rainy night in Louisiana, somewhere around Shreveport. I remember warning my driver about the slick roads, I remember falling asleep in the front seat, and I remember a thump and a bump and a crash and excruciating pain. We slipped off the road into a tree. The tree wound up in my seat, and because I wasn't wearing a seat belt—a seat belt would've killed me—I was thrown out of the car. Instinct had me raise my right arm to protect my face. As I flew out of the car, that arm caught the top of the windshield; my flesh was cut so deep, a big chunk of skin was hanging off me; I could see all the way back to the white of my bone. Luckily, the cut missed my main artery or else, according to the surgeon, I would have bled to death before the ambulance rushed me to the hospital.

Once in the hospital, the presence of pretty nurses lifted my spirit. While the doctor dug glass out of my arm and sewed me up with 163 stitches, I flirted with the nurses. Even in times of terrible pain—*especially* in times of terrible pain—thank God for women. My right arm might have been aching, but my left arm was working, and I made the gig that night like a million other nights. The name of the game is making the gig.

As the grind of the road ground down my emotions, I tried to lift myself up by learning new things. I try to learn something new every day. Since I was a boy, I've been blessed with good teachers. As an adult, the same was true. My friend James Wilson was the first to get me into reading newspapers. As a country boy and tenth-grade dropout, that came late to me. I never realized the information contained in the papers—simple stuff like TV listings—until James pointed that out.

My overall tutor and teacher was Hampton Reese, who recently died. Hamp was a brilliant arranger who started out on trumpet and wound up on violin. He was my confidant and role model. He gave me the Schillinger Method of Musical Composition books that I still use today. That's how I improved my reading skills—not that they're all that great—and how I learned some music theory. I also started fooling with clarinet and violin. I got where I was a pretty good sight reader on clarinet and could play scales on violin. The electric bass, of course, was something I picked up a lot easier 'cause it's first cousin to the guitar. Also liked fooling with different keyboards.

Hampton Reese encouraged all this. His thing was books, books, books. If you don't know something, go to a book. Don't sit around feeling sorry for yourself; don't feel inferior; pick yourself up, get to a library, find the book, and learn what you need to learn. Until Hamp, I really didn't understand what research was all about. Didn't know that there's a world of information just waiting for you. When computers came in, I got involved as soon as I could. They made learning even easier. But in the beginning, it wasn't easy at all.

It was in the sixties, for example, when I wanted to learn to fly. Happened in a funny way. I was working the Chicago area. Sue was with me and I thought we'd take off a couple of days to spend some quiet time on Lake Michigan, fishing, relaxing, and getting romantic. Couple of friends—one a bass-playing schoolteacher and the other a deputy sheriff—mentioned they'd be in the area. Asked me if I wanted to watch 'em do some "touch-and-go." "What's that?" I wanted to know. "We rent us two small airplanes," they said, "and fly over this noncontrolled airport. It's a ball. Why don't you come along?"

I was fascinated. I cut short the romantic time with Sue and went out to watch. Because these guys had soloed as student pilots, they were allowed to rent planes. Well, that afternoon the sky was blue and the weather was warm and watching 'em take off and zip and zoom around and come back in for these smooth landings made me mighty jealous. Man, I wanted to do it myself. I knew it took some brains; I knew the schoolteacher was smart, but the deputy sheriff seemed dumb as me. *If that dude can fly,* I figured, *so can I.*

I was all set to get an instructor when Hampton Reese stopped me. Hamp said, "B, if you're serious about flying, you could learn a whole lot by just reading." Hamp took me to a used bookstore where we bought a pile of texts on meteorology, flying small craft—the whole business. "Study," said Hamp. And study I did. Studied, studied, studied until I knew the stuff. Found me an instructor who was impressed with how much I already knew. I'd practically completed the ground instruction on my own. That boosted my confidence.

Still, I had some scary moments. Landing by myself for the first time, I nearly caught the top of a tree. Flying around Midway Airport in Chicago, I'd forgotten my map. The tower said jets were in the area. I told the tower I was in trouble. But my solid instruction and sense of direction led me out of there. I overcame my fear and learned to love to fly. Flying solo was a thrill. In short hops, I flew cross-country from one small airport to another. I had conquered something that, only a year or so before, seemed beyond me. When my music career was going sideways, it was good to have a feeling of accomplishment doing something else.

The best part was the clear blue sky and the peace that comes with sailing over the earth. Sure, you need to be alert and prepared and aware of your instruments, but there's also a point—a magical point—when you're floating free over the worries and stress of the land below. You feel alone, but you also feel the presence of a spirit, a calm that lifts you above your cares and lets you feel a force at the center of things that's powerful and strong and completely still. I call that force God. It's the force that says everything's all right; the planets are spinning in space, the universe is in sync, and a little plane flying through a puffy bank of clouds is as graceful as an eagle heading home.

I flew for years, for the sport and the kick and the meditation. Flying chilled me out. But flying can be dangerous. Everyone remembers the terrible crash when Buddy Holly, the Big Bopper, and Ritchie Valens went down in 1959. And when we lost Otis Redding and his band in a small-plane crash in 1967, people around me started to worry. Kept after me to find another hobby. The insurance company got even more insistent. Said I'd have to stop. So I did.

The road never stopped. The road led back to the Regal in Chicago, the black theater I'd played hundreds of times before. Johnny Pate, a wonderful arranger and producer who'd been hired by ABC, wanted to record the concert. I said fine. The year was 1964. I thought my band had a good feel. Bobby Forte was on tenor, proving himself one of my all-time great sidemen. Duke Jethro was on piano, playing a whole mess of blues. By then, my repertoire was pretty set. I'd open with "Every Day," slide into "Sweet Little Angel," move to "My Own Fault," and strike back with Leonard Feather's great "How Blue Can You Get," which climaxed with the lines: "I gave you a brand-new Ford, you said you wanted a Cadillac; I bought you a ten-dollar dinner, you said, 'Thanks for the snack'; I let you live in my penthouse, you said it was just a shack; I gave you seven children and now you want to give 'em back!" The last line always gets good response, and that night the audience was hot.

When the record came out as *Live at the Regal*, the critics went a little wild. Called it my best ever. A bunch of writers talked like they were "rediscovering" me. But I didn't know I had disappeared, didn't know I'd been hiding. I thought I'd been out there night after night, year after year. Some of the writers described *Live at the Regal* like I was playing way over my head. Well, I ain't one to argue with praise. I like and welcome praise whenever it comes my way. Go on and heap on the praise. But I also know I got to keep my head about me. And even though the *Live* album was cool, I've probably played hundreds of better concerts than the one taped at the Regal. But who am I to argue with critics?

If I have beefs, I usually keep them to myself. There was a time when I decided to change my show around. Happened at the Apollo. Opened without the band—just me and Lucille—sitting on a stool. I wrote a script about my musical history and, as I played, Hampton Reese read my words from the wings. It was my way of reaching out to the people by telling my story. The crowd liked it, but the next day a critic wrote how B. B. King had hired some slick writer to work up this script and, even worse, B. B. King was playing some watered-down blues. Man, that stung. First of all, what does B. B. King know about watered-down blues? I don't think I could play watered-down blues if I tried. I took calling me "some slick writer" as a compliment, but the critic didn't mean it that way.

Critics can be plain mean, even when they mean to be nice. Sometimes critics say, "B. B. King is a good *blues* musician." They'll emphasize "blues." Or they'll say, "I'm pleased and amazed that B. B. also plays a little jazz." Well, that makes me feel like only geniuses can play jazz, while anyone can play blues. Some see a blues musician like a follow-the-dots painter. Like any fool can do it. But simplicity is deceptive. And feeling is something that's not easy to evaluate. Lightnin' Hopkins may not have known many notes, but he knew all the right ones, and he knew where to put 'em. Some genius with four Ph.D.s in music theory might never be able to do in a lifetime what Lightnin' did in a minute—tell the truth.

The truth is that, as the sixties rolled on, I was a different bunch of guys. I was a road dog, running from town to town, struggling to stay afloat. I was a flat-footed bluesman on the soul shows no one especially wanted to hear. I was a recording artist for ABC, where my records, for all these new producers, still weren't hits. I was an artist who seemed to be getting some recognition from white blues bands popping up in England and America. And I was a husband with a wife who was unhappy to see me gone so much.

The thing with Sue went up and down. We'd go from misery to ecstasy in a quick second. I admired her ambition and thirst for knowledge. She studied French at UCLA, she studied business, she even learned banking and became an expert in finance. I sure could have used an expert at finance, but something kept stopping me from making Sue a full-time road companion and business manager. My temperament told me marriage and business should stay separate. My temperament probably told me wrong, but my temperament was strong. So we compromised. I made a vow to work less, something that's not easy for me.

Friends have asked me whether I'm addicted to work, gambling, and sex. Gambling and sex have sure complicated my life and put me through some changes. I admit to that. I enjoy gambling and sex, but they're both pleasures I feel I can control. Work is a different matter. Work controls me. The pattern might go all the way back to the plantation and picking cotton and driving tractors. Might go back to wanting to get by and get over and get something better. Might just be in the blood.

If I feel like I'm gonna miss a gig, my blood starts boiling. It might be unavoidable; the bus broke down or the plane's grounded or the highway's covered with ice. But I'll find a mechanic or charter a plane or brave the ice rather than disappoint a promoter and let down a crowd. That's just me. Sue understood; Sue said she even admired that quality, but Sue wanted a husband who was home a reasonable amount of time. I couldn't blame her. I said, "Sue, I'll schedule gigs on weekends and promise to be here, say, Monday through Wednesday." That was the plan, but the plan fell through.

All through the sixties, the IRS remained a noose around my neck. Can't blame the feds—it was my messy money management that was bringing me down—although the feds didn't give me much of a chance to breathe. For a while, I wondered whether it was because I was a black entertainer. But later I decided it wasn't race so much as me being naive. I didn't know what I was doing. Didn't know, for instance, that you could hire a tax attorney to work out a deal with Uncle Sam. So I just went on, putting one foot in front of another, plodding my way through.

Good things were turning bad. Like winning at keno, the numbers game I loved playing in Vegas. One big win would only encourage me, which meant I'd wind up losing even bigger. I didn't want to lose Sue. I loved her with all my heart. I wished we could have had children, but in the beginning she miscarried, and later I learned from the doctors that my own sperm count had weakened to the point where I could no longer impregnate.

My relationship with Sue was growing joyless. The end came when I couldn't honor my commitment to stay home for longer periods of time. The IRS came down on me so hard, I saw no choice but to keep working like I'd always worked—every night I could get. I was back to 340 one-nighters a year.

Looking back, I see my mistakes. If I were a different man, I would have let my wife manage me and run the business. God knows, she'd do better than this old fool. If I were a smarter man, I'd have found a tax expert to negotiate my way out of misery. If I were a different artist, I would have found a way to have hits like Percy Sledge or Wilson Pickett or Sam and Dave. But I was just B, struggling to stay alive.

20

How Do You Lose a Bus? How Do You Lose a Wife?

The bus broke down in Augusta, then Atlanta, where my man Cato Walker left it with a watchman while he went to Memphis for a tow vehicle. When Cato got back, the watchman and the bus were gone with the wind. The cops thought they had a beat on it, but then the cops lost it, and finally me and Cato just gave up. I'd also given up theft insurance some time back. It'd been too costly. Now, in 1966, I felt doubly foolish.

I found transportation, though, and kept my band together. My band's always been together, in good times and bad, although for a while I cut it back to just Kenneth Sands on trumpet, Bobby Forte on tenor, Duke Jethro on organ, Wilbert Freeman on bass, and the brilliant Sonny Freeman on drums. What we lacked in size, we made up in sizzle. That small band could cook.

I guess the thing that cooked my goose was a $78,000 lien on my income by the IRS. Since I had never stuck with a consistent plan to pay Uncle Sam, I figured this was coming. What I hadn't figured on, though, was being sued by Sue, who hired a divorce lawyer and let me have it. Many years later, I can understand her action. She was fed up with my lifestyle and disgusted that I'd broken my promise to stay home. My reason seemed sound to me—I couldn't relax my schedule till my tax problem was resolved—but I could see where Sue didn't buy it. She figured I'd never cut down on travel. In a contest between her and the road, Sue reasoned the road would win. And rather than reason with me anymore, she turned it over to a lawyer. Now that makes sense.

Back then, it stung like hell. I resented her action. I wondered how she could take legal action against me, knowing that the IRS had just done the same. I remember winning a big game of keno in Vegas. Hit for $50,000. Put the money in a safe-deposit box. Few days later, I learn the IRS has put a lien on the box. Those dudes were practically following me to the bathroom, waiting for me in the next stall.

I lost Sue. I lost this wonderful woman, and I'm still singing the song that says, "It's my own fault, baby." When we were married, I was so convinced it was a lifetime thing, I even bought us adjoining plots at Forest Lawn Cemetery. That was a dream I had to bury. But at least the suit got settled with no mudslinging. We got divorced and, after a few years, we could even go back to being friends. There's no lady I respect more.

I kept talking to myself, kept saying, "Things are getting better, B. Your career is getting better." But cold hard reality says I'm back on the road, it's a bitter cold Friday night, and I'm in Beaumont, Texas. It's a black club called Blue Buddies and I'm playing my blues, trying to keep my spirit strong, giving the less-than-capacity crowd something to remember me by.

I'm lost in my music when I look up and see four white men wander in and congregate at the bar. I silently sigh. I figure it's the IRS, here to check the kitty.

When my set's over, one of the guys approaches the bandstand. He's different than the others. He's an albino, a skinny dude with long hippie hair. He's carrying a guitar and asks me if he can sit in. Well, I ain't sure. I don't like strangers sitting in with my band. How do I know if he can play? I hate to make the crowd suffer for my ignorance. But I think about it. If I went to an all-white club to sit in with a white band, I might think they'd be racists to turn me down. I don't want this dude to think I'm racist, so I turn my mind around and say yes.

So the kid gets up and plays. And plays. And plays some more. Plays him some blistering, burning blues. Fact is, he plays so much, the crowd gets up and gives him a standing ovation. I take note 'cause I'd never gotten a standing ovation in a club like that in my life. But I'm happy for the kid; he deserves it. Afterward, he's gracious and grateful to me. Calls himself Johnny Winter. Years pass before I bump into him again, and by then I'm the one who's grateful.

I was increasingly grateful to a whole school of new blues players who kept calling me by name. Paul Butterfield had a band in Chicago with some bad white boys who said I had inspired them. Paul was a protégé of Little Walter, and Little Walter, along with the original Sonny Boy Williamson, is my favorite harp player. Paul was no slouch himself; his harmonica had all the grit and grind of the old masters. Paul went down to the South Side, taking along guitarists like Mike Bloomfield. They'd get up there and play with Muddy Waters and Howlin' Wolf; they'd live the life of the bluesmen they loved. They were serious students.

Mike Bloomfield was a special friend. He was a Jewish boy from a wealthy family with a father who didn't appreciate his son's appreciation of black blues. I believe Mike suffered from that conflict—all sons want Daddy's respect—and poured his pain into his playing. He developed into a beautiful musician and authentic interpreter of big-city blues. I loved Mike. When we ran into each other on the road, we'd sit and talk. I saw him as a son. Encouraged him all I could. He played with Bob Dylan and got his own band together called the Electric Flag. Mike became a star in the world of hippie rock 'n' roll. Every time anyone interviewed Mike, he'd talk about B. B. King. Musicians like Mike and Elvin Bishop and Johnny Winter acted like my press agents. I believe their only motive was love.

I detected a change in the wind. Hippies were wild about black music, and hippies represented the mainstream youth market. Even better for me, their taste went beyond current R&B, back to the source. The Rolling Stones, for example, wouldn't stop talking about the bluesmen who inspired them. Keith Richards and Mick Jagger were scholars of black music. I think they felt the same way I did—that bluesmen deserved a wider audience. Through sheer conviction on their part, they helped introduce that audience to B. B. King.

It happened slowly. There were folk festivals in the sixties that included artists like Muddy Waters and my cousin Bukka White. But the promoters thought my blues weren't "folky" enough. I saw myself falling in the cracks again. But this time there was change, partly brought about by a book by Charles Keil called *Urban Blues*. Using me and Bobby Bland as two examples, Keil said modern blues were being overlooked by the critics. He said it was silly to call us "impure." He interviewed me, put my picture on the cover, and wrote about my music in flattering ways. A white college professor himself, Charles took on the white establishment and changed many minds. In the media world where writers mold opinion, he brought me attention and maybe even some respect.

I still had my beefs with categories. From the day I'd started out, I'd been called a rhythm and blues artist. I thought that description fit me. But somewhere in the sixties they dropped the "rhythm," and I became blues only. That label stands today. I don't mind. Long as you come to my concerts and buy my records, you can call me grand opera. But I can't help wondering what happened to my "rhythm"? Did I lose it along the way? I think the original label still says it best. I still see myself as a rhythm and blues man.

Couple of times a year, ABC got me in the studio and issued my albums on a regular basis. For a while, I still used Maxwell Davis. No one understood me like Maxwell. No one kept as sharp on my music. Maxwell could read my soul and interpret my sound. Even though he had the better musical mind, he let me lead. In the fifties, I was in charge; in the sixties, I was produced. ABC put me with producers I didn't know. Because these producers brought me songs, I wrote less in the sixties. There was no need to create my own material. Besides, the sixties was the age of the producer. Record companies felt like producers, not artists, knew how to get hits—and getting a hit, a genuine across-the-board hit—was something I'd never had. So I accepted the situation.

I didn't always like the situation. A bluesman can't be produced like a rock band. A bluesman has to be true to his blues. Producers can suggest and bend and slightly alter your approach. I'm always altering my band's approach so it sounds current and clean. But I'll only go so far. When the sound is getting away from me, I put on the brakes.

The low point came when I cut a record and later learned the producer was using another guitarist to play the instrumental breaks. Man, that ticked me off. Me and Lucille are like ham and eggs. We go together. I don't have to tell you that I appreciate many other guitarists, but none of them can complement my singing better than Lucille. I don't even wanna name the producer or the record. I'd rather forget him. I still have bad feelings about that session and promised myself it'd never happen again. It hasn't.

Other bad moments haunt my mind. Touring the South during the civil rights era was no picnic. It might have been worse than the early days because the tension was so high. Racists resented our demands. The era brought out the best in some people and the worst in others. Can't even begin to remember how many times we stopped at restaurants where owners or waiters looked at us like dirt and refused to serve us. My style was to walk away. My band members didn't always share my temperament and there were confrontations and fights. There was nothing I could do. I didn't try to change anyone's mind. If a band member was angry, he had a right to be angry, and he didn't need no sermon from me. For my part, though, I loved listening to the sermons of Reverend Franklin and Dr. King; I still believed that the best resistance I could offer was passive.

As the sixties rolled on and I looked at the militants, I couldn't buy their program. I understood rage, but I was a practical man. Practicality told me that brutal force wouldn't bring victory. Besides, brute force didn't correspond to the feelings of my heart. My heart wanted change, wanted respect. I didn't want to bust anyone's head open.

The men I respected most were doers, not talkers. My friend and fellow Mississippian Medgar Evers showed me more courage than a thousand pistol-wielding militants. I was close to Medgar. He wasn't interested in proving his manhood. He recruited plantation workers into the NAACP. I knew those plantations. And I knew how plantation owners lorded over their land like absolute dictators. They could do anything on their land they wanted to; they could get away with murder. So to come on a plantation, to walk right into the lion's den and openly say, "Here I am. I'm an organizer. I'm here to change the ways things have been done for hundreds of years" . . . man, that took guts. I didn't have those kind of guts, but Medgar did. Medgar had more guts than anyone. Remember, he was doing this back in the fifties and early sixties. They called him an agitator, but I called him a hero. I worried for his safety. I feared for his life.

Medgar was assassinated in 1963 and Dr. King in 1968. Those murders crushed me. In memory of Medgar, I've gone back to Indianola the first week of every June to play a four-day music festival for free. Been doing it now for nearly thirty years. It helps heal some hurt. It helps to see thousands of little black and white kids playing together, to see the big crowds so happy to hear blues that feels good to everyone. I like when the children come running up and call me B. B. like they've known me forever. I like reminding them of the bravery of a man like Medgar.

I held Medgar and Martin both to my heart when, later in my career, some militants called me Uncle Tom. That hurt, but it didn't destroy me. I felt I was doing all I could by bringing people together through music. I had a clear picture of courage, and it had nothing to do with style or muscle or hip political slogans. You didn't have to be a genius to realize brute force wouldn't work. Mama always talked about kindness and self-respect. Daddy was about work, about feeding his family. In my mind, the two go together. Respect requires work. Medgar Evers and Martin Luther King worked fearlessly so our people could realize respect. That's why they died. And why they live on.

21

Vision

I had dreams, but no real vision. Didn't even know what vision meant. Dreams came naturally to me. Dreams of moving to Memphis or making a record or playing the Apollo. Dreams of having a bus or having a band or having more and more people enjoy my music. Dreams stayed with me. And many of the dreams came true.

But sometimes beautiful dreams turn into mixed-up nightmares. And I believe I was deeply frustrated around 1968 because my career was still slowly going nowhere. I could always find work, but the venues were the same, record sales were slim, and promoters kept trimming my cut. After all these years, I had to admit I was a lousy businessman. Lou Zito was managing me, and Lou was a decent and diligent guy. He tried his best to keep me on the road. But Lou wasn't doing anything differently than Robert Henry had done years before. They both kept me going from one gig to another. It was all about survival.

Lou used a New York City accountant named Sidney Seidenberg. Sid was a wizard with numbers. I liked talking to Sid. He was exactly my age—forty-three—and had been stationed at Camp Shelby in Hattiesburg, Mississippi, the same time I was there. Naturally we hadn't met each other because of segregation. But I felt like I'd known Sid all my life. In some deep way, we were connected. He reminded me of other good men I'd met along the way, like Johnson Barrett. Sid seemed fair. And smart. More I knew him, the more I'd ask his advice, until one day I decided he'd be a good manager. I asked him to take over. He was reluctant. Said I already had a manager. But I wasn't happy with my progress. I needed someone who thought big.

"It'll cost you money," said Sid. "I don't work for free."

"I don't expect you to," I explained. "Besides, if you make money, I'll make money."

I talked Sid into taking me on. It was the single best business decision of my life. With Sid, everything started to change. Sid had vision. He saw way down the road. He said, "B, we're going to initiate five-year plans. We'll project ahead and see where we want to be five years from now. It's all about expanding your market, getting your music to people who don't know about B. B. King."

Those words excited me. They were the words I'd been waiting to hear for years. Beyond Sid's good common sense and his ability to think big, he also worked as hard as me. To this day, he thinks about my career more than I do. He's obsessed with promoting B. B. King. It takes an obsession to break through barriers. And one of those biggest barriers, of course, was me.

Sid set me straight in lots of ways. He knew I loved to gamble, so he said, "B, when you want gambling money, always write yourself a check. That way, you'll see exactly what you're doing." Sid believed in self-knowledge. He also believed in respecting my personal life—he never asked questions or interfered—and understood my burning need for professional management.

One of the first things Sid did was introduce me to Joe Glaser, president of Associated Booking. "B," said Sid, "I want to get you the best booking agency in the country." I've always been shy around big businessmen, but Sid insisted I come along. Sid knew Glaser—he'd worked for him—and I knew Glaser had a reputation as one of the toughest guys in show business. Word was, Glaser always made sure his acts got paid. He was the force behind Louis Armstrong. Louis Armstrong himself gave Glaser credit for making him an international star. Because Associated Booking booked Fats Domino, Fats had also mentioned Joe Glaser as a powerhouse.

Meeting him made me nervous. Sitting out in the waiting room, I was ready to hide behind Sid. When we were announced, we walked through the door and I saw this intense man with burning eyes looking right through me. Mama had said staring was impolite—I'd been trained not to look anyone directly in the eye—so this was something new. Never had seen anyone stare so hard as Joe Glaser was staring at me.

"Sit down," he said.

I sat. I saw a pile of checks on his desk written to artists for huge sums of money. Couldn't help but be impressed.

"Do you know Louis Armstrong?" asked Glaser.

"Yes, I do," I said.

"And Fats Domino?"

"Know him, too."

"Well," Glaser continued, his eyes still fixed on me, "if you can get your career going like them, you'll be all right."

I liked hearing that. I liked being compared to two artists I admired. I thought of Louis and Fats as superstars.

"Superstars," said Sid, "deserve super advances." And with that, he signed me to Associated Booking and renegotiated my deal with ABC Records. Here again, Sid had vision. He didn't think in terms of tens of thousands of dollars; he thought in terms of hundreds of thousands. He said to ABC, "You've got a major artist in your midst, and you better start treating him like one." When Sid talked, ABC listened. I finally had someone fighting for me.

Sid said, "B, some jobs may pay you less but give you better exposure. Better exposure will mean more money later on." Sid helped widen my own view of the business world. I realized that after nearly twenty years of trying to make it, I could relax and leave management to someone else. I heaved a sigh of relief, knowing the one area where I was weak—planning— was Sid's strength.

It also comforted me to know Sid was an accountant. Because of those skills, he worked out a deal with the IRS. It still took years to settle the matter, but at least I had a reasonable payment schedule. And Sid saw to it that I never missed a payment. He imposed fiscal discipline. Because I knew it was important to my survival, I listened to Sid. In the area of business, I was smart enough to know I wasn't smart; I let Sid lead.

The road was leading me to new venues. Sid understood that white superstars like Mike Bloomfield and Keith Richards were valuable allies. They were among the rock 'n' rollers who had helped educate a new audience—young and white—

about my music. It was time, said Sid, to take my music directly to that audience.

Bill Graham was the man. He ran San Francisco's Fillmore West, where all the hot hippie bands like the Jefferson Airplane and the Grateful Dead carried on. It was the height of hippiedom; the Summer of Love was going strong. The kids were wearing beads, smoking dope, and making love, not war. I liked all this, but I sure didn't feel a part of it. As a country boy from the Delta, the changes were still strange for me. It wasn't the politics; I hated war as much as anyone. I just wasn't sure I understood the hippies, and I wasn't sure they understood me. That's why, when my bus pulled up to the Fillmore, I had butterflies in my stomach.

Funny part was that I had played the Fillmore many times before. But in the old days it was a black club. After Graham bought it, he booked acts for the flower children. Soon as I got off the bus, I saw longhaired kids in tie-dyed outfits seated on the stairway leading up to the door. Felt like I was in the wrong place, but my road manager assured me it was the right place. Went up to my dressing room, covered with psychedelic posters. Saw Graham and said, "Man, are you absolutely *sure* you want me in this place?" "Sure I'm sure," said Bill. "You need anything, B?" I needed a drink. I was scared. Bill said he didn't sell booze, but he sent out for a bottle. Quickly, I threw back a couple of stiff belts.

Waiting for showtime made me even more jittery. When the moment of truth arrived, I took another swallow and followed Bill to the bandstand. It wasn't like any club I'd seen before. Hippies were seated on the floor, covering every inch of the place. A cloud of sweet-smelling marijuana hung over the room. There were no chairs at the Fillmore, and getting to the bandstand meant walking over people. Well, where I come from, walking on someone's shoe or foot can cause a fight. But the vibes were mellow in the Fillmore and no one minded. The hippies were chilled out.

At the microphone, Bill Graham gave me a straight-to-the-point introduction. "Ladies and gentlemen," he said, "the Chairman of the Board, B. B. King." By the time I strapped on Lucille, every single person in the place was standing up and cheering like crazy. For the first time in my career, I got a standing ovation *before* I played. Couldn't help but cry. With tears streaming down, I thought to myself, *These kids love me before I've hit a note. How can I repay them for this love?* The answer came in my music. I played that night like I've never played before. Played "Rock Me Baby" and "Sweet Little Angel" and "You Upset Me Baby" and "How Blue Can You Get," played all my stuff with all my heart while they stayed on their feet, screaming and stomping for nearly three hours. It was hard for me to believe that this was happening, that the communication between me and the flower children was so tight and right. But it was true, it was probably the best performance of my life, the one performance that showed me I was finally moving in a new direction.

I took direction from Sid, who thought it was important to put me together with new producers in new situations. I hooked up with Al Kooper, a great blues-rock musician who'd played organ with Bob Dylan and who formed Blood, Sweat and Tears. And I also got together with Quincy Jones, who had me sing "You Put It on Me" for the movie *For Love of Ivy*. That was something new for me. Wrote a song with the wonderful poet Maya Angelou called "Get Myself Somebody" and had an

R&B hit with something I called "Paying the Cost to the Boss." My sound was changing. The blues was still the heart of the matter—that would never change—but the arrangements reflected some of the newer horn sounds that pleased my ear. I was trying to be flexible.

I was also listening to other guitarists. The fashion was for wah-wah pedals, a treble boost that creates an envelope of sound that might remind you of a baby crying. It gives the guitar a vocal quality. I liked the wah-wah effect. I'd heard it years before it became popular. Dude named Earl Hooker could make the thing talk, and that was in the fifties. In the sixties and seventies, I did some experimenting with the pedal myself. Used it on the album *Lucille Talks Back*, but it didn't feel right to me. Truth is, it felt like cheating, like a robot was doing the work for me. I was so used to trilling and bending with my hand and fingers that the use of a machine to create another voice was almost too easy. Felt unnatural.

I liked it on others, though. Jeff Beck was a wizard at wah-wah. And so was Jimi Hendrix. I'd known Jimi when he was with Little Richard and the Isley Brothers. Later on, when he went to England, he made more sense out of the wah-wah than anyone. He had his own approach. Jimi was based in the blues, but he went farther out on a limb. I liked that. I liked that he created a style the kids liked. Jimi was one of the main guys that turned the guitar into the main instrument of rock. In one way, Jimi was like the new Elvis: Because of Jimi, millions of kids wanted to play guitar. And when the guitar is the center of musical attention, that's good for my business.

I liked Jimi doing "Foxy Lady," "Wild Thing," and "Hey Joe." I was flattered when he played my song "Rock Me Baby," though, to be honest, I would have rather heard it by Muddy Waters. That's not to take away from Jimi, but Muddy was a lot closer to the way I saw the world. The world of Jimi Hendrix was definitely the world of the future. Guitarists like Jimmy Page with Led Zeppelin were virtuosos. They were showmen and musicians and rebels creating a new brand of theater.

I was impressed, but I also admit I'd get disturbed seeing a group like the Who smash their instruments against the speakers. I'm sure it's got to do with my upbringing and my dues-paying, but, man, I get cold chills just thinking of hurting Lucille. Don't even like anyone touching her when she's sitting in her stand in my dressing room. The idea of smashing her to bits against a wall or an amplifier makes me sick.

But that's me and my generation. I'm a big believer in making room for the new generation. Pete Townshend and Eric Clapton won my respect because they could play. Didn't matter if they wore crazy clothes and led crazy lives. I'd been leading a pretty crazy life myself. I was just glad that the new generation was accepting me, even if I was wearing three-piece suits and doing my usual down-to-earth show.

In 1968, though, I was definitely not conducting business as usual. I made up my mind to give up California as a home base. If my career was changing, I wanted to change my personal life as well. California represented the past—my collapsed marriage and my long-suffering financial state. I was never able to get it together in California. I didn't like Governor Reagan and I sure didn't like the state tax board and don't even mention the IRS. If California was a symbol of the American dream, my dream never came true there. I was ready to get out. I wanted a new start and new address. The address I chose was

10 West 66th Street, just off Central Park, in the middle of Manhattan. I liked the idea of being close to Sid Seidenberg. I was ready to live where I'd never lived before, in the center of the most exciting city in the world.

22

Someone Asked Me About Oral Sex

And it got me to thinking. I went back to the beginning of my fascination with women, to the time when I was six years old and Peaches was my honey. I loved the way females felt, their smooth soft skin, their sweet smiles and gentle ways. To have a woman simply caress my cheek or stroke my forehead or hug me tight was a comfort and a thrill. I've been lost in the love of women my whole life, and I'm not complaining, not changing my attitude that I need women as much as I need water to drink and air to breathe. Without women, I'm lonely and unhappy and unable to cope. With women, seems like life makes sense and the stress goes away.

But I'm a man of my time. Coming up, sexual activities had certain limitations. When the fellas got to talking, hardly anyone mentioned performing oral sex on a woman. It was okay if a woman did it to us; we might like it, but reciprocating was another matter. I was hesitant myself. So hesitant, in fact, that it wasn't until after my second divorce that my mind was liberated to the point where I felt free to please a woman in the most intimate ways.

At the end of the sixties and the start of the seventies, liberation was in the air. Even though I wasn't part of the new generation, I can see how I was influenced by some of their attitudes. Things were looser, freer. I wanted to be free of the feeling that I had failed in another marriage, and I made up my mind that marriage wouldn't work for me. I haven't been married since.

I kept up with my children as best I could. I supported them and their mothers. I wanted to be there for them all, but now that my career was finally taking off, there was no going back. I looked for love where I'd always looked—on the road, in Minneapolis on one night and Detroit on another. I enjoyed my sense of sexual liberation. I made it clear to my women that my lifestyle meant moving on. I didn't lie. In certain cities, I had girlfriends who seemed to understand. Once in a great while, I might even enjoy an orgy. During the wild sixties, I went to three or four. But I wouldn't bring a girlfriend to an orgy, and I wouldn't force myself on any woman who wasn't willing or even eager to be with me. I wouldn't wanna manipulate anyone. What tears me up most is when a woman says I've lied. Maybe that's the Virgo in me, but just the sound of the accusation—even if it isn't true, and I try never to lie—makes me cringe.

As I grew older, I was more willing to ask women what stimulated them. I'd let them make suggestions. And I wanted to be told what was thrilling them and what wasn't. In one way or another, things usually worked out. One time, though, they didn't. Happened in a hotel in Atlantic City.

It's noontime and I'm asleep after a beautiful night of love-making. A voluptuous lady is by my side, our arms intertwined. We're both naked as the day we were born. Suddenly I'm startled out of my deep sleep by a voice that's shouting, "B. B.!" I look up. So does my companion. Standing over the bed looking down at us, eyes all red and crazed, is a former girlfriend of mine. My first thought is: *She's gonna shoot us both dead.*

The uninvited visitor is a woman who had a nervous breakdown. She's a sweet but disturbed lady, and I don't know what to expect. I'm defenseless.

"How'd you get in here?" I ask.

"I told 'em I'm Mrs. B. B. King," she said.

I can feel my bed companion shivering and shaking. With great effort, I stay composed. I tell the intruder, "You know you shouldn't be here. This isn't right."

"I don't care," she says. "I ain't leaving."

"Look," I suggest, "why don't you go in the next room while we get dressed. Then we can talk things over."

My bed companion doesn't wanna talk over nothing. She's hiding under the sheets while the uninvited guest reaches into her purse. I'm scared shitless she's about to pull out a pistol. Instead, thank God, she pulls out her lipstick and smears some on. Helluva time for makeup, but I ain't arguing, I'm reasoning. I'm saying, "I know you're upset, but we can work this out."

"How?"

Good question.

"By backing off a little," I answer.

"I wanna be with you," she says.

"You are. We're all together."

I suggest that I order breakfast for all of us. Meanwhile, my bed companion is kicking me under sheets and my uninvited guest is growing impatient. It takes another half hour of coaxing on my part, but the infuriated former girlfriend finally loses her fury and agrees to meet me downstairs so we can talk it over. We do, and I'm happy to say reason prevails.

When it comes to women, I've always tried to follow reason, but haven't always succeeded. Reason has sometimes made me suffer. After I moved to New York, for instance, I was at a party where I met a gorgeous female friend, a beautiful black woman, who felt like drinking that night. After downing a lot of spirit, she came up to me and said, "B, I'm not feeling well. I don't feel like going back to my hotel, and I'd like to stay at your place if you promise not to bother me." I promised. She kept drinking until I practically had to carry her out of there. Took her home with me, and when she fell asleep I undressed her and put her in bed. Her body was a breathtaking work of art. Over the years, my mind goes back to that scene, and I hate myself for making that promise. But I honored that promise, just as I've tried to honor all my promises. I've lived according to the principle learned as a boy in the South: My word is my bond.

During this same period, I was going with a pretty white woman from a well-off family. We'd been seeing each other for some three years. I loved when she came to New York to visit. She'd stay with me and we'd enjoy each other in all sorts of wonderful ways. We had a good understanding—no strings attached, no head games, just good companionship and sensational sex. Everything stayed cool until one weekend when she came to say she'd found a rich guy who wanted to marry her. It was in her best interests, she said, to accept the proposal. I understood. But did I understand, she asked, that it would mean never seeing me again? That hurt, but it was something

I accepted. After our final fling, she left. Since then, she's never called me and I've never called her. I respect her for her honesty and straight-ahead approach, and I'm hoping she's happy.

Other women haven't been so straight-ahead. Some have said, "Man, you're just using me for sex." I say, "Well, baby, you're using me the same way." I like honesty. If a woman says, "Why can't we just hold hands? Why can't we just walk in the park?" I'll say, " 'Cause I can do that stuff with my aunt." Friendship is fine, but sex is even finer, and when the two come together, I'm a grateful man. I can't—and don't—pretend that all I want is a woman's companionship. I want her body. And I state my position openly; I let her know I want sex.

New York living was exciting. It gave me a charge I've never found anywhere else. The energy on the streets is unlike any energy in the world. The city never sleeps and I never got tired of the bright lights and skyscrapers and nonstop action. I'd never lived in a penthouse apartment with a spectacular view before. It all felt glamorous, like my life was taking off.

Not long after moving to the city, I took some time off to record in a Manhattan studio. Bill Szymczyk was producing, the same man who'd later produce the Eagles. Even though I was moving into the future, my musical mind was combing the past. I have a feeling that's true of a lot of us—professionals and fans alike—who fell in love with music at an early age. The music of our childhood never ceases to excite us. I was still excited about hearing Walter Brown sing "Confessin' the Blues" with the Jay McShann big band twenty-five years earlier, and now I wanted to record my own version.

I'd also been fascinated by a tune Roy Hawkins did on my old label, Modern Records, back in the fifties called "The Thrill

Is Gone." Something about the song haunted me. It was a different kind of blues ballad, and I carried it around in my head for many years. I'd been arranging it in my brain and even tried a couple of different versions that didn't work. But on this night in New York when I walked in to record, all the ideas came together. I changed the tune around to fit my style, and Bill Szymczyk set up the sound nice and mellow. We got through at about 3 A.M. I was thrilled, but Bill wasn't, so I just went home.

At 5 A.M. Bill called and woke me up. "B," he said, "I think 'The Thrill Is Gone' is really something."

"That's what I was trying to tell you," I said.

"I think it's a smash hit," Bill added. "And I think it'd be even more of a hit if I added on strings. What d'you think?"

"Let's do it."

The string session was thrilling. Bert DeCoteaux wrote the arrangement. I'd call it icing on the cake. Made it really irresistible. By January 1970, "The Thrill Is Gone" started climbing the charts. Black radio stations played it right away. I wasn't too surprised. But when the pop stations picked it up, I felt wonderful. The more they played it, the more people liked it. Before the end of the winter, it broke into the Top Twenty. It stayed there awhile and became the biggest and only real hit of my career.

When I say "real," I mean across-the-board. I'd always dreamt of hearing my music played in all parts of the country by all kinds of people. In the fifties, the hitmakers were singers like Frankie Laine or Rosemary Clooney or Patti Page. In the sixties, the public liked Andy Williams or Diana Ross or Neil Sedaka. All these artists had something to offer, but I did too. I wanted the widespread appeal that would let me hear my song coming out of the car radios and restaurant loudspeakers. So when I heard "The Thrill Is Gone" practically everywhere I went, I felt triumphant. The song got me my first Grammy.

I felt especially proud 'cause the song was true to me. "The Thrill Is Gone" is basically blues. The sound incorporated strings, but the feeling is still low-down. The lyric is also blues, the story of a man who's wronged by his woman but free to go on with his life. Lucille is as much a part of the song as me. She starts off singing and stays with me all the way before she takes the final bow. People still like to ask me why I don't sing and play at the same time. I've answered that I can't. The deeper answer, though, is that Lucille is one voice and I'm another. I hear those voices as distinct. One voice is coming through my throat, while the other is coming through my fingers. When one is singing, the other wants to listen.

I was listening to other blues guitarists who were having crossover success like me. I was happy for those successes. Among the greatest was Albert King. Just about my age, Albert had been out there a long time before he finally got some hits on Stax Records out of Memphis in the late sixties. He had his "Crosscut Saw," "Born Under a Bad Sign," and "I'll Play the Blues for You." Albert was born in Indianola, he called his guitar Lucy, and for a while he went around saying he was my brother. That bothered me until I got to know him and realized he was right; he wasn't my brother by blood, but he was sure my brother in the blues.

Albert had a beautiful way of making these big bends on his guitar. He was left-handed and played his guitar upside down, hardly ever using a pick, just his bare thumb and fingers. He was a big strong dude who developed a guitar cry that could cut you in half. Albert attacked the guitar. I liked the major scales, and he liked minor. He had his own sound that, far as I can see, had more influence on guys like Jimi Hendrix than I did. Sometimes I'd hear little pieces of myself in bluesmen like Buddy Guy, who I also love, but I think the heavy rockers looked to Albert as a main model.

Seemed like the heavy blues guitarists were finally getting some overdue credit. Freddie King was another monster player, another man related to me not by kin but by spirit. Freddie had a strong association with Leon Russell, the writer and piano player who produced Freddie singing "Palace of the King." I liked Leon myself. On the album following up "The Thrill Is Gone," Leon played piano on one of his tunes—"Humming-bird"—and one of mine—"King's Special." I called the record *Indianola Mississippi Seeds*. Even though I'd just crossed over, I wanted to remind myself—and my audience—about my real roots. At the same time, I was excited about new talents and new directions. On one song, for example, "Chains and Things," which I cowrote, Carole King played electric piano. She had a beautiful bluesy feeling and, it turned out, was in the middle of making her own album called *Tapestry*. *Indianola Mississippi Seeds* was also one of the only times I sat down at the piano, playing a little snippet of blues that said, "Nobody loves me but my mother, and she might be jiving too."

Sid was quick to take advantage of my new audience and book me into rock festivals. I'd never played venues of this size before, never played before an audience so large that when you looked out from the stage you saw an endless ocean of people. I was excited by these crowds and glad to get the gigs. Some of them were amazing. The most amazing gig of all might have been in Macon, Georgia.

The band was already there when I flew in from California.

A limo took me from the airport to the rock festival, which was out in the country. The crowds were pouring in, the roads were clogged with hippie vans and trailers and cars. It was blazing hot summertime. We were stuck and it was getting late. Couple of Hell's Angels roared by and looked in the limo. Seeing my dilemma, they said, "Hey B. B., jump on back and we'll get you there in no time." So I did. We weaved through the long line of vehicles and made it backstage. When I walked into my trailer, my band members were giggling. I wondered why.

"Y'all tickled 'cause I came up on a motorcycle?" I ask.

No reply.

"What's happening?" I wanna know. "Is my fly unzipped or something?"

"No, everything's cool, B," they say and leave.

Outside my trailer I still hear them laughing. And I'm still wondering why when I take Lucille out and start practicing. I always like to get in a few hours of practice a week. Now there's a knock on the door. "Come on in," I say without looking up. I'm running my scales.

When I do look up, I'm shocked. Standing before me is a young white woman in her early twenties without a stitch of clothing. "I'm your escort for the festival," she says.

Apparently it was a custom at certain hippie festivals to assign escorts to the artists. Sometimes the escorts were naked girls. The women weren't there to offer sex, but, in the spirit of the flower children, to show love. It was a new way of welcoming musicians to the gig.

Well, I can still hear the guys laughing, but, man, I'm nervous. I'm nervous because this is Georgia, and I'm nervous because I really don't know how to act. Don't wanna be rude;

don't wanna insult the lady; but I sure do wanna stare. What does a gentleman do in a situation like this? I try thinking in artistic terms. Try not to see her as a sex object, but more as a piece of perfect sculpture. I wanna show my appreciation without acting the fool. I think I manage, but it feels funny inviting a naked lady to sit down and relax while I go in the bathroom to change my clothes.

The changing times were confusing and exciting. And the more I hung out with hippies at the rock festivals, the more I liked them. They were people who didn't judge. Didn't matter how old or young or ugly or beautiful you might be. Seemed like they were interested in gentleness and beauty and the power of music to give good feeling. They gave me a feeling of acceptance. After growing up in a segregated world of uptight attitudes and prejudices—some hidden, some out in the open—it was nice entering a world of young people ready to embrace me just the way I am.

I suppose you could say that as the sixties turned into the seventies, I had finally crossed over. Reading the words—"crossed over"—gives me a strange feeling. Naturally I was happy to have a bigger audience and wider acceptance. I was about to take my blues around the world. That was fine; that was wonderful; I like when doors open and, looking back, I can see I managed to open a few doors for younger bluesmen who came after me. All that is gratifying. But I'm still amazed how the public suddenly fell in love with my blues, which, in most ways, was the same blues I was playing twenty years before. What caused it all? The young people helped. In popular music, the young people lead the way. But I started seeing all sorts of people at my concerts, all sorts of colors, all sorts of ages.

I welcomed these new people. I entertained them. But I can't say that I became a new person myself. I didn't think of B. B. King as a crossover artist. The truth is that I kept my music on a steady course. I saw that the world of music was changing. Television was available to me when it hadn't been available before. Venues were changing. Concerts were being held in big arenas and ballparks. New markets were opening up overseas. I left the marketing to my manager. I did what I've always done—forged ahead, worked nearly every night, caught the bus, caught the plane, showed up, made the gig, put on my show. I might have been more popular, but as an artist and a man, I was still the same guy.

23

There's Something About Being in Prison

Maybe it's the stone walls, maybe the electric fences or the guard towers or the sound of those huge iron doors slamming behind you. There's something final and scary and rock-hard about being on the inside of a prison. I was a guest performer at the Cook County Jail, I'd come to entertain the men, and I couldn't help but feel the oppression. My heart was heavy with feeling for the guys behind bars. It didn't matter that I'd never been in criminal trouble myself. I'd known men who'd gone to prison and understood how the circumstances of their lives led them there. It's not that I don't feel for the victims and it's not that I don't believe in personal responsibility. I do. But I worry about the correctional facilities and their capacity to help rebuild souls, rather than destroy them.

My involvement with prisons started, of all places, at Mister Kelly's, a prestigious Chicago jazz spot on Rush Street. I believe I was the first bluesman to play the club. It was part of Sid's plan to broaden my appeal. Rock fans were one thing; jazz fans were another. Jazz and jazz festivals were popular all over the world and we were just starting to break into the market.

During my stay at Mister Kelly's, a man named Winston Moore came to see me. He was the first black to be appointed head of the Cook County Correctional Institution. "B," he said, "it's a first for you playing Mister Kelly's and a first for me supervising prisons. Now I'd like for the two of us to do another first. Would you come play for our inmates?"

I thought it over. Thought how the inmates could use the blues in a good way—as something to get positive about, a way to show them the outside world cares. I decided to do it. Sid liked the idea and, always thinking, he suggested we cut a live record and bring in the press. If you listen to *Live in Cook County Jail*, you hear the inmates booing when the officials are introduced. That made me a little uneasy. But once I warmed up and got my groove going, the men were warm and gracious. Looking out in the yard, seemed like 70 percent of the dudes were black. That made me sad and glad—sad that so many brothers were behind bars, glad that I was reaching out to my own people.

The press interviewed many inmates, and the *Chicago Tribune* played it up big. The reporters did a beautiful job, learning how prisoners were frustrated by the fact that the time spent waiting for trial—and that could mean years—didn't count as jail time. They wanted to be compensated. The newspaper publicity caused a stir and eventually the law was changed. Made me feel good that my Cook County Jail concert helped spotlight a legitimate gripe and give the guys some justice.

Prisons became a regular part of my routine. For the past twenty-five years, I've played forty-seven different jails, never for money but only the satisfaction of touching souls needing to be touched. In Jackson, Michigan, in a prison thought to be one of the toughest, the touching got a little scary. After the show, the inmates gathered around the band and started pushing and shoving until I felt uneasy. The vibes were angry. But we got out of there, just a few days before a riot broke open.

Also remember riding in helicopters with F. Lee Bailey and landing in the yard of great granite fortress prisons. They felt like scenes out of movies, with everyone running to greet us like we were the Second Coming. Bailey became a good friend. We both loved small planes—he's a real pilot—and he also helped me start an organization championing inmate rehabilitation.

In the early seventies, I was going to all sorts of new places, including *The Ed Sullivan Show* television studio in midtown Manhattan. This was another Sid Seidenberg idea. National TV was a novelty for me, and the idea of appearing on *Sullivan,* the biggest show in the country, was frightening and thrilling. Two days of rehearsals meant lots of waiting, waiting, waiting. The rock 'n' roll and soul stars were used to national TV; they'd been playing *American Bandstand* for years. When it came to television, though, I felt like a virgin. This was live TV and I was jumpy as a live wire. For forty-eight hours, I sweated it out. I was also squeezed between a bunch of other acts. George Burns was there, and the Carpenters, and Tony Bennett, and I can't remember who else. Couldn't concentrate on the comedy or the music 'cause I was too busy worrying how I'd do. I did fine. The applause was good. Afterward, I was hoping Ed Sullivan would come over and shake my hand, a sign of respect. He never did, but by then I was just glad the ordeal was over.

For me—now and then—every performance is like meeting your in-laws for the first time. Until you win them over and make 'em feel like you're family, you're scared they won't like you.

If Ed Sullivan hit one audience, the Rolling Stones hit another. Sid was determined to cover all bases. The Stones had Ike and Tina Turner opening for half their tour and me opening the other half. It wasn't that me and Mick and Keith hung out like old buddies, but they were cool. They told me how they named themselves after a Muddy Waters tune and they showed me respect. But I wasn't used to being around rock 'n' roll stars. I wasn't comfortable. It was another new situation that had me worried about fitting in. I felt like I was being forced on the fans, like I was going to someone's house without being invited. But I was glad to open the show 'cause after the Stones' "Ruby Tuesday" and "Jumpin' Jack Flash" and "Honky Tonk Women," I wouldn't wanna follow.

Same was true for the Marshall Tucker Band when I toured with them a little later. Hard-core rockers were there to hear them play "Take the Highway," not B. B. King's "Three O'Clock Blues." But I managed and picked up a few new fans along the way. I liked Troy Caldwell, the group's guitarist and singer, who told me about his big new house with a bedroom designed just like a room at the Holiday Inn. "Been on the road so long, B," he said, "I need the feel of a motel before I can fall asleep." I understood.

I was traveling more than ever, although the trips were different. Sid had me running to California to be on the Mike Douglas or Merv Griffin TV shows. *The Tonight Show* was a different case. I'd been bumped a couple of times because of overbooking. I didn't get mad; I figured it's just showbiz. I finally got on when Flip Wilson was substituting for Johnny Carson. Later Johnny had me on himself. At first, though, he didn't invite me over to the couch after I'd played. Friends wanted to know why he didn't talk to me. Well, maybe he didn't have anything to talk to me about. Was I angry? No, I was happy to get a national shot at selling my songs. I also saw Johnny as the kind of guy who needs time to warm up to you. After a year or two, he did invite me over to the couch and, from then on, we had nice chats. I liked Johnny's wit, and I appreciated that he had me on the show twenty-seven times.

National TV was part of Sid's five-year plan. And so was a showcase Sid set up at the Hotel Peabody in Memphis. I performed along with Roy Clark, one of my favorite country artists. It was strange playing the Peabody, a place that, for much of my life, only allowed blacks in the back door—and just those blacks wearing white coats and ready to serve. This time, though, we were serving up our music to a roomful of college kids in charge of booking concerts on their local campuses. Sid said, "This is a market we gotta get." We got it. Over a two-year period, we did over two hundred college concerts. New worlds kept opening up.

Then, for the first time in my life, I played overseas. In 1971, I went to Tokyo, amazed that the Japanese were buying my blues. I toured Australia. And Sid even got the State Department to send me to Africa—Ghana, Nigeria, Chad, and Liberia—where I saw faces and heard rhythms that drew me back to my earliest childhood. I was almost too excited to play.

My first trip to London was thrilling. Always in my corner, John Lennon had been telling everyone how much he loved "The Thrill Is Gone," and when I finally arrived they snapped my picture in front of 10 Downing Street like I was the Prime Minister. Everyone was amazed I drank tea, and I was surprised Ringo Starr wanted to play on my *Live in London* album, produced by Ed Michel and Joe Zagarino. Ringo's rhythm was right there. Gary Wright played on some tracks, along with Dr. John, Jim Keltner, and Steve Winwood. England was beautiful to me—the Old World of guys wearing bowler hats and bow ties and the wild world of Carnaby Street fashions and Mods and Rockers. I'd been hearing 'bout the British interest in blues for years, but to see and feel it up close was amazing.

Back in the U.S.A., I cut a big production album with a big band and called it *Guess Who*. The title tune, "Guess Who," had been a hit for the great crooner Jesse Belvin back in the fifties. It was written by Jesse's wife, Jo Anne. They were a loving couple, and when they were both killed in a car wreck in 1960, it broke my heart. "Guess Who" reminds me of their love for each other and of my love for my fans. I'm still singing it at concerts.

One song I ain't singing is "Summer in the City," recorded on the same album. It was a hit for the Lovin' Spoonful, and the producer thought it'd be a good tune to cover. It wasn't; it didn't fit my style and I wish I'd left it off.

Stevie Wonder understood my style a lot better. Stevie understands rhythm and blues. Stevie *is* rhythm and blues. He and Syreeta Wright wrote "To Know You Is to Love You." I liked the song so much, I titled my next album after it. Stevie was blazing hot, but he took off the time to come in the studio and play behind me. To see him rocking back and forth at the piano, smiling his radiant smile and sparking the session, was a big-time thrill. He said I'd inspired him, but that night he was the one with the ideas and the energy. Playing with Stevie wasn't like playing with the rock stars, where I could be edgy and uncomfortable. Stevie and I locked in right away. Musically, we were coming from the same place. So were Wayne Jackson and the Memphis Horns, who also played on the session. I remember recording "Respect Yourself," a hit for the Staple Singers, a gospel group I loved not only for their lead singer Mavis Staples, but for Pops Staples's soulful guitar. Pops had a wonderful way of being tasteful and funky at the same time.

In the early seventies, I was listening to a lot of the funk by Sly and the Family Stone and George Clinton's Funkadelic. I liked that sound. I heard funk as a hopped-up variation on blues. Showed me how blues could adapt to modern times without losing its essence. I picked up on some of the seventies' style. Let my hair go natural. I couldn't be me and wear one of those big blow-out Afros or crazy bell-bottoms—I still preferred suits—but I appreciated the new styles.

What I appreciated most was the opportunity to record a double-album date with Bobby Bland. I've already told you that Bobby's my man. We've been through the wars together, even had heartache with some of the same women and same IRS agents. I never thought I was in Bobby's category as a vocalist, but I always wanted to sing with him. When he was signed to ABC, the pieces fell into place. Because we knew each other so well, we didn't wanna plan anything formal. We cut the thing live in L.A. and made it up as we went along, singing a mess of blues, everything from "Black Night" to "Driving Wheel" to "Goin' Down Slow." It went down easy and mellow and, man, I loved it better than practically any album I'd ever made.

One critic for a national magazine didn't agree. He rode me and Bobby hard. Said the album was a mess and called the music nothing. That bothered me. It's one thing if a critic says he doesn't like you, but another to call your music nothing, especially if he can't make music himself. I don't like arguing with critics, so I didn't. I waited. Waited to see the fans' reaction. Well, the fans loved it; *B. B. King and Bobby Bland . . . Together for the First Time . . . Live* went platinum. By then, I couldn't contain my emotions anymore, so I wrote the magazine, saying, "Please let the critic who criticized my album criticize all my albums. With the success of my record with Bobby Bland, the man is bringing me luck." Never heard back from the magazine. But I did hear from ABC, who said they wanted me and Bobby to cut another album, which we did a couple of years later. So much for critics.

By the mid-seventies, I had a few new ideas rattling around my head. New York had been good to me, but New York was crowding me in. The cold winters were getting colder. I dreamt of sunshine and space, a big spread where my children could come and be comfortable, where I could gather my family together and have a real home. I'd already lived in California and didn't wanna go back. The place I liked most was probably the place I needed least. At least that's what my manager Sid said. I wanted to move to Las Vegas.

24

Luck Is a Lady

And like a lady, luck can be a sometime thing. Luck can haunt you, tease you, please you, give you joy, or drop you cold. Like a lady, luck is the one thing a gambler's always looking for. Without luck and a lady, gambling and loving are awfully lonely.

I've looked for both. I've found some luck at the tables in Vegas, had me some big scores, only to lose a lot more than I'd ever win. Fact is, I feel like I've paid for at least one of those fancy chandeliers at the Hilton Hotel on the Strip. That's why Sid was so upset when I said I was moving to Vegas. He thought I'd lose control. But I didn't.

I'm not saying I didn't have bad spells. I was still working to straighten out my IRS mess well into the seventies. My discipline over money management wasn't anything I could brag about. In addition to my own indulgences, my family—the mothers of my children, my children themselves, and my large extended family—knew I liked indulging them. But Sid was smart enough not to lecture me. He knew to leave me alone and let me find my own way. When I announced my decision about relocating to Vegas, Sid never said another word about it. I'm glad I made the move in 1975. Been living there ever since.

Vegas was more than a city to me. It represented the ultimate in American entertainment. It was lavish and rich and reached out to everyone. The whole world loves Vegas. If Vegas embraces your music, the world will follow. To me, Vegas was about an artist like Liberace, a man who turned his art into a grand spectacle. Only met him a few times, but Liberace struck me as a kind and gentle man, a showman willing to take it all the way. I also liked what Liberace said when the scandal sheets started calling him names—that he was crying all the way to the bank.

Don't get me wrong; I didn't have illusions about putting dancing girls or fancy lights or wild costumes in my show. My show is my show, and my blues are my blues. That wouldn't change. But I had always liked taking my blues to Vegas and having them accepted.

I'd started out playing all-black clubs on the edge of Vegas. That was back in the fifties. By the seventies, Sid was able to slip me into Caesar's Palace, thanks to Frank Sinatra, who was headlining. They asked Sinatra whether it was all right for me to play Nero's Nook, the lounge. "Hell, yes!" he said. Not just yes, but "Hell, yes!" That meant a lot to me.

Meant even more to meet the man. I saw him as the singer's singer; I'd been studying Sinatra since the forties. I knew Jilly Rizzo, Frank's friend, who set up the get-together. It was postponed a couple of times because Sinatra's mom was sick.

Sammy Davis and Nancy Wilson filled in for him. Meanwhile, we'd already been playing the lounge and doing great business. In the middle of the week, Rizzo came over and said, "Frank's ready to see you."

It was 3 A.M. and we'd finished our last set. I was ready. I rode the elevator up to the penthouse. Big double doors, big entryway. Inside lots of gorgeous girls milling around an enormous suite overlooking the Strip, a billion watts of neon aglow below. "Frank just flew in from Palm Springs in his private jet," said Rizzo. "He'll be out in a second."

I waited, a little uncomfortable, a lot excited.

Finally Frank appeared, a couple of guys at his side.

"Hi, B," he said. "I'm happy to see you."

"Happy to see you too, Frank."

"Hear you're packing 'em in downstairs."

"Things seem to be going well, Frank."

"Look, B," he said, "I'm dead tired. I need to go to bed. But I got some booze and some broads. Help yourself."

And with that, the man was gone.

I didn't take advantage of his generosity. It wasn't exactly my crowd, but I believe Sinatra's offer was sincere. As a guy in a room talking to me face-to-face, he had a presence and a power I couldn't help but admire.

That was my first venture into big-time Vegas. My second involved Elvis. Like Sinatra, Elvis encouraged the hotel to book me in the lounge while he was in the showroom. When Elvis played the Hilton, it was a combination of Mardi Gras and New Year's Eve. Flags and flowers, people everywhere, parties without end. By then, our lounge act was strong. If it had been any entertainer other than Elvis, we might have even drained business away from the showroom. We were popular enough to stay for a month-long stint, and soon Sid got the Hilton to give me a multiyear contract, my first ever.

Vegas was opening its arms to me, so in 1975 I decided to go all the way. I loved Vegas for the nonstop action and the bargain meals. No city has a better breakfast at a cheaper price. I bought a big corner house. Phyllis McGuire, who sang with her sisters and went with Sam Giancana, lived right behind me. The neighborhood was filled with tall trees and big lawns. Tourist buses rolled by with guides pointing out the stars' homes. It felt prestigious to have my home on that tour. I was the first black in the neighborhood. Later I heard the people who sold me the house caught hell, but no one said a word to me. I'm sure that's because I'm an entertainer. If I was an unknown black man, they might have burned a cross on my lawn.

My dream was to draw my family together. I wanted my children to know each other. Because of their similar backgrounds and problems, I was hoping they could help each other. I wanted to provide shelter for them from a world that could be cold and cruel. To some degree, I succeeded in protecting them. In other ways, I failed miserably.

I also wanted to house myself, to provide shelter for me and my books and records. Ever since I'd started deejaying back in Memphis, I'd built up a collection of materials relating mostly to music, but also other subjects like aviation. I had amassed thousands and thousands of albums in the field of rhythm and blues and jazz. The Manhattan penthouse couldn't house them as comfortably as my expansive spread in Vegas. I needed to stretch out.

Funny, but I hadn't read more than half the books I bought. I hadn't heard all the records I owned. Yet having them in my possession gave me a good feeling. I liked living in a place that looked like a library. Liked living around reams of information. Maybe it's 'cause I quit school in the tenth grade, but I'm comforted by published works and piles of research.

As videotape recorders developed, I became a fanatic. I taped everything, not just the daily TV soap operas—I loved those stories—but old movies with Spencer Tracy and Robert Mitchum and my man John Wayne. When films on tape became available, I started collecting black movies, things like *Stormy Weather*, cowboy adventures with Herb Jeffries, and the TV show *Amos and Andy*. Even on the road, I'd carry those video recorders with me—still do—to tape shows being broadcast while I'm performing. I like the educational channels, and I also confess to a fascination with pornography. Especially now in my old age, pornography seems a safe stimulant and substitution for the real thing. I love illustrated instruction books like *The Joy of Sex*.

The real challenge of living in Las Vegas, of course, was the joy of gambling. Was Sid right to worry as much as he did? Was I about to do myself in on keno or craps? The truth is that by being in the gambling capital of the world, gambling became less of a lure. It was so available, so easy, so everywhere, I tended to cut down. I'm not saying I wouldn't go to the casinos. I would, and I did, but never to any degree of self-destruction. It was Sid who said, "B, when you perform in Vegas, don't draw on your salary." I never did. Never would endanger the salary of the men in my band. That's one reason, I believe, musicians tend to stay with me for decades at a time. I never mess with their money. I kept accounts with the Hilton and Caesar's; I'd get in trouble from time to time, but I slowly learned to walk away. I gave myself limits. After taking it on the chin a number of times, I knew when to wave a white flag. I cut my losses.

I cut out of Vegas soon as my house was furnished and went back on the road. I never left the road for any real period of time. Even after moving into the house, I doubt if I was ever there more than two weeks a year. During any twelve-month period, it was still unusual for me to work less than 330 dates.

Maybe it was the distance between Las Vegas and New York, or maybe the fact that Sid Seidenberg had expanded his agency and was involved with Gladys Knight and the Pips, a group I loved. Either way, things were changing with me and Sid. He was opening new offices and divisions to his company. I was used to dealing directly with him, but now someone else from his agency was contacting me. A stranger was telling me what to do. I didn't like that. So I decided to go back and manage myself. Since we'd always had nothing more than a handshake deal, there were no legal hassles. Sid didn't stand in my way.

Over a year's time—this was 1976—things were getting a little loose. The touring wasn't so smooth, the scheduling wasn't tight, and I felt myself losing control. Little by little, I was falling into the kind of money messes I'd fallen into before. I remember being down in Mississippi with my good friend Charles Evers. Charles is Medgar's brother and took over the state NAACP after Medgar was killed. Charles is a good friend, an educated and good-hearted man who became mayor of Fayette, Mississippi. He's the first black man to hold such a post in a racially mixed city in the South since Reconstruction. Charles is someone I could always count on.

"You look down, B," said Charles.

"I feel like the finances are getting away from me," I explained, reminding myself that once a lousy businessman, always a lousy businessman.

"You know what you need, don't you?" he asked.

"What?"

"Sid."

A few seconds of silence passed before Charles restated his point. "You need Sid," he said, "and Sid needs you."

"You think I should go back to Sid?" I asked.

"Yes, and let the man do his thing."

I took Charles's advice. Saw Sid and said, "Let's work this out. Only this time I wanna deal directly with you and no one else."

Sid was all smiles. He was back in my corner, where he's remained ever since.

The next year, 1977, I was in New Haven, Connecticut, about to receive an Honory Doctorate of Music from Yale. That was frightening enough. But when I went up to spend the weekend and was invited to the home of university president Kingman Brewster and found myself seated alone in a book-lined study with Secretary of State Cyrus Vance—him in one big armchair, me in another—I wondered what the hell I had to say to this man. I swallowed hard and remembered what I always try to remember in new situations: *Be yourself.* Being myself made the conversation flow. He wondered about playing the blues and I wondered about playing politics and we got along great.

Sid was great at playing politics. But when he came up with a plan to blow up my international profile with an extensive tour of the Soviet Union, I was skeptical. I didn't think the Russian government was interested in B. B.'s blues, but Sid kept selling them. When they hesitated, Sid said, "Go hear B. B. in concert. Go see him at Lake Tahoe." Officials of the Soviet Union cultural office came to the show. They wanted to check me out, make sure, I suppose, that my songs were acceptable. It was an audition. Well, after hearing three or four blues, I guess they decided that all blues sound alike 'cause they got up and left. Next thing I knew, the trip was on and I was off to Russia.

Didn't know anything about the country, so I read a long book about the Russians. That helped me understand the complicated cultures and enormous diversity of the Soviet Union. My understanding really kicked in, though, when I saw the place itself. Man, we went all over. Started out in the south, in Azerbaijan. In the dingy hotel, huge lights from the Russian troll boats would sweep through my little room every five minutes, keeping me up all night, reminding me that I was only fifteen minutes away from Iran and a world away from the Delta.

We went up through the Republic of Georgia. The airplanes were old and rickety and, even worse, on the runways I saw the broken-down remains of demolished aircraft. When you're flying around, you don't like seeing crashed airplanes left out to rot.

One of the guys accompanying us from the U.S. government made me even more nervous. As we flew over Russia, he'd sit next to me, leaning over and taking photographs with a super-small camera. Every airport we passed over—*click, click, click*; every city or military base—*click, click, click*. If he wasn't a spy, I ain't a bluesman. "Hey, man," I said, "put that camera away. They're gonna think I'm your partner." But he kept on—*click, click, click*—and I kept praying no one would charge us both with espionage.

As we made our way to Moscow, we switched from a plane to a bus. The roads were dirt, the going was rough, and I kept looking out the window, seeing sights that reminded me of my childhood—open fields, farmworkers, tractors, crops grown and crops harvested, the steady rhythm of life tied to the soil. Living off the land is a common link, whether it's rural Russia or rural Mississippi. Driving through rural Russia, I felt this strange connection to a people I didn't know.

At the concerts, I was surprised to see the young kids knew about B. B. King. The adults, though, were in the dark. The adults seemed to be sitting on their hands. When we finally made it to Moscow, I was determined to get the audience going. I wanted some reaction. Opened my show with "Every Day I Have the Blues," played with all the fire at my command. I wanted to really rouse the crowd, to see 'em smile and shout and show me they got the message. Still no signs of appreciation. Went into "Rock Me Baby," hoping to rock their socks. Nothing. "Sweet Sixteen" and "How Blue Can You Get" didn't get 'em either. I did everything but buck-dance, and still no response. After another half-dozen tunes, nervous desperation gave me an idea.

I offered my guitar pick to a woman sitting in the front row. She was shy at first, but I urged her on. She approached the foot of the stage and accepted my gift. She looked it over and then—miracle of miracles—she smiled at me before turning to the audience and smiling at them. I had a few extra picks and gave them away as well. Now people were starting to rush the stage; I finally got 'em out of their seats and involved with the show. I took that as a sign. From then on, at the end of every performance, I always give away dozens of picks to fans. It's become my trademark.

If I could get through to the people in faraway Russia, maybe I could get through to anyone. Russia represented a breakthrough. It proved to me that, no matter how foreign or strange or remote a country, folks still feel the power of the blues. For years, I talked about the blues as universal music. But that was talk—talk I believed, but talk that was untested. Russia was the acid test. When the Russian government invited me back several more times over the years, I knew they were hungry for even more blues. As the years went on, as Sid booked me everywhere from Italy to Israel to New Zealand, I was honored to carry the blues all over the world. The color of the people didn't matter; the politics of their country didn't matter; what mattered was the sound of our music, born in the American Deep South and brought up through the big cities. Everyone in the world seemed to love the blues.

As my markets kept expanding and my trips kept widening, I might have gotten cocky or prideful. I didn't—and for a good reason. I knew I was there, carrying the blues message around the globe, only as a result of good timing and happenstance. Others before me—Blind Lemon or Lonnie Johnson—would have served as better messengers than me. They were more original talents. T-Bone Walker should have been the worldwide symbol of the blues. T-Bone was the sure-enough guru; I was just his disciple. But T-Bone was born too soon. The international marketing of music hadn't kicked in. The influence of American culture hadn't seeped in. But I was lucky. By the time I got ready to make my move, all systems were go. And, most important of all, I had someone with the smarts to build me up and sell me around the world. That someone was Sid.

25

Circumcision Is No Laughing Matter

joke about it now, but at the time it was serious business. Moving out of middle age into senior status, I finally admitted to a medical problem. It was a delicate one 'cause it involved my penis. I wasn't circumcised, and over the years my foreskin gave me problems. In cold weather, the skin would tighten and sometimes break. Occasionally, bacteria would set in and swelling would occur. Urinating could be painful and sometimes sex was ruled out. For years, I'd put off the inevitable—the idea of circumcision gave me cold chills—but finally I figured I had to do the right thing.

It happened in Houston. My doctor down there assured me he'd minimize the pain. In the waiting area, another male patient told me he was going in for a triple bypass and asked about me. I was shy, but finally told him, "I'm being circumcised." "Oh, shit," he said, "that's a piece of cake." I tried to keep his words in mind as they wheeled me into the operating room.

I remember feeling self-conscious around the pretty nurses—they all knew why I was there—but I flirted with them all the same. Needed women around me, even when I was at my most vulnerable—*especially* when I was at my most vulnerable. Female faces whirled around me as the drugs knocked me out and I drifted off to sleep.

Woke up hours later, feeling drowsy but okay. *Hmmmm*, I thought to myself, *that wasn't bad*. But a few minutes later, I felt like someone had dumped burning hot coals on my joint. I yelled for the nurse, but the nurse said my blood pressure was low and all she could do was give me pills. No shot. I wanted a shot. I wanted the pain to go away, but I had to live with the pain another hour—one of the worst hours of my life. Finally the pain subsided and my penis, thank you very much, has been in good working order ever since.

The order of my work was the same in the eighties as it was in the fifties—the road, the recording studio, back on the road, back to the recording studio. ABC Records sold out to MCA, but that made little difference. They kept my contract and Sid kept negotiating good advances. I also got with a good producer—Stewart Levine—who put me with good jazz musicians to change the formula a bit.

I loved recording and performing with the Crusaders, whose jazz sounds gave me the lift I was looking for. We cut the album *Midnight Believer*, which had me believing in new combinations for my blues. Couple of the tunes—"When It All Comes Down (I'll Still Be Around)" and "Never Make a Move Too Soon"—got good airplay, but nothing like "The Thrill Is Gone."

Another Stewart Levine production, *There Must Be a Better World Somewhere*, featured my homeboy Hank Crawford and his former colleague from the Ray Charles band, David "Fathead" Newman. The album won a Grammy. So did *Blues 'n' Jazz*, where Calvin Owens, my trumpet man from the old days, wrote a bunch of beautiful charts, using jazz greats like Woody Shaw, Don Wilkerson, Fred Ford, Arnett Cobb, Lloyd Glenn, Major Holley, and James Bolden, another trumpet player and mainstay of my band today. James has been with me nearly twenty years.

Weird, but *Blues 'n' Jazz*, one of my least traditional albums, won a Grammy for Best Traditional Blues Album. I ain't complaining, and I ain't giving back the Grammy. I say thanks for the awards—I love 'em all—but I'd be lying if I didn't tell you those categories sometimes seem pretty silly.

My musical family got tighter with the addition of my nephew Walter Riley King. Walter had been raised by my sister and my daddy. At a young age, he showed an interest in music, so I bought him a trombone. I was always buying instruments for the kids in my family, but Walter was the first one who stuck with it. Later he switched to sax. He became the first King to graduate from college—he majored in music at Tennessee State—and that made me exceptionally happy. He taught music in high school before joining my band, where today he serves as my musical director. Walter is a helluva musician—jazz, blues, you name it—and a wonderful writer. He's done his old uncle proud.

I also felt proud when Ray Charles asked me to do a duet with him. He's one of my favorite singers and piano players. For forty years, we'd been playing some of the same shows, encountering each other on the road. But we'd never recorded together. Ray's idea was "Save the Bones for Henry Jones ('Cause He Don't Eat No Meat)," a song Johnny Mercer made popular in the forties. Johnny had cut it with Nat Cole and his trio. When Ray said he wanted it to cut it with me, I was ready— but not quite ready for his rearrangement of the melody. In the studio, Ray's in control of everything; Ray's a perfectionist. If he doesn't get it like he hears it, he gives you a hard time.

Suppose you could say Ray gave me a hard time. I kept flubbing the phrasing and Ray kept insisting I get it right. I couldn't. Finally Brother Ray had to give up on me and try me out on another tune, James Taylor's "Nothing Like a Hundred Miles." This time I came through, and Ray was so happy, he got to slapping his side and screaming, "That's it, Brother B, you got it now!" I was relieved that I gave the Genius what he wanted.

My musical flexibility is a funny thing. I believe my ability to trim my sails got me through some rough musical storms. To some extent, I adapted in the fifties and sixties. I wasn't rock 'n' roll and I wasn't strictly soul, but I made enough adjustments to keep me fresh. When disco came storming through the seventies, I hardly had a disco sound, but by then I had a loyal audience who liked their blues strong and straight-ahead. My almost exclusively black audience from the early days had turned predominantly white. That left me conflicted.

Can't tell you how many times a young black person would come up to me and say, "Mr. King, I'd like your autograph. It's not for me, but for my mother. My mother loves you." Or someone might even say, "The autograph's not for me, it's for my grandmother. My grandmother loves you." That approach hurt me. I'd want to say, "How about *you?* How do *you* feel about

the blues? Didn't your mama teach *you* to love the blues?" But
I kept my mouth shut and gave them whatever they wanted. I
understood they meant no disrespect. They were just trying to
make their mother or their grandmother happy.

Seems like the English or French or even the Australians
and Japanese were loving the blues more than my own people.
I understood how some blacks have a bad association with the
blues. The blues represent a painful past; for some, the blues
stand for a time when we didn't have pride and hadn't made
progress. No one likes opening up old wounds. But in my
mind, my blues always had dignity. That's why I modeled my
presentation after Nat Cole and Duke Ellington. They had class;
they represented their people with distinction and presented
their music without ridicule or shame. I wanted my own people
to feel like I'd done the same with the blues, the one form that's
followed our path from slavery to freedom. I can't help but wish
that, even today, I had a young black following.

On the other hand, I like today's young black music. I've
liked black music from Blind Lemon to Prince. When Prince
sang about partying like it's 1999, that stroked B. B. King real
good. I like hip-hop and I like rap; I'm not among those who
want to bring 'em down. I don't like a lot of the cursing, but I
like a lot of the grooves. I respect the rhyming genius of these
brothers and feel rap is filled with creativity. It's a new kind of
poetry. When I was a kid, adults were putting down boogie-
woogie, another young form created by young people. That
was our time, an era when we were experimenting with new
ways of expression. Boogie-woogie and, later on, T-Bone's
soaring electric guitar fit our lifestyle. Same's true today. Now
is the era of the rappers, and they're entitled to the freedom to
express themselves and find their artistic way. I like their de-

termination, and I feel, underneath it all, their rhythm is that same rhythm that drives me; it's the rhythm of life. Their blues have taken a different shape than mine. But they're still talkin' 'bout heartache and love and fear and hope and the mysteries of making it in a world that don't care nothin' 'bout you.

I was sixty-three when my career hit its hottest stride. I don't wanna discredit my own hard work and tenacity. I'm proud that I kept on keeping on all these years. But the truth is that something bad happened to Sidney Seidenberg that turned out good for me. Wish it hadn't been that way, but it was.

In the mid-eighties, Gladys Knight and the Pips parted ways with Sid. That hurt me 'cause I knew Sid had helped their career. Sid adored Gladys. I didn't ask details, it wasn't my business, but I saw the disappointment in Sid's face and felt him making an even stronger commitment to me. Sid's attitude was "Now I'm gonna show the world what I can do. I'm gonna put all my energy into B. B. King and make him a bigger star than anyone ever dreamed possible."

Sid worked on my career so hard that once, when he discouraged his wife Edie from coming along on a road trip because of hazardous conditions, Edie got mad and told me, "You know, B, Sid may sleep with me, but he's married to you."

It was Sid who got me film projects like John Landis's *Into the Night*. I wrote music for the score, which I composed on guitar as I looked at pictures in the editing room. That was a new and exciting creative experience for me. I also sang the theme song, which became my first MTV-styled video. That was fun 'cause the film's stars, Jeff Goldblum and Michelle Pfeiffer, were my bandmates, along with Eddie Murphy and Steve Martin. I'd started appearing on TV shows as well—guest shots on sitcoms like *Bill Cosby* and even a couple of segments of *General Hospital*, one of my favorite soaps.

Sid was also looking for greater exposure. That's why he hooked me up with U2. I'd heard their *Joshua Tree* album and knew they were among the biggest rock groups in the world. I could relate to rock. I heard its blues roots and felt its connection to my music. I could see its popularity had grown like wildfire since Elvis started shaking his pelvis in the fifties. Opening for the Stones and Marshall Tucker had been important for my career. But it took Sid—and not me—to think of a way to introduce myself to still another young generation.

"We're going to Ireland," said Sid, "and U2 is coming to the show. So why don't you ask Bono, the guy who sings lead, to write a song for you?" Sounded like a good idea, but I wasn't sure Bono would be interested. I also hate to impose myself on anyone else. When it comes to business, though, I make myself do certain things, even if they might go against my nature.

After my Dublin concert, Bono and his boys showed up in the dressing room and we had a nice relaxed chat. They acted more like old friends than superstars. Before Bono left, I mentioned how I'd like him to write a song for me. All he said was "Okay, I will." A year passed, maybe more, and I'd forgotten the whole thing when Sid said Bono had been looking for me. U2 was playing Fort Worth, Texas, and wanted my band to open the show. Sure thing.

When I got there, Bono was all smiles. Said he'd written the song, but it was a duet for the two of us. I was flattered but frightened. Wasn't the kind of material I was used to. But he was cool and patient and showed me how it went. More I heard it, more I was convinced our styles would blend. He called it

"When Love Comes to Town." The story surprised me; the lyrics weren't what I'd expected. Didn't think someone so young would write something so deep. In a rock tune, he'd written about the Crucifixion of Jesus. The song was solid and the rhythm was right, and that night, after my show and after his, Bono called me back out in front of forty thousand screaming U2 fans and we sang "When Love Comes to Town" as the crowd stood and cheered. It was a great moment.

It was also great going out with U2. We taped a video that got heavy airplay and won an MTV Video Award. "When Love Comes to Town" was the hottest single off the album. Produced by Jimmy Iovine, we basically used the live version with some adjustments made in the studio. After the song came out on their album *Rattle and Hum* and hit big, U2 carried us around the world for over three months. We hit Europe and Japan and came back home, playing huge football stadiums and giant arenas to sold-out crowds. Bono treated us with absolute respect. He never made us feel like an opening act. I was given a hotel suite as big as his in every city I played. And in every concert, I felt a new energy coming from audiences who brought with them a fresh appreciation of the blues.

I'll never know how many new fans I made on that tour. But I believe my music was heard by still another new generation of young people who seemed to feel the same thing I'd felt when I first heard the blues sung by my Uncle Jack hollering in the cotton fields outside Indianola—raw emotion.

26

Indianola Sunset

finally got what I wanted: worldwide acceptance. I wish I could have had another "The Thrill Is Gone"; I wish my family life could have stabilized. I wish for lots of stuff. But the idea that my blues have been accepted gives me peace of mind. My finances finally worked out. Me and the IRS are on good terms. I don't say this to boast, but the truth is that I've become a millionaire. I'm proud of that fact because, as you know by now, it wasn't easy. Solid investments, thanks to Sid, have given me security in my old age.

Sid likes to say B. B. King has turned into a conglomerate. We've franchised the B. B. King blues nightclubs in Memphis and L.A. Others should be opening soon in Nashville and Orlando. Gibson started a line of B. B. King guitar strings made of Swedish steel. There's B. B. King casual clothing and B. B. King food products—B. B. King barbecue sauce, B. B. King salad dressing, B. B. King salsa, and B. B. King bean spreads.

We're even thinking about B. B. King frozen catfish. I'm most comfortable with the catfish. I haven't eaten meat since almost ten years ago when I watched a TV show about the slaughter of chickens and cows.

That had me thinking about more than the cruel circumstances of the creatures' deaths. I thought about my own childhood when I was so close to the animals. I recalled talking to them after Mama died and feeling how only they understood my pain. In my little boy's mind, I felt they had souls. As an adult, I'd lost that connection. The TV show brought it back. So I decided to change my diet. I call myself a semivegetarian because I do eat fish and eggs. But I don't wanna give you the impression I'm a purist. When Dave of Wendy's restaurants asked me to do a commercial, I agreed. Made me think of my days back on WDIA, selling Pepticon. I've always liked selling products, and I tell folks that if I did eat meat, I'd go to Wendy's.

I've enjoyed doing lots of commercials over the past ten years. It's against my nature to turn down money. I'm flattered that big-time products like M&M's want me as a spokesman and Budweiser beer uses my music. Biggest compliment of all, though, came from Northwest Airlines, who not only put me in their TV spots but, for my seventieth birthday, painted Lucille on one of their jets and wrote HAPPY BIRTHDAY, B. B. KING all over the plane.

I've gotten enough trophies and plaques to fill a garage, but nothing was as big as receiving the Kennedy Center Honors from President Clinton last year, along with honorees Neil Simon, Sidney Poitier, Marilyn Horne, and Jacques d'Amboise. The President reminisced about seeing me and Bobby Bland on the same bill in Little Rock. Back in 1990, Lee Atwater, an assistant to President Bush, was the first politician to carry me to the White House. Lee, another young man who died before his time, was one of those blues-loving white boys who came to see me when I was playing roadhouses down in Georgia. Lee was a blues player himself, and he worked hard to get rhythm and blues recognition in high places.

Through Lee, George Bush was the first President to invite me to the White House. Man, I was excited. I received the Presidential Medal of the Arts, one of the highest awards, I've been told, the country can bestow upon a private citizen. I chatted with the President for a while and later was invited back for a private lunch with Vice President Quayle. He said he just wanted to get to know me. The same thing was said by the American ambassadors to Germany and Japan and by the presidents of Turkey and Latvia. They've all come backstage to chat with me. They said they were fans.

Queen Elizabeth and Prince Philip of England once invited me to a garden party they were throwing in Washington, D.C. I put on my best suit and flew in for the afternoon. Tea with the Queen sounded like fun. The place was swarming with big shots—movie stars, famous politicians, business titans. I greeted the Queen and Prince and started mingling in the crowd. I felt a little uncomfortable, so I found a quiet corner under the tent where I sat and drank my tea. Before I knew it, lots of people were congregating around me to say hello. This wasn't my intention; it just happened. As the line to greet me grew longer, I heard the Reverend Jesse Jackson say, "Looks like more people are lining up to see the King than the Queen."

I'm always excited to hear that men and women in important positions want to meet me. And I always worry a little that I'll disappoint them. But the truth is that they hear and see the same B. B. as the average fan looking for an autograph or a

Polaroid. I make plain conversation, try to be diplomatic, and stay simple. I find that most people, especially the important ones, respond positively to someone who doesn't act important. Chances are, I'll ask more questions than I'll answer, because I realize I'm with someone who has something to teach me.

Years back, I sold my big house in Vegas and moved into a smaller place in a quiet part of the city. Colonel Parker lives across the street. My home is piled up with a million records, books, and videotapes. I'm still working 250 to 300 nights a year, so I'm not home that much. Only two stoplights stand between my house and the airport. I've got a Mercedes and a Rolls, but it's my GM low-rider truck that gets my loving attention when I have time to kill. I take her out in the desert, goose her hard, and, feeling every bump in the road, forget my troubles.

That might be the only time you'll catch me wearing jeans. Nowadays, you'll see kids wearing torn-up jeans with the butts hanging out and their knees showing. It's okay with me if they think that's cool. Fashions are funny, but I spent too many years wearing ripped jeans because I had nothing else. Torn-up jeans will never be my fashion.

In the same way, I want Lucille to shine and look her best. I'm playing Lucille #16 these days, a beautiful Gibson with ultrasensitive pickups, fine-tuning capability on every string, gold-plated tuners, and a crank that lets me change a broken string onstage in no time flat. Lucille #17 is sitting on a stand right behind me, soaking it all in so when she's called into action she'll know what to do.

Back in the eighties, I got into computers. Apple seemed friendly, so I got one to use with my music. I thought the

Omega was even friendlier—I liked all the icons—and then I went from the Commodore to the Toshiba laptop. Now I travel with two laptops. I use them for games—solitaire's got me hooked—but also for general information, courses on music theory and even mathematics. Anything to keep my aging mind from getting rusty. I recently started fooling with CD-ROM—even did a CD-ROM version of my life story—and jumped on the Internet. I like stumbling around the world of high-tech.

High-tech medicine helped me learn I had diabetes, which I watch carefully. Gave up smoking twenty-five years ago—those menthol Kools were doing me in. Gave up drinking nine years ago. Now I hold a cold can of Diet Coke in my hand and pretend it's a beer. At age sixty, I saw my willpower wasn't as strong as it used to be, and I started putting on weight. For the first time, I couldn't control the way I looked. Now I fight back by checking into the Pritikin Center for Longevity every year for a couple of weeks. That's a health resort in Santa Monica, California. When I first arrived, I was nervous 'cause I didn't know the routine. But once I saw the schedule—the exercise program, the nutrition classes—I got with the program and learned to eat right. Slimmed down from 290 to 250. The battle ain't over; the battle of the bulge rages on forever.

I feel great about my current band, my best ever. These guys knock me out night after night. Most of them have been with me for fifteen years or more. My lineup is Walter King and Melvin Jackson on sax, James Bolden on trumpet, the fabulous Leon Warren on guitar, Michael Doster on bass, James Toney on keyboards, Tony Coleman and Calep Emphrey, Jr., on drums. I'm also blessed with great support from my road manager Burnett Fogg, tour manager Sherman Darby, and personal assistant Joe McClendon. I can always count on Willie King and

Edris Banks and my main man who's been with me through what seems like several lifetimes—Norman Matthews.

I wouldn't ever want a pickup band. I care too much about my music being right, my groove being solid. So in order to keep a band as good as mine, you need to provide the guys with steady gigs. That's one reason I stay on the road. My men need to work; they have wives and children and grandchildren and mortgages. I'm proud to provide them with a medical plan and health insurance. I wish more bandleaders would do the same.

The other reason I'm still working so hard goes back to lessons learned from the old days. If you don't get much airplay—and I still don't, you don't see much B. B. King on MTV or VH1—you generate more press and sell more records by playing for the people. Record companies are quick to make videos for pop artists, but not blues acts. Videos are a great promotional tool and, without them, I have to work my personal appearances even harder. If I don't keep presenting myself to the public, the public has no reason to remember me. That's especially true in Europe, where I do as much TV as I can. When those shows are replayed, the exposure is good and so are the residuals. In recent years, I've earned as much abroad as at home.

I'm still amazed that certain foreign countries, like Israel, treat me like a native son. After I slipped on a steep stone stairway in Jerusalem and fell, busting my lip real bad and bruising my hand, I floated in the Dead Sea, thinking the salt was good for the wounds. Then Sid rushed me to the Hadassah Hospital, where the doctors gave me royal treatment, stitching me up in no time. I played and sang that night like nothing had happened. While I was waiting in the hospital, I watched a woman have a miscarriage as she was walking into the building. The image was far more painful than the pain in my lip. I also recall an Arab man who'd been bit by a snake being treated by a Jewish doctor. I wondered if it's the people of the Middle East who don't get along, or if it's their governments.

Israel made me wonder about many things. In Jerusalem, visiting the holy shrines of Christianity, Judaism, and Islam, I felt a quiet thrill in my heart. I couldn't help but think about the close links tying those religions together. As a guitar player, I look for harmony among notes. As a human being, I look for harmony among people. I rode all over Israel, fascinated by the agriculture. I kept comparing it to Mississippi, where the land is so fertile. In Israel, land is arid and the fertility man-made, the irrigation phenomenal, and the advanced mechanized technique for picking cotton, for example, something I couldn't have imagined as a little boy.

As a grown man, I appreciate Israeli women. Over the years, I've fallen for two. The first was a Sephardic Jew, dark and beautiful and absolutely enchanting. The other was a sexy gemologist. Neither relationship proved permanent. As usual, my schedule and temperament got in the way.

I carry other memories of Israel. In the early seventies, the Israeli Defense Force flew me to a secret camp near the Suez Canal to entertain the troops. The general in charge was no older than twenty-four. We lunched on olives, chickpeas, cucumbers, and tomatoes. The sun was blistering hot, and I remember thinking that the soldiers looked so young. It broke my heart—it still does—to think of the fighting that rages on in that part of the world, where God seems so near.

I guess we all live somewhere between heaven and earth. I see God in the creation of the sky and sea, but I don't hear

Him, as some say they do, in the silence of the mind. I still look for signs or miracles, but I don't see them. That doesn't mean I don't believe. I do. Given the wonder of the world, I'd be a fool not to believe. But God, like life or death itself, is a miracle and a mystery that I'll never fully explain or understand. I'm content to accept things the way they are, express gratitude for my blessings, and move on to the next gig.

Folks ask me if I'd change anything if I could. Well, I wish I'd finished high school and gone to college. And I wish I'd waited till I was forty to get married. Down South, we say a man doesn't have any sense till he's forty. In my own case, I didn't start reasoning with myself too well till I hit middle age.

I'm still excited about what I do. I still love music more than ever. Some say I have corny taste for calling Willie Nelson's "You're Always on My Mind" and Lionel Richie's "Three Times a Lady" my favorite songs, but who cares? I like what I like, and I love Luciano Pavarotti, even if I don't know what his words are saying. Hearing him one night in Buenos Aires was enough to hook me for life.

After seventy-four albums, I still look forward to the next session. Still thrilled to pick up Lucille in the privacy of my hotel room or at a public concert and have her soothe my troubled mind. Still looking for the right blue notes and right blue sounds that paint private feelings words can't describe. Can't describe, for example, how excited I was to go on tour with a special superband a few years back that included Gene Harris, Ray Charles, Ray Brown, Plas Johnson, Urbie Green, Sweets Edison, and my favorite jazz guitarist, Kenny Burrell. Listening to Kenny every night was like a lecture from a great university professor. Felt just as excited taking my own band to Beijing, China, where we opened the Hard Rock Cafe.

I'd like the excitement to keep coming till I die. I don't fear death. I wish I had firmer faith in an afterlife—that it's gonna be all milk and honey—but I'm not worried. It's the here and now that concerns me most. Been trying to get my will in order. I'm insisting that my grandchildren and great-grandchildren go to college in order to get an inheritance. That's how much I want them to benefit from the kind of education I missed.

When I think of death, I have three preferences: that I die in my sleep, or holding Lucille while playing onstage, or holding a woman while making love. After all these years, I'm still obsessed with women. After nearly thirty years of being single, I'd like to get married. I realize my two marriages were ruined, at least in part, by my work. I still can't compromise my work. But in a few years from now, when I can sock a little more money away, I'd like to try. I'd like to cut down my touring, say, to 175 or 200 dates a year. I think I'll be ready to take off an occasional weekend with someone who's ready to relax with an old man. That's the lay-back I'm looking forward to.

Recently I've met two or three ladies I'd marry. But I'm afraid the old pattern is still there. They want me home more than I'm willing to stay home. So I decided to let some other lucky guy enjoy their company. I'm also funny in another way: I don't want a woman as old as me. She doesn't have to be twenty-five or thirty. Fact is, I prefer mature ladies who know life. She can even be sixty or sixty-five. As long as she's a year younger than seventy.

At my age, I know it's a rare thing for a young woman to truly care for B. B. King. A lady meeting me after my show may like me 'cause I've got a good name and make good money. Maybe she thinks she can show me off to a friend; maybe she imagines I'll die soon and leave her well-off. I don't mind that thinking. But I'd be crazy to believe she really loves me for the way I look. I know I'm no Prince Charming. I try to see my love life realistically. I'm not easy. I like to be mothered, but not too much; I like to be smothered, but not too much. Women who've been able to understand me have remained my friends throughout my life. I still want to make one woman happy with my affection; I want her to be comfortable. But the question is the same one that's haunted me forever: Can a lady marry a guy whose marriage to his work is the only marriage that's ever worked?

It's been over ten years since my father passed away. I still miss him very much, just as I've missed Mama every day of my life. They both had their limitations—we all do—but they gave me what I needed to get through. In their own way, they both demonstrated courage to deal with a world that didn't exactly welcome or want them. My parents taught me to cope.

Folks ask me about progress. As I think about leaving the world, is it a better place than when I came in? I don't know. War and famine and injustice still rage all around us. Maybe they always will. I'll get down and depressed about all the drive-by murders and senseless violence when suddenly someone comes by and does something unusually kind or brave and my heart fills up again with the belief that people are good. But is that progress? I can only answer the question from the narrow perspective of my own life.

If someone asked me to give a state-of-the-blues address, I'd say the blues are prospering. When I think about the audience for the blues when I was a kid and the audience for the blues now, I can't help but be amazed. When I was a kid, only black people loved the blues—and many other black people were prejudiced against them. Today, the world loves the blues. To my mind, the blues have never been in better shape. I've watched the blues travel from the rural roads of Mississippi to practically every point on the planet. When I play in Sydney or Oslo or Osaka, I get the same feeling I used to get in Osceola, Arkansas; people are grooving on the blues because the blues are universal. The rockers and rappers and soul-singing children all come out of the blues. The blues is the grandfather watching over his children.

Many brothers have taken the blues torch from my generation and carried it proudly. My good friend Albert Collins, who died not long ago, came up after me and built a beautiful career on true blues. So did Junior Wells. Buddy Guy has become a superstar—and so has Robert Cray, though I've never heard Robert describe himself as a bluesman. Taj Mahal is a walking encyclopedia of blues; he can sing and play up a storm. I like Little Milton, Luther Allison, Joe Louis Walker, and dozens of others, like Lucky Peterson, born a generation or two or three after me.

Because this country is so predominantly white, it's only logical that white boys have had the most impact in keeping twelve-bar blues alive. Englishman Eric Clapton is devoted to the blues and never stops paying tribute to his masters. For that, I pay tribute to him. Eric is the number-one rock guitarist in the world and plays the blues as well as anyone and better than most. Bonnie Raitt is a white woman who has devoted her career to boosting black blues. She's a tireless fighter for blues pioneers and a great performer who happens to be the best slide guitarist out there, bar none. Jeff Healey, out of Canada, is also a helluva bluesman.

Of all the white guys, though, Stevie Ray Vaughan earned a place of his own. I loved him. Stevie came through in the early eighties, just after Mike Bloomfield died an early and tragic death. I remember thinking that another white boy nurtured by black music was going to keep the faith. Stevie did more than that. He played with such incredible technique and genuine soul that he became the boldest guitarist of his generation. He was a superstar with the potential of Elvis. What Elvis did for rock 'n' roll, Stevie might have done for the blues.

When his brother Jimmy, another great guitarist, introduced us, Stevie said, "B. B., I feel like I've known you my whole life." He treated me like a son treats a father. And I came to love him as I had loved Mike Bloomfield. These *were* my sons; these were the children who'd not only learned my craft, but improved upon it. They could play everything I played—and much more. They brought the blues to a new generation of fans. They spread the word wider than I could have ever spread it myself.

When Stevie died in a helicopter crash in 1990, I was devastated. I'd lost part of myself. The world had lost the man destined to become the greatest guitarist in the history of the blues. I still miss Stevie—and miss Mike—and wish both boys could have lived long, prosperous lives. They deserved kinder fates. Something happened not long ago, though, that made the mourning a little less painful. I was playing Portland and listening to the opening act, an eighteen-year-old kid named Kenny Wayne Shepherd. The boy could play blues, and after my show he told me how his idol had been Stevie Ray. It was beautiful to see Stevie Ray's legacy living through a teenager, just as I like to think T-Bone's legacy is living through me. The point was made again when I met Nathan Cavalieri from Australia. Nathan is a highly proficient blues guitarist with a good sense of the instrument's dynamics and diverse history. The kid is thirteen.

I'm impressed that even older forms of the blues are alive and kicking. There are black guys like Keb Mo' and white guys like Kelly Joe Phelps who play acoustic country blues and make 'em sound new and fresh. Every blues style—backwoods or big-city—has kept its own vitality. Maybe when they look back five hundred years from now, hip historians will give the blues the credit it deserves—as the backbone of the American music.

Despite its popularity with the public, the blues are still treated like an orphan by most major record companies. They still won't give us the advertising, the videos, and the marketing muscle they give to pop or country. I'm not sure why. If they argue that blues sales don't justify the promotion, we argue back that the promotion will boost sales. It's which comes first, the chicken or the egg? In my heart of hearts, I still believe there's prejudice against the blues. Record executives won't say it to your face, but I think they secretly feel blues is too simple, too old-fashioned, too basic to have super-mass appeal. In my mind, it's the simplicity of the blues that keeps them alive and makes them timeless. The blues will never die.

While the blues may be more popular than ever, I think they could be even more popular. I've spent a lifetime trying to prove that point. I'm still not where I want to be, but I do think that me and my blues have made progress. But what about race relations? People are always asking me—maybe because I'm old and look like I should know something—whether I see progress along those lines. I don't have any easy answers, just a few memories.

*   *   *

In the fifties, the B. B. King blues tour is storming through Louisiana. We've been riding since Alabama and we're dead tired and we're starving; we're hungry enough to eat a horse. We stop at a roadside restaurant and walk inside. We don't know what to expect. Angrily, all the white people walk out, but when the white owner recognizes me, he announces, "It's okay, folks. This is B. B. King the singer. Y'all come back in." Hesitantly, they come back in. And every time a new customer walks in, the owner is quick to point to my table and say, "He's all right. He's B. B. King the singer." I feel good 'cause me and the band are finally getting to eat; I feel bad 'cause the prejudice is still there, still thick enough to cut with a knife.

In the seventies, the B. B. King blues tour is storming through Holland on the Berlin Express. The train stops in a little town and the conductor says we have an hour to eat. There's a café next to the station. The moment we walk in, everyone walks out. It's Louisiana all over. But when someone tells the owner who I am, he gets all excited and, in a language I don't understand, starts talking to the people who walked out. Now they're walking back in. Now they're pointing and staring and suddenly everything's cool.

Or is it?

Can you change people's hearts? Can you erase centuries of blind hatred and ignorance? I've tried to stand for something, tried to let people see I'm a human being with human feelings just like everyone else, but have I made any real difference in the grand scale of things?

I'd rather think on a small scale. Rather remember a time not long ago when I returned to Indianola. I still see the sun as it starts to set, the sky all pink and blue. I'm not standing in the cotton fields. I'm not following the mule or driving the tractor.

I'm not a kid or a teenager or a young adult dreaming of glory. I'm an adult, an entertainer known as B. B. King. I'm sitting on the porch of a big house on a big hill on the white side of the tracks. The lady who owns the house is Miss Jessie Lee, one of the wealthiest citizens in the city. She and I and maybe a hundred other guests are sipping tea and eating cake and watching the light of day slip away. The guests are about evenly divided between whites and blacks. They've been invited to greet me. I know many of these people; I've known them my whole life. Some are deeply prejudiced—whites who don't like blacks, blacks who don't like whites. Some of the conversations are strained. Some of the guests are uncomfortable. But everyone seems to be trying. Everyone senses something good in the air.

I look over the small community of my childhood and think that this is a magical dusk, a magical moment. Here in the place where the White Citizens' Council was born, a tenderhearted lady has brought together folks who have never been together before. Miss Jessie Lee hasn't invited the press. Her motive isn't publicity, but simply the joy of doing something to promote kindness and understanding.

I feel privileged to be there.

I feel blessed to be part of the change—even if it's only for a single afternoon, even if it lasts only as long as it takes the shimmering sun to melt into the dark Mississippi soil.

Being with B

BY DAVID RITZ

B is sick as a dog. His forehead is burning hot, and he's coming down with what looks like a nasty case of flu. Back in his dressing room, I'm waiting for him to cancel the show, call the doctor, and spend a week in bed. Instead, he asks his valet to fetch his luminous green-and-orange tux jacket, his black trousers and black patent-leather shoes. Without saying a word, B steps into his clothes, combs his hair, sprays on his Furyo eau de toilette, and heads for the stage. He walks with the unhurried and distinguished gait of a diplomat.

He performs from nine to nearly eleven, when he returns to his dressing room, naps for a half hour, and then plays a second show from midnight till two. Both performances are strong; both crowds haven't the slightest notion that B is suffering.

At 3 A.M. after patiently signing autographs, B instructs the bus driver to take off for the hotel, nearly ninety minutes away.

"David," says B, calling me back to his private compartment, "you ready to go to work?"

He's ready to be interviewed, while I, exhausted from merely watching the man, am ready to collapse.

"Sure, B," I say, "let's talk."

And talk we do—on the bus and in limos, in cars and planes and hotel suites and TV studios, in the Pritikin Center, in his home in Vegas, wherever he is working because B is working all the time. We talk for months and months, talk during a grueling tour of the West and the Midwest, talk when he's fighting a long-lasting flu in Southern California, talk on a slow-moving ferry crossing the Puget Sound, talk in the tiny closet of a dressing room in the Blue Note jazz club in New York's Greenwich Village. For all this talking, talk doesn't always come easy to B. He's friendly to a fault, but cherishes privacy and long spells of repose. Travel is his quiet time. But because he is first and foremost a worker, and because he understands our work involves dialogue, he talks, even when drained and dreaming of silence.

For all my work in cowriting the memoirs of musicians, I've never experienced a collaborator like B. B. King. Before beginning, I go back to my own beginning with B. B.'s music and trace the paths that brought us together.

The first time I saw him was in Dallas. I was fourteen, B was thirty-two. I was a kid in the crowd, B the star onstage. The venue was the Longhorn Ballroom, which looked more like an enormous barn than a ballroom. It was one of those places that switched genres and races: Sunday was white with country and western, Monday was black with rhythm and blues. Rhythm and blues was a recent discovery of mine. I'd only moved to Texas a year before; back East, I'd been listening only to jazz. Jazz hit me when I was eight or nine, turning me into a young elitist. I looked to *Downbeat* magazine to validate my taste. I looked to Monk and Miles as deities of high art. I bought R&B records by Bill Haley and His Comets and LaVern Baker, but felt ambivalent about doing so. I paid my dues in the peanut gallery in Birdland, intoxicated by the hard-bop energy of Art Blakey's drums, the sweetness of Clifford Brown's trumpet, the lyricism of Red Garland's piano.

Dallas changed all that. Texas felt like the desert until someone said there was a jazz session in South Dallas at the American Woodmen Auditorium. That's where I heard and met Hog Cooper and Fathead Newman and James Clay—Dallasites, members of the Ray Charles band, and brilliant jazz musicians who helped me redefine my understanding of jazz. On a Sunday afternoon, they played Miles Davis–style jazz. On a Saturday night, with Ray Charles, they played tight rhythm and blues, mixed with twelve-bar blues, mixed with jazz, mixing me up to the point that the categories started to fall. Ray Charles was chiefly responsible for that fall. His reckless disregard of genres, blending gospel with soul and country with blues and jazz with everything else, reformed my orthodoxy and left me looser to simply ingest the beauty of black music.

Charles's live performance prepared me for King's live performance, just as, decades later, writing Ray's book ultimately led me to B's. For some, Ray represented jazz. I heard his jazz voicings and knew about his jazz foundation. But in his voice I heard a far more ancient cry—a field holler, a spiritual, a gospel shout, the unmistakable mark of country blues. Ray led me back to blues, something my New York upbringing had missed. Texas turned out to be the perfect training ground. Freddie King was in Dallas, Lightnin' Hopkins in Houston, and practically every week the road shows rolled in with Jimmy Reed or Bobby Bland or B. B. King.

The elements of B's art that struck me as a kid are the elements that sustain me as an adult—the piercing sound of his guitar, the full-throated sincerity of his singing, the deep grooves in which he moves, and his towering emotional commitment to his audience. At fourteen, I was flabbergasted, not only by the ritual blues show—the booze, the smoking, the dancing, the fancy dresses and slick suits and ultrahip attitudinizing—but by the quality of B's band. Like Ray's band, the musicians could go both ways; when they weren't playing blues, they were playing jazz, Basie–style charts that allowed the sidemen ample space to stretch out and show off. Unlike Ray, though, the centerpiece of B's show was B's twelve-bar blues, basic Delta blues refined, filtered, and recharged through the electricity of a dynamic big-city band.

The sound stayed with me and so did the dilemma that, I later learned, stayed with B: Academic critics, whom I read religiously, gave him scant respect. They were irritated by the very thing that excited me—B's electricity and the great volume of his sound. They slammed him for being too loud, too crass and commercial, while I marveled at what seemed to me his subtle dynamics. I disagreed, but never found a champion until my senior year in college when I read Charles Keil's *Urban Blues*. Keil took on the academicians he called "moldy figs," scholars busy saving blues from its impurities by denigrating electric bluesmen as compromisers and corrupters. Keil defended B. B. King, Bobby Bland, and Ray Charles as keepers of the flame of vital blues; he viewed them as righteous representatives of their communities' material hopes and spiritual souls. The book inspired me to write a fan letter to its author, who was engaged in ethnomusical research in Africa.

Fate intervened, and a year later Keil and I were colleagues at the State University of New York at Buffalo—I as a teaching fellow in the English Department, Charlie as a professor in American Studies. We became fast friends. Charlie inspired me to write my first essay on soul music, and we collaborated on a rhythm and blues book that never saw the light of day. Charlie was also responsible for my first meeting with B. B. King.

A decade had passed since I'd seen B's live show. In Buffalo, he seemed more fiery than ever. When Charlie took me backstage to meet him, I wondered whether he'd show signs of bitterness. After all, rock 'n' roll had neglected him in the fifties, while soul music was skipping over him in the sixties. In 1967, his crossover success still hadn't come. We shook hands, and I sat and listened as he politely thanked Charlie for having written *Urban Blues*. "When you came 'round interviewing me," B told Charlie, "you were a college kid. Now look at you—you're a full-grown man!" Good cheer and politeness were his most impressive qualities. Other aspects of his being were not apparent. I saw him as a charming though inscrutable gentleman.

My relationship to musicians and music literature radically changed when, eight years later, I began working with Ray Charles. Trained in traditionally academic ways, my first instinct was to write a biography of Ray in *my* voice. I'd taken no college courses on cowriting memoirs. My sole familiarity with the genre, though, was a strong one—Billie Holiday's *Lady Sings the Blues*, written with William Dufty, a tome I still cherish. As I approached Ray, my loyal and world-wise agent Aaron Priest made it clear that readers, not to mention publishers, were far more interested in what Ray had to say about Ray than what I had to say about Ray. But how does the collaboration work?

I learned by doing, and it wasn't easy. Ray could be demanding. He'd call me to talk at 4 A.M. or not call me for weeks at a time. It took months to read his moods right; it took soul-searching on my part to understand what questions to ask and when to ask them. He could be gracious or cold or short-tempered or reflective. I soon saw that my job was more than listening with my ears and my tape recorder; to get to his soul, I had to listen with my heart. And to elicit his candor, I had to win over his confidence.

Even more trying were the transcripts. When I typed out our conversations, his literal words on paper lacked the sound and fury of real-life speech. I began to understand that the eye hears much differently than the ear. The rhythm of his locution got lost in translation. How to find it? The answer was in moving away from the tapes and going back to the listening heart. The challenge, like writing poetry or fiction, was one of imagination. I had to imagine myself as Ray Charles. And I needed Ray's help as a cowriter in telling me which phrases sounded real and which sounded fake. Two years later, when Ray read our final manuscript and said, "I like it, it's me," I felt relieved.

I fell in love with the genre. I began thinking of all the autobiographies I would have loved to have cowritten: Charlie Parker, Lester Young, John Coltrane, Sam Cooke. The idea of working with these people for years at a time, hearing their stories, being true to their sensibilities and helping give them a literary voice seemed completely wonderful. Criticisms of collaborative books begged the question.

When Billie's *Lady Sings the Blues* was attacked by scholars for being inaccurate, for example, I didn't care. *Lady* is the closest I'll ever get to sitting in a room with Billie and hearing her speak. The fact that she exaggerates, omits, or mythologizes merely reinforces the very essence of storytelling. We each have the freedom to see ourselves any way we want. Myth-making is a sacred right. And when I put myself in the place of the reader and asked the question—In whose voice would I want to hear Sam Cooke's story, Sam's or some writer's?—the answer was always Sam's. Well, if it was too late for Sam Cooke, then it wasn't too late for Marvin Gaye.

Like Ray, Marvin presented distinct difficulties. He didn't sign contracts, he'd miss appointments by months, he'd be in Hawaii when he'd agreed to meet me in L.A., only to skip to Belgium by the time I got to Honolulu. His moods were wildly volatile, now sweet and loving, now depressed and remote. Fortunately, my determination proved stronger than his whimsy. Although the process took five years instead of two, and although his tragic demise required the narrative to be con-ceived in my voice, his voice remains the centerpiece of the story.

And so I've learned to live with—and even enjoy—the id-iosyncrasies of my collaborators. With Smokey Robinson, it was conducting interviews in a golf cart while he worried over his next chip shot. With music producer Jerry Wexler, it was ne-gotiating his proclivity for fancy English and flowery words. With Etta James, it was working around her long periods of self-imposed isolation and, at times, her rage. I'm not complain-ing. These are all people whose art I admire and whose personalities I came to love. I also came to feel that, because these books were born out of an emotional chemistry stirred up by my subject and me, my own contribution as the invisible "I" was a source of tremendous gratification.

It was Etta James who brought me to B for the third time.

In 1993, they were, by coincidence, both staying at the Pritikin Center in Santa Monica, California, working to lose weight. Etta asked me to dinner. When I arrived in the dining room, I thought I had mistakenly wandered into some suburban country club. I hadn't. The Pritikin Center has that look. I spotted Etta seated at a faraway corner table. I was surprised to see her with B. B. They didn't seem happy, and I soon saw why. On each of their plates was a skimpy piece of plain fish, a boiled potato, and a stick of broccoli. Dinner conversation was minimal. An unspoken understanding said we all would have liked a sizzling hot pizza.

I would have liked to talk more with B. B., but Etta was my focus. I was still writing her book. B was affable as ever, but there was no time to get to know him. That time came after Etta's book came out and B, on the advice of his manager Sid Seidenberg, decided to write a book of his own. After Sid read Etta's story, he arranged for me to meet his man and, in short order, we were in business.

I worried at first. I'd read Charles Sawyer's *The Arrival of B. B. King,* a work of considerable scholarship. In the past, my books had all broken new ground. This was the first time I was writing an autobiography after a biography had been published. As expected, though, Sawyer chose to write the story from Sawyer's point of view—not B's. B's voice is barely audible.

I also worried that B's temperament was too elusive, too even. I was accustomed to temper tantrums and indomitable egos. I was concerned that there wasn't enough conflict or psychology, concerned B's politeness would impede candor. But I was wrong. And it didn't take long—in fact, it happened in our first meeting—before I got a taste of the special character of this collaboration.

"How are you, David? Let's get started" are B. B. King's first words to me.

When I go into a long rap about the importance of candor, B cuts me off at the pass. "Whatever you ask," he says, "I'll try and answer."

It's that simple.

"And whenever you come out on the road with me," he adds, "I'll make time for you."

I'm so used to tiptoeing around unpredictable moods and screwy timetables, our working rapport seems too good to be true. But as the months roll by, it proves that good. B is a man of his word.

Our dialogues progress at a slow but steady pace, much like the progress of his career, much like the road trips we're taking, much like the very cadence of B's life. B puts one foot in front of the other and rarely trips. He wants to like everyone and wants everyone to like him, but if they don't, he's happy all the same—and even happier if hostilities are avoided. Civility is the cornerstone of B. B. King's character.

Musically, he lives in certain grooves; personally, he moves in certain routines. These routines are set. When he travels, his assistants lug an enormous amount of equipment B uses for information and entertainment—audio and video recorders, computers, monitors, books, tapes, compact discs. He travels with a virtual library of material.

Not a day passes when he doesn't give me my time. His favorite time is the afternoon, especially in his private compartment on the bus, and especially when the ride is long. As I knock on the door, I hear the strain of blues. I'm happy to report B. B. still loves blues—and still listens to blues—as much as the most fanatical blues devotee. If he plays the blues for money most every night, he listens to the blues for love every day. No matter where in the world he finds himself, he is never without cases of cassette tapes that contain a sampling of un-adulterated blues.

His deejay background is evident in the sequencing of his tapes. He'll move from a Mance Lipscomb lament to a Little Milton romp, alternating tempos and moods to keep his inter-est. His loyalty to his original heroes is clear. A week doesn't pass without B. B. spending hours with Leadbelly, Lonnie John-son, Django, Charlie Christian, and T-Bone. They are the pillars holding up his cathedral. Beyond the foundation of blues, how-ever, his tastes range far and wide. During the Christmas sea-son, for example, he puts together a tape of yuletide songs featuring the Whispers, the soul-singing close-harmony vocal quintet. When I arrive in his private compartment on any given day, he's listening to Louis Jordan or Amos Milburn or Pee Wee Crayton or Jimmy Rushing or Joe Turner. The period of his musical coming-of-age—the mid to late forties—still fascinates him most.

"Listen to this," he says to me one afternoon as we wind our way through Arizona.

It's Ray Charles's famous jazz sessions with Milt Jackson from the fifties. "No album," he says, "has ever had a better title. They called it *Soul Brothers.*"

We don't speak until the last precious note is played.

On another day, this time barreling down a lonely highway

in Iowa, I realize the quality in B that I value most—his absolute sincerity. The most memorable musicians I've profiled have displayed the ability to simply say what they mean. Sincere expression, beginning in speech, is the basis of B's music. I love hearing the patterns of his speech in his music and the patterns of his music in his speech. The two are deeply intermingled and wonderfully complementary. I'm also moved by B's insistence that he has a speech impediment, in spite of his apparent fluency. My own stutter is still alive and well, and I wonder whether his identification of himself as a stutterer is his way of reaching out to me.

The way B describes pain—feelings of being misunderstood by his children, sadness about the collapse of two marriages, hurt suffered from racial insensitivity—flow from him like spontaneous music. His stories seem to carry the same theme as his blues: "Mistreatment," says B, "makes me sad." But, in telling the tale, his rhythms turn grief to joy and his suffering sounds like a song.

B can be testy. His testiness is triggered when someone undervalues the blues. Every night after every show, I watch him patiently entertain dozens and sometimes hundreds of well-wishers. Autographs, photos with fans, and souvenir guitar picks and pens are never refused. One night an observer says, "I heard you playing jazz guitar out there tonight, Mr. King. Man, you were great! I knew you played blues, but never dreamed you could actually play jazz." "Thank you" was B's only reply.

The next morning, riding the bus to Wichita, Kansas, B is still upset about the man's comment. "He made it sound like playing blues is nothing," says B. "How does he think that makes me feel? Does he think anyone can pick up a guitar and play some blues? Is it like washing the dishes or mowing the grass? Oh, well," B concludes, calming himself. "Everyone's entitled to an opinion."

B is usually calm. I spend hundreds of hours looking at B looking out the window of the bus. As the countryside zips by, the ride is calming. One gig has been played and another looms ahead. I watch the light of day slowly creep across B's face. Sometimes his features remind me of his fellow Southerner and dear friend Dizzy Gillespie—the expressive eyes, the broad nose. Sometimes I see him through a portrait he has shown me of his father. In his ability to stay on the road, I wonder how much is commitment and how much is compulsiveness. He's surely addicted to work, but his addiction is uniquely calm. He appears uniquely patient—with my endless questions, with the length of these trips, with the very process of living.

Everywhere we go, B is visited by family—children, cousins, sisters, nieces, nephews. I get the impression half the world is related to B. B. King, who describes himself as "free-hearted." Every family member, no matter how busy B might be, is granted an audience. And no one leaves empty-handed. No one knows exactly how much B doles out, but the amount must be staggering. He's famous for not refusing. And everyone— including Sherman the tour manager and Sid the personal manager—understands that B's generous relationship with his relatives is a private matter not to be questioned.

In Oklahoma City, we leave early in the morning for an all-day trek into Texas. Last night's show was over at 2 A.M., and only a few hours later the bus is departing downtown. Everyone is groggy. B arrives a little late and, instead of going to his private compartment, sits up front. "Can you go find the sight of the bombing?" he asks the driver, referring to the Federal Building, which was blown up in 1995. The sight is marked by a makeshift memorial to the fallen children. Their toys and clothing and pictures are placed against a chain-link fence surrounding the barren parcel of land. B leaves the bus and stands alone, looking at the children's pictures. When he returns, he says nothing; he's shaking his head back and forth, his cheeks stained with tears.

He adores women and will frequently ask a woman for a hug. "Just for the warmth," he says. "Just to make me happy for the rest of the day." His need to charm and be charmed by women is as visceral as his need to play the guitar. After two arduous shows, I watch his eyes get happy as a lovely female enters his dressing room. Suddenly his fatigue is gone and his smile is back. Even when ladies aren't present, the very subject of the feminine gender makes him happy. I've never seen him aggressive with women, only appreciative and eager for companionship.

His most loyal companions are the members of his entourage and band. He pays generously and never fails to acknowledge their contribution in private and public. In a business where bandleaders are notorious skinflints and exploiters, B's reputation is stellar. His payback comes in the performance of a group of men whose devotion is absolute.

One day I get on a kick. I decide to figure out how many gigs B has played and how many miles he's clocked since starting out in the fifties. B and I start figuring, and the numbers get crazy—an average of some 330 one-nighters over forty years with an average of 250 miles between each gig. But that doesn't take into account Europe and Asia and South America and Africa and soon the calculations get away from us. I ask him whether he, the most modest of men, thinks any other entertainer in the modern era has worked as much. He reflects for a second. "Maybe not," says B with only a hint of satisfaction in his voice.

B doesn't like surprises, doesn't like changing personnel or established ways of working. His show, for all its refinements, remains much the same show as I saw as a fourteen-year-old in Dallas. B. B. King comes onstage with his band kicking him hard; he plays the hell out of Lucille; he sings his heart out; and he leaves his fans feeling good.

"I look at every show like a test," he says one night as the bus sweeps up Interstate 55 toward Chicago. "I want the audience to feel like they're at a homecoming. But can I make the people out there feel like family? Can I make 'em feel how much I love the blues? Can I make 'em feel that the blues loves them? If the answer is yes, I've done my job. But if not, I'm out there the next night, trying a little harder."

Toward the end of our long journey together, we wind up in Vegas. B drives me from the Desert Inn, where he's performing, to the townhouse where he's lived for the past ten years. The place is overloaded with memorabilia, closets of clothes, reams of records, stacks of souvenirs, trophies, priceless old pictures, and the biggest hat and cap collection I've ever seen.

B and I sit around his kitchen table. We're both hungry, so he heats up some beans and cornbread, sticks a slab of butter on top, pours on milk, and mashes it all up. Tastes great.

"When I was a boy," says B, "I made me many a meal like this. That was after Mama died. Now sometimes when I get off the road, I come in here and pretend I'm back there, just doing for myself. Gives me a feeling of comfort. I know I've changed a lot, but I also know I haven't changed at all. Thinking of it that way, my life starts to make some sense."

SELECTED DISCOGRAPHY

The following are currently available on cassette tapes and/or compact discs. All are available on MCA, except where noted. The four-CD/cassette box, *King of the Blues*, provides the best overview of B. B.'s career.

The Fifties

Singin' the Blues/The Blues (Flair/Virgin)—his first two original albums on one CD.
Do the Boogie! B. B. King's Early 50's Classics (Flair/Virgin)
The Best of B. B. King, Volume One (Flair/Virgin)
The Best of B. B. King, Volume Two (Flair/Virgin)
Heart and Soul (Ace)
My Sweet Little Angel (Ace)

The Sixties

Live at the Regal
Blues Is King
Lucille
Live and Well
Completely Well

The Seventies

Indianola Mississippi Seeds
Live in Cook County Jail
Live in London
Guess Who
To Know You Is to Love You
B. B. King and Bobby Bland . . . Together for the First Time .
   Live
Midnight Believer

The Eighties

Now Appearing at Ole Miss
There Must Be a Better World Somewhere
Love Me Tender
Blues 'n' Jazz
Six Silver Strings

The Nineties

Live at San Quentin
Live at the Apollo . . . with the Philip Morris Superband (GRP)
There Is Always One More Time
*Blues Summit**
Heart to Heart . . . with Diane Schuur
How Blue Can You Get . . . Classic Live Performances . . .
    *1964–94***

---

*Duets with Robert Cray, Katie Webster, Buddy Guy, John Lee Hooker, Koko Taylor, Etta James, Lowell Fulson, Albert Collins, Ruth Brown, Irma Thomas, and Joe Louis Walker.

**Includes the Crusaders and duets with Bobby Bland, Joe Louis Walker, Gladys Knight, and Ruth Brown.

AWARDS

Honorary Doctorates

1973 Tougaloo College (Mississippi) (L.H.D)
1977 Yale University (D. Music)
1982 Berklee College of Music (Boston) (D. Music)
1990 Rhodes College (Memphis) (D. Fine Arts)

Honorariums

1990 Presidential Medal of the Arts, presented by President George Bush
1991 National Heritage Fellowship, National Endowment of the Arts
1991 National Award of Distinction, University of Mississippi

1995 Kennedy Center Honors
Founding Member, John F. Kennedy Performing Arts Center
Cofounder, Foundation for the Advancement of Inmate Recreation and Rehabilitation (FAIRR)

W. C. Handy Awards (Blues Foundation)

1983 Hall of Fame Classics of Blues Recordings (Albums): *Live at the Regal*, "The Thrill Is Gone"
1985 Hall of Fame Classics of Blues Recordings (Single Recording, including Album Tracks)
1987 Keeping the Blues Alive (Radio): *The B. B. King Blues Hour*
1988 Keeping the Blues Alive (Radio): *The B. B. King Radio Hour*
1991 Blues Band of the Year: The B. B. King Orchestra

MTV Video Music Awards

1988/89 Best Video from a Film: "When Love Comes to Town," from *Rattle and Hum*, U2 with B. B. King

NAACP Image Awards

1975 Best Blues Artist
1981 Best Blues Artist
1993 Best Blues Artist

National Association for Campus Activities Awards

1986 Blues Act of the Year

NATRA Golden Mike Award

1969 Best Blues Singer of the Year
1974 Best Blues Singer of the Year

French Academie du Jazz Award

1969 Best Album of the Year: *Lucille*

Grammy Awards

1970 Best Rhythm and Blues Vocal Performance, Male: "The Thrill Is Gone"
1981 Best Ethnic or Traditional Recording: *There Must Be a Better World Somewhere*
1983 Best Traditional Blues Recording: *Blues 'n' Jazz*
1985 Best Traditional Blues Recording: "My Guitar Sings the Blues," a track from *Six Silver Strings*
1990 Best Traditional Blues Recording: *Live at San Quentin*
1991 Best Traditional Blues Recording: *Live at the Apollo*
1993 Best Traditional Blues Recording: *Blues Summit*

B. B. King has been nominated for seventeen Grammy Awards through 1995. In 1970, King's *Indianola Mississippi Seeds* won a Grammy Award for Best Album Cover, an award for art direction.

Halls of Fame

1974 Ebony Blues Hall of Fame
1980 Blues Foundation Hall of Fame
1987 Rock 'n' Roll Hall of Fame
1995 *Performance Magazine* Touring Hall of Fame

Lifetime Achievement Awards

1987 Grammy Awards Lifetime Achievement Award
1990 Songwriters' Hall of Fame, Lifetime Achievement Award
1991 The Orville H. Gibson Lifetime Achievement Award (Gibson Guitar)

Humanitarian Awards

1973 B'nai B'rith Humanitarian Award, Music and Performance Lodge of New York

Walks of Fame

1989 Rock Walk
1989 Amsterdam (Holland) Walk of Fame

1991 Hollywood Walk of Fame (Between Milton Berle and Vivien Leigh)

Downbeat

1970 Best Rock/Pop/Blues Group (International Critics' Poll)

1971 Best Rock/Pop/Blues Group (International Critics' Poll)

1972 Best Rock/Pop/Blues Group (International Critics' Poll)

1973 Best Rock/Pop/Blues Group (International Critics' Poll)

1974 Best Rock/Pop/Blues Group (International Critics' Poll)

1975 Best Rock/Pop/Blues Group (International Critics' Poll)

1990 Blues/Soul/R&B Musician of the Year (Readers' Poll)

1991 Blues/Soul/R&B Musician of the Year (Readers' Poll)

1991 Blues Artist of the Year (International Critics' Poll)

1992 Blues Artist of the Year (International Critics' Poll)

1992 Blues Group (International Critics' Poll)

1993 Blues/Soul/R&B Group (Readers' Poll)

1993 Blues/Soul/R&B Musician of the Year (Readers' Poll)

1993 Blues Group (International Critics' Poll)

1993 Blues Artist of the Year (International Critics' Poll)

1994 Blues/Soul/R&B Group of the Year (Readers' Poll)

1994 Blues/Soul/R&B Musician of the Year (Readers' Poll)

1994 Blues/Soul/R&B Album of the Year: *Blues Summit* (Readers' Poll)

1994 Blues Group (International Critics' Poll)

1994 Blues Artist of the Year (International Critics' Poll)

1994 Blues Album of the Year: *Blues Summit* (International Critics' Poll)

1995 Blues Group (International Critics' Poll)

Ebony

1974 Best Male Blues Singer
1974 Best Blues Instrumentalist
1974 Best Blues Album: *Live at the Regal*
1975 Best Male Blues Singer
1975 Best Blues Instrumentalist
1975 Best Blues Album: *To Know You Is to Love You*

Guitar Player Magazine

1970 Blues Guitarist of the Year
1971 Blues Guitarist of the Year
1972 Blues Guitarist of the Year
1973 Blues Guitarist of the Year
1974 Blues Guitarist of the Year

Performance Magazine Readers' Poll

1985 Blues Act of the Year
1987 Blues Act of the Year
1988 Blues Act of the Year

Melody Maker

1973 Best Blues Artist of the Year (World Section)

Blues Unlimited

1973 Best Blues Guitarist

Jazz & Pop

1968 Best Male Jazz Singer of the Year

INDEX

INDEX

SONG PERMISSIONS

"How Blue Can You Get" by Leonard Feather, © 1946, Renewed 1977, Model Music Co.

"Miss Martha King" by Riley B. King, © 1991 Careers-BMG Music Publishing, Inc (BMI). All rights reserved. Used by permission.

"Three O'clock Blues" by Riley B. King and Jules Binari, © 1952 Careers-BMG Music Publishing, Inc. (BMI) and Powerforce Music. All rights administered by Careers-BMG Music Publishing, Inc. All rights reserved. Used by permission.

"You Upset Me Baby" by Riley B. King and Jules Binari, © 1954 Careers-BMG Music Publishing, Inc. (BMI) and Powerforce Music. All rights administered by Careers-BMG Music Publishing, Inc. All rights reserved. Used by permission.

"Sweet Little Angel" by Riley B. King and Jules Binari, © 1956 Careers-BMG Music Publishing, Inc. (BMI) and Powerforce Music. All rights administered by Careers-BMG Music Publishing, Inc. All rights reserved. Used by permission.

"Sweet Sixteen" by Riley B. King and Jules Binari, © 1959 Careers-BMG Music Publishing, Inc. (BMI) and Powerforce Music. All rights administered by Careers-BMG Music Publishing, Inc. All rights reserved. Used by permission.

"Sneakin' Around" by Riley B. King and Jules Binari, © 1957 Careers-BMG Music Publishing, Inc. (BMI) and Powerforce Music All rights administered by Careers-BMG Music Publishing, Inc. All rights reserved. Used by permission.

"I Want To Get Married" by Riley B. King and Jules Binari, © 1957 Careers-BMG Music Publishing, Inc. (BMI) and Powerforce Music. All rights administered by Careers-BMG Music Publishing, Inc. All rights reserved Used by permission.

"It's My Own Fault Darlin'" by Riley B. King and Jules Binari, © 1953 Careers-BMG Music Publishing, Inc. (BMI) and Powerforce Music. All rights administered by Careers-BMG Music Publishing, Inc. All rights reserved. Used by permission.

"What Can I Do" by Riley B. King and Jules Binari, © 1955 Careers-BMG Music Publishing, Inc. (BMI) and Powerforce Music. All rights administered by Careers-BMG Music Publishing, Inc All rights reserved. Used by permission.

"Beautician Blues" by Riley B. King and Jules Binari, © 1953 Careers-BMG Music Publishing, Inc. (BMI) and Powerforce Music. All rights administered by Careers-BMG Music Publishing, Inc. All rights reserved. Used by permission.

B. B. KING hit the road in 1951 and has been on it ever since. He is the recipient of uncountable honors and awards, including an honorary doctorate from Yale University, a Presidential Medal of the Arts, an MTV Award for Best Video ("When Love Comes To Town"), and seven Grammy Awards (with sixteen nominations). He is a member of the Rock-and-Roll Hall of Fame and the Blues Hall of Fame, and has more than 74 albums to his credit.

DAVID RITZ is the critically acclaimed author of the bestselling biography *Divided Soul: The Life of Marvin Gaye,* and co-author of the autobiographies of Smokey Robinson, Etta James, and Ray Charles. His book *Rhythm and the Blues,* co-written with Jerry Wexler, won the 1993 Ralph J. Gleason First Prize for Best Music Book of the Year. Mr. Ritz has written several novels, including *Blue Notes Under a Green Felt Hat*; song lyrics, including "Sexual Healing"; and in 1992 he won a Grammy for writing liner notes for Aretha Franklin.